WALBANK, F. W. Polybius. California, 1973 (c1972). 201p bibl
(Sather Classical Lectures, 42) 72-189219. 8.50. ISBN 0-
520-02190-8
Polybius is one of the authors whom everyone praises but very few read;
it is not surprising, then, that the present work, the latest of the Sather
lectures, is the only book-length study in English. Walbank, as author
of a three-volume commentary (two volumes so far published; v. 2,
CHOICE, Sept. 1968) is clearly the leading English Polybian scholar.
This is definitely a scholarly work, provided with full documentation,
multi-language bibliography, and two indices. Walbank deals with the
life of the author, the Hellenistic historiographic background, Polybius'
sources and principles, and problems of composition. The book will be
valuable to every serious student of ancient historiography; the less
specialized reader will probably find the last two chapters, on Polybius' treatment of the Roman constitution and his attitude toward Rome,
the most rewarding. Since its usefulness to undergraduates will be
slight, Walbank's study is recommended chiefly for university and
larger college libraries.

SATHER CLASSICAL LECTURES

Volume Forty-two

POLYBIUS

POLYBIUS

by F. W. WALBANK

UNIVERSITY OF CALIFORNIA PRESS
BERKELEY, LOS ANGELES, LONDON

UNIVERSITY OF CALIFORNIA PRESS
BERKELEY AND LOS ANGELES, CALIFORNIA
UNIVERSITY OF CALIFORNIA PRESS, LTD.
LONDON, ENGLAND

© 1972 BY THE REGENTS OF THE UNIVERSITY OF CALIFORNIA

ISBN: 0-520-02190-8

LIBRARY OF CONGRESS CATALOG CARD NUMBER: 72-189219

PRINTED IN GREAT BRITAIN
AT THE UNIVERSITY PRINTING HOUSE, CAMBRIDGE
(BROOKE CRUTCHLEY, UNIVERSITY PRINTER)

BERKELEIENSIBUS CETERISQUE
SANCTI FRANCISCI SINUM
HABITANTIBUS AMICIS
D.   D.   D.

Contents

Preface

Many of the ideas in this book have emerged over the years that I have spent working on a historical commentary on Polybius. Writing a commentary is a discipline which occasionally begins to feel like a strait-jacket; and every commentator, I suspect, sooner or later feels the urge to break out and write a more general book about his particular author, something, as Polybius would say, more σωματοειδής. When, or indeed whether, left to myself, I should eventually have got round to doing this, I cannot say. Fortunately, I had my mind and resolution suitably concentrated when the University of California at Berkeley honoured me with an invitation to deliver the Sather Lectures for 1970/71.

This book is the fruit of that invitation and it is a pleasant duty to acknowledge debts incurred in its writing and publication: to the University of Liverpool for releasing me from my normal duties to take up the Sather Professorship; to Mr M. H. Crawford for his kindness in reading the manuscript and the proofs to my considerable advantage; to my wife for help with the index; and to Mr August Frugé and his colleagues in the University of California Press and to the staff of the Cambridge University Printing House for their expedition and invariable help and courtesy while the book was in their hands. I thank them all warmly.

The lectures are printed almost as they were delivered in Dwinelle Hall in the winter quarter of 1971. It was a time that will remain memorable for the pleasure of living and working in Berkeley (hic ver adsiduum atque alienis mensibus aestas!) and even more for the kindness and hospitality which were constantly shown to my wife and myself by Professor W. S. Anderson, the Head of the Classics Department, and his colleagues in the Classics and History Departments (and their wives) and by the members of my graduate class. It therefore seems fitting that the book should be inscribed to them and to our other friends, old and new, in the Bay Area who in countless ways helped to render our stay in California so enjoyable.

F. W. W.

University of Liverpool
July 1972

[ix]

I

The Man and his Work

I.

In the middle of the second century B.C., when Polybius set out to describe the rise of Rome to world power, the writing of history had already been practised for three centuries as a discipline with its own aims and methods, and a well defined area of study.[1] Herodotus was the first to formulate the concept of an enquiry into individual secular events and their explanation on a strictly human level;[2] and Thucydides had sharpened the focus, limiting the field to what was contemporary and political.[3] The purpose of both was to understand and explain the world they were describing, not simply to relate what had happened but also to indicate the reasons. Thucydides went further. He used particular incidents as a basis for generalisations which, by their universal validity, would be of help to his readers in similar contexts.[4] This notion of what history included and what it could hope to achieve was inherited by Polybius. But as well he inherited a more diffuse and more frivolous attitude towards the past which was to be found expressed in the works of a host of other historians who drew on traditions going back behind Herodotus[5]—to the epic stories in which fact and myth were not clearly differentiated, and to the poets and tragedians for whom pleasure and emotion were

---

[1] Virtually nothing is known, however, of its treatment in theoretical works. See below, pp. 36–7, for the treatises of Theophrastus and Praxiphanes.

[2] Cf. Collingwood, *Idea*, 25–8.

[3] Cf. M. I. Finley, 'Myth, memory and history', *History and theory*, 4 (1965), 300; and two articles, there quoted, by A. Momigliano ('The place of Herodotus in historiography', *Secondo contributo*, 29–44; 'Storiografia su tradizione scritta e storiografia su tradizione orale', *Terzo contributo*, i. 13–22; English translation in *Studies*, 211–20).

[4] Jacqueline de Romilly, 'L'Utilité de l'histoire selon Thucydide', *Histoire et historiens*, 41–81.

[5] See my discussion in 'History and tragedy', *Historia*, 9 (1960), 216–34.

[I]

ends as legitimate as truth and utility. This further legacy was one against which Polybius struggled consciously; nevertheless it has left its marks here and there upon his work.[6]

Polybius' importance rests to no small extent upon the importance of his theme—the rise of Rome. Yet this too links closely with the works of his predecessors, in which from the outset the impact of the non-Greek world upon Greece had played a significant part. Herodotus' *History* had grown out of the attempt to explain why Greeks and Persians fought each other and, as he says,[7] to preserve for posterity a record of the great and wonderful deeds performed on both sides. Despite the discursive character of the early books the Persian Wars lay at the centre of his work; indeed, it may well have been contact with the Persian empire that had made the Greeks especially alert to the outside world and so furnished one of the main incentives to create the science of history.[8]

Salamis and Plataea banished the Persian danger from mainland Greece; but the Peloponnesian War brought Persia back into Greek politics. It is one of the many disconcerting aspects of Thucydides that he is so strangely uninterested in Persia; and it has been plausibly argued that one of Theopompus' aims was to restore Persia to her due place of prominence in the historical scene and to draw attention to the threat she presented to Greece.[9] Theopompus looked to Greek unity, eventually under the leadership of Philip II of Macedonia; but this solution was violently controversial. In the eyes of many Greeks, such as Demosthenes, Macedon represented a greater threat than Persia. This was an argument fought out both in rhetoric and, ultimately, on the battlefield. Its echoes were still to be heard two centuries later when Polybius, contemplating the rise of Rome, was reminded, he tells us,[10] of Demetrius of Phalerum's remarkable prophecy in his

[6] For examples see below, pp. 39–40.

[7] Herod. i introd.; on this see Strasburger, *Wesensbestimmung*, 16 ff., who distinguishes between τὰ γενόμενα ἐξ ἀνθρώπων, men's achievements in general, i.e. 'cultural history', and ἔργα μεγάλα καὶ θωμαστά, 'the great deeds of individuals' (which take us back to the Homeric epic and forward to political and military history as it later developed).

[8] Cf. Momigliano, 'Fattori orientali della storiografia ebraica postesilica e della storiografia greca', *Terzo contributo*, ii. 813–18.

[9] Cf. Momigliano, 'Teopompo', *Terzo contributo*, i. 367–92. See also A. Andrewes, 'Thucydides and the Persians', *Historia*, 10 (1961), 1–18, for the undervaluation of the importance of Persia by Thucydides.

[10] Polyb. xxix. 21; see below, pp. 26–7 nn. 133–4 and p. 62 n. 179.

treatise *On Fortune*; just as the Macedonians, virtually unknown fifty years before, had overthrown the mighty Persian empire, so in due course the Macedonians in their turn would be defeated by Fortune and yield their mastery to someone else—a prophecy, the fulfilment of which Polybius believed that he had witnessed in his own lifetime.

In this way the impact of the outside world upon Greece became the centre of Polybius' history as it had been that of Herodotus's. But the form it was to take brought him into conflict with another more recent writer, Timaeus of Tauromenium, who in his history of the west could already claim to be regarded as the first historian of Rome.[11] Polybius' relationship to Timaeus is devious and complicated, and I shall return to it in more detail in the next chapter.[12] But one of his main objections to the Sicilian historian is the western context in which everything is set.[13] To Polybius the affairs of Sicily were a mere storm in a teacup—καθάπερ ἐν ὀξυβάφῳ as he says,[14] criticising Timaeus' account of Timoleon. The real significance of Rome is only to be apprehended in a universal, an oecumenical, context—which to Polybius means first and foremost in relation to mainland Greece and Macedonia. Timaeus' western history fell outside the main tradition represented by Herodotus, Thucydides and Theopompus, and if a universal history, like that of Ephorus, of which Polybius approved,[15] naturally went beyond Greece to take in the east and the west, it is still primarily the history of the city-states grouped around the Aegean.

Polybius writes with both a Greek and a Roman public in mind. His Roman readers are mentioned here and there. For instance, in his account of the Punic treaties he specifically hints at the need

[11] According to Dionysius (*Ant. rom.* i. 6. 1) Hieronymus was the first writer to deal with Rome's early history; but Hieronymus will hardly have done more than touch on the Roman background of the war with Pyrrhus. After him came Timaeus, who included τὰ ἀρχαῖα τῶν ἱστοριῶν in his general history, and was regarded as the first historian of Rome (for Lycus of Rhegium, whom Agatharchides mentions along with him (*FGH* 570 T 3), seems to have been an ethnographer rather than a historian). See, on the importance of Timaeus, Momigliano, 'Atene nel III secolo A.C. e la scoperta di Roma nelle storie di Timeo di Tauromenio', *Terzo contributo*, i. 44–53; Walbank, 'Polemic in Polybius', *JRS*, 52 (1962), 10.   [12] See below, pp. 48 ff.

[13] Cf. Momigliano, art. cit. (n. 11), *Terzo contributo*, i. 38–9.

[14] xii. 23. 7; cf. 26 b.

[15] See v. 33. 2, where Polybius praises Ephorus for having been the first man to attempt a universal history.

felt by Roman senators for accurate information;[16] and he excuses himself for any shortcomings in his account of the Roman constitution that may be apparent to those brought up at Rome.[17] But these passages are on the whole exceptional. Moreover, the most striking reference to Roman readers, in which he seems to suggest that they are his main public, when read carefully indicates the opposite. This passage is to be found in a discussion of the integrity of Aemilius Paullus, inserted in a kind of obituary in book xxxi, where, after observing that Aemilius died a poor man despite all his opportunities for gain, Polybius continues: 'If anyone considers what I say to be incredible he should bear in mind that I am perfectly well aware that the present work will be perused by Romans above all people, because it contains an account of their most glorious achievements, and that it is impossible that they should be either ignorant of the facts or disposed to pardon any departure from the truth.' It is surely apparent that in this passage Polybius is addressing a Greek audience, and mentions his Roman readers only as a kind of guarantee that what he is saying about Rome is the plain unvarnished truth: as he goes on to add, 'this should be borne in mind throughout the whole work, whenever I appear to say anything extraordinary about the Romans'.[18] That he is writing primarily for Greeks rather than Romans can be seen in many asides and references to internal Greek affairs;[19] and

---

[16] iii. 21. 9, ἵνα μήθ' οἷς καθήκει καὶ διαφέρει τὸ σαφῶς εἰδέναι τὴν ἐν τούτοις ἀκρίβειαν, παραπαίωσι τῆς ἀληθείας ἐν τοῖς ἀναγκαιοτάτοις διαβουλίοις—perhaps with a hint at the critical debates in the Senate before the Third Punic War. Von Scala, 289, believes that the remark (iv. 18. 10) that the temple of Artemis, which lies between Cleitor and Cynaetha, ἄσυλον...νενόμισται παρὰ τοῖς ῞Ελλησιν is meant to purvey information to Roman readers; but more probably it is intended to throw doubts on the Greekness of the Aetolians who violated it.   [17] vi. 11. 3.

[18] xxxi. 22. 8. There seem to be no grounds here for von Scala's hypothesis (290) that the Greeks were increasingly alienated from Polybius in his later books, and that these were therefore written rather with a Roman audience in mind; Pédech, *Méthode*, 566, taking this passage at its face value, draws the same conclusion. When Polybius inserted the account of the geography of Sicily in book i (42. 1–7)—and Pédech, *Méthode*, 565, argues convincingly that this was after the voyages and journeys of 152–146—he still has Greek readers primarily in mind, since the position of Sicily relative to Italy is compared to that of the Peloponnese relative to the rest of Greece. Granted, Polybius has many harsh things to say against Greek leaders in his later books; but many of his readers no doubt shared his prejudices.

[19] For hints at his Greek readers, or references to them, see i. 3. 3–8 (ignorance of Greeks about Rome); ii. 35. 9 (dangers of a Gaulish attack on Greece);

there are several other indications of which I will mention just one. Polybius' *Histories* proper, as distinct from the two introductory books, open with Olympiad 140, covering 220–216 B.C., but since in this Olympiad the various strands of world history have not yet become interwoven, as they were afterwards to be, he does not here adopt the annalistic method of treating events which he uses later, but instead he narrates the affairs of Syria and Egypt, Greece and Macedonia, Rome and Carthage and several other subsidiary theatres of war in long continuous passages which overstep the separate Olympiad years. In order to orientate his readers on the chronological connection between these sections, he includes from time to time a synchronism, linking up the various sets of events.[20] These synchronisms—there are eight or nine in all (depending on how one calculates them)—work out at two for each year, and it is significant that they are all inserted in the parts dealing with Greek events. A recent hypothesis[21] suggests that they are designed to provide points of reference within each half Olympiad year and are based on the somewhat improbable convention that Polybius treated any events occurring within each such period of six months as synchronous. This is, I think, far too subtle. In fact Polybius explains[22] that these synchronisms, relating outside events both to the Olympiad year and to contemporary happenings in Greece, will make his narrative clear and easy to follow. There is nothing recondite about them, and the kind of events mentioned are the battles of Trasimene and Raphia, the Peace of Naupactus and Hannibal's attack on Saguntum. But the point I want to emphasise is that the first four of these syn-

---

iii. 59. 8 (his object is to inform the Greeks about Africa, Spain, Gaul and those parts); 72. 12 (the strength of the Roman legion); 87. 7 (distinction between dictator and consuls); 107. 10 f. (organisation of legions); vi. 3. 1–4 (Rome's constitution is complicated compared with those of Greece)—indeed book vi is clearly designed primarily for Greeks; x. 4. 9 (use of the *toga candida* at elections); 16–17 (procedure in the Roman army when plundering); xiv. 3. 6 (on the sounding of trumpets in night-watches); xxi. 2. 2 (the *supplicatio*); 13. 11 (function of the Salii). See further von Scala, 289, and Petzold, *Studien*, 41, who observes that 'nirgendwo...gewahren wir in seinem Werk eindringlicher seine innere Verbundenheit mit der Heimat als in den erschütternden Ausführungen zu der Katastrophe des Jahres 146 (xxxix. 1–5)'.

[20] They are: iv. 27. 1–28. 1, 37. 1–7, 66. 7–67. 1; v. i. i–4, 29. 5–8, 101. 3 (taken with 105. 3), 108. 9–10, 109. 4–6 (cf. 111. 1).

[21] Pédech, *Méthode*, 468–73; I hope to discuss this hypothesis in detail elsewhere.

[22] v. 31. 3.

chronisms, running from autumn 220 until spring 218,[23] are closely linked with the spring and autumn entry into office of the Achaean and Aetolian generals—a somewhat odd focal point in a universal history.

2.

Primarily, then, Polybius is writing for Greeks. His purpose in writing is repeatedly stated:[24] it is to be of use, to produce a history that will be χρήσιμον. In the frequent didactic digressions in which he explains his purpose and his methods Polybius conveys an impression of great candour; and this has sometimes misled his readers into thinking that he presents no problems.[25] In fact, his candour is not that of Herodotus; it is the apparent candour one sometimes finds in a man who has persuaded himself of the truth about matters in which he has a strong personal commitment, and is not prepared even to envisage the possibility that there may be another point of view.

Given Polybius' background and experiences, such a commitment is not altogether surprising. His life involved him in several ups and downs, and events forced him to make more than one violent personal adjustment—though his later years, as far as we know, were passed in tranquillity. Born, it would appear,[26] about

[23] iv. 28. 1 (cf. 29. 1), 37. 4, 66. 8–10 (cf. 67. 1); v. 1. 1.

[24] For his repeated emphasis on utility and the rhetorical contrast between χρήσιμον and τερπνόν cf. i. 4. 11; vii. 7. 8; ix. 2. 6; xi. 19 a. 1–3; xv. 36. 3; xxxi. 30. 1.

[25] Cf. Howald, 87, 'Es gibt keine Polybiosfrage, wie es eine Herodot- und eine Thukydidesfrage, aber auch eine Sallust- und eine Tacitusfrage gibt'.

[26] See my Commentary, i. 1 n. 1; the evidence is indecisive. Pédech, 'Notes sur la biographie de Polybe', LEC, 29 (1961), 145–56, would put Polybius' birth as early as 208, and D. Musti, 'Problemi polibiani (1950–1964)', La parola del passato, 104 (1965), 381–2, in 205. An argument for an early date is Polybius' activity about 180, when he was nominated to a more or less honorific embassy to Ptolemy V, and served on a commission to regulate the boundaries between Megalopolis and Messene (xxiv. 6. 5; Insch. Olymp. no. 46); but it is not impossible that a young man with Polybius' family connections should have begun to hold such posts at 20. Polybius' meeting with Chiomara, the wife of the Galatian chieftain Ortiagon, is not to be regarded as evidence that Polybius served under Manlius Vulso in the campaigns in Asia Minor of 189 (Musti, loc. cit. against Pédech, loc. cit.; see also Lehmann, Untersuchungen, 273 n. 269); this meeting (xxi. 38. 7), when Chiomara impressed Polybius by her φρόνημα καὶ... σύνεσις (not her beauty: so Pédech, loc. cit.), is likely to have been later. Habicht, 'Über die Kriege zwischen Pergamon und Bithynien', Hermes, 84 (1956), 99 n. 1, considers favourably the view of van Gelder, Galatarum res, 258, that Chiomara was interned in Sardes after Ortiagon's fall in 183, following the support he gave to Prusias against Eumenes. However, Gelzer, Kl. Schr.

200 B.C., or a year or two before—the date is uncertain—he spent his first thirty or so years in a political milieu in Achaea, whose central problem was that of maintaining satisfactory relations with the ever more ubiquitous and oppressive power of Rome. He may just have remembered Flamininus' proclamation of Greek freedom at the Isthmian Games of 196,[27] and the departure of the legions two years later.[28] His boyhood will have been coloured by the growing tension that preceded the war with Antiochus and the Aetolians and characterised the difficult time that followed.[29] From his earliest years conversation with his father, the Achaean statesman Lycortas, and other eminent men, must have familiarised him with the political and military problems that confronted the Achaean confederacy. Friction with Sparta and constant uncertainty about how far one could go within the framework of the Roman alliance[30] were the two realities dominating Achaean politics throughout the twenty-five years that separated the Second from the Third Macedonian war. Already the young politician must have been devoting much thought to the problem of co-existence with Rome. The war with Perseus brought these issues to a head, not only in Achaea but in most other Greek states as well. The results were disastrous except to those statesmen firmly committed to obsequious collaboration with Rome; and this was not the policy of Lycortas' party. In the year 170/69 Polybius held the post of cavalry leader,[31] the office next below that of federal general. To avoid involvement was impossible, and though he has left a detailed defence of his policy and behaviour[32] the Romans took a different view. In their eyes, Achaea was under an obligation to respect the interests of the Roman people, and from 167 to 150 Polybius was one of a thousand Achaeans who had to adjust

---

iii. 202, following Ziegler, col. 1461, would date the meeting to sometime before 169.

[27] xviii. 46. 5 ff.

[28] Livy, xxxiv. 52. 1–2 (based on Polybius)

[29] Aymard, *Rapports*, gives a detailed account of the period down to 189, and Errington, *Philopoemen*, is useful down to 183.

[30] There had been collaboration between Rome and Achaea since October 198, when the Achaeans switched their support from Macedonia to Rome, but no *foedus* was made until (probably) 192; cf. Badian, 'The treaty between Rome and the Achaean league', *JRS*, 42 (1952), 76–80 (for other suggested dates see Deininger, 45 n. 25).

[31] xxviii. 6. 9.

[32] Cf. xxviii. 13. 9–13; xxix. 24. 1–4, 7–8.

to a life of internment in Italy, without any charge being made or any opportunity for defence being offered.[33] His fellows were banished to the country towns of Italy for safe keeping; but either as a special privilege (for he may already have made his acquaintance with the family of Aemilius Paullus in Greece)[34] or—a less probable suggestion[35]—in order that the government might keep an eye on so prominent a politician, Polybius was allowed to remain at Rome. There he very soon established himself as the intimate friend and, one might say, tutor of Scipio Aemilianus, a privileged position which must have afforded him exceptional opportunities for observing Roman affairs. Yet if we can judge from his discussion of the Roman state in book vi,[36] he was perhaps better at interpreting the more mechanical aspects of the constitution than he was at understanding the basic unwritten customs, such as patronage and clientship, and the obligations they imposed, which together determined the way the Roman nobility made the constitution work. Despite a close personal relationship with Scipio, one can detect in Polybius some degree of failure to sense the nuances of public life at Rome and the values which held the esteem of the Roman aristocracy.

Polybius goes out of his way to emphasise his friendship with Scipio:[37] in a sense it forms part of his credentials as the interpreter of Rome. But Scipio will not have been his only contact in influential Roman circles; indeed he was only seventeen or eighteen when Polybius came to Rome,[38] and hardly in a position to wield much influence until he entered the senate towards the end of the fifties. There will however have been other acquaintances dating back to Polybius' youth and the years of his political activity at

[33] xxx. 13. 1–11, 32. 1–12; Paus. vii. 10. 11; Livy, xlv. 31. 9.

[34] This is not excluded by Polybius' account of how his intimacy with Scipio Aemilianus arose ἔκ τινος χρήσεως βυβλίων (xxxi. 23. 4), i.e. from the 'loan' or 'use' (either meaning is possible) of books—probably from the library of Perseus, which fell into the hands of Aemilius Paullus' sons after the battle of Pydna (Plut. *Aem.* 28. 11). See further Gelzer, 'Über die Arbeitsweise des Polybios', *Kl. Schr.* iii. 178 n. 133.

[35] So Roveri, *Studi*, 153; but there must have been many exiles more eminent and potentially dangerous than the young Achaean, yet we do not hear that any of them was kept at Rome.

[36] vi. 3–10, 11–18, 43–58.

[37] Cf. xxxi. 24. 12, οὐκέτι τὸ μειράκιον ἐχωρίσθη τοῦ Πολυβίου, πάντα δ' ἦν αὐτῷ δεύτερα τῆς ἐκείνου συμπεριφορᾶς.

[38] Cf. Astin, *Scipio*, 245–7, for the dates of Scipio's birth and death; he died in 129 and was born probably in 185, but perhaps in 184.

home, when Romans were frequent visitors in Achaea[39] and will certainly have enjoyed hospitality in the households of leading citizens. There is no reason to suppose that while in Rome Polybius suffered restrictions or that he was boycotted. Indeed there is strong evidence that during the later years of his detention he was allowed to travel in Italy and even abroad.[40] Nevertheless, his situation was ambiguous. He had come to Italy under a cloud and he stayed on under compulsion. It would not be surprising if he chose for preference the company of fellow-Greeks, whether exiles with whom he could share his misfortune or Greek envoys with news from his own land. There is in fact one passage, dealing with an event of 162 and probably composed shortly after its occurrence, though later incorporated in book xxxi of the *Histories*,[41] which furnishes evidence of Polybius' close relationship with another detainee, the future King Demetrius I of Syria—so close indeed that it was apparently at Polybius' instigation[42] and as a result of his careful planning[43] that the Seleucid hostage succeeded in boarding a convenient ship at Ostia and sailing off to recover his kingdom. There was another reason too why Polybius may have

[39] We know of an embassy consisting of Q. Caecilius Metellus, M. Baebius Tamphilus and Ti. Sempronius (Gracchus or Longus) (xxii. 6. 6, where 'Ti. Claudius' is probably an excerptor's error for Ti. Sempronius; cf. Livy, xxxix. 24. 13, 33. 1), which visited the Peloponnese in 185, of visits by Ap. Claudius Pulcher in 184 (xxii. 12. 9–10; Livy, xxxix. 33. 5–8, 35. 5–37. 21; Paus. vii. 9. 3–5), by Q. Marcius Philippus and others in 183 (xxiii. 4. 16, 8. 1–7; Livy, xxxix. 47. 11, 48. 5–6, 53. 10–11), by T. Quinctius Flamininus the same year (xxiii. 5; Plut. *Flam.* 17. 6)—according to Valerius Antias he was accompanied by L. Cornelius Scipio Asiaticus and P. Cornelius Scipio Nasica (Livy, xxxix. 56. 7; cf. Plut. *Flam.* 21. 14), by M. (?) Claudius Marcellus in 173 (Livy, xlii. 5. 10–6. 2). But this merely covers official embassies; during both the Aetolian War and the Third Macedonian War especially there must have been many others.

[40] See my *Commentary*, i. 4, for criticism of Cuntz, 55–6, who argued that as a detainee Polybius would not have been allowed to leave Latium.

[41] xxxi. 11–15; the reference to Carthage as if it were still in existence in 12. 12 supports the view that this passage was composed before 146, and indeed probably as a memorandum, shortly after the incidents described (cf. Gelzer, 'Über die Arbeitsweise des Polybios', *Kl. Schr.* iii. 161, and the earlier works there quoted in nn. 8–9).

[42] It was plausibly suggested by Nitzsch, 60, that a senatorial group—presumably connected with Aemilius Paullus—stood behind Polybius' action; so too Susemihl, ii. 85 and Ziegler, col. 1452.

[43] Bruno Lavagnini, 'Polibio, ovvero la storia maestra della vita', Est. dagli *Atti della reale accademia di scienze lettere e arti di Palermo*, ser. 4, II. 2 (1941), pp. 1–13, propounded the ingenious theory that Polybius organised the escape of Demetrius following that of Hannibal from Carthage in 196 as a model.

spent more time in Greek company than he indicates. In the exiles and in the members of the countless embassies sent by their states to negotiate or plead with the Senate, the historian had an unparalleled source of information not only about current events but also about what had happened in previous decades. Since therefore most people who mattered at this time would turn up sooner or later in Rome, Polybius' exile gave him an opportunity which he would never have had in Achaea to learn not only about Rome but also about Greece and the Hellenistic kingdoms.[44]

In 150 under pressure from Aemilianus and with the acquiescence of Cato, the Senate at last agreed to let the Achaeans go;[45] of the original thousand a bare three hundred were still alive.[46] These survivors were no doubt getting on in years and suitable material for Cato's harsh jest about handing them over to the ministrations of Greek undertakers.[47] For the next five years Polybius found himself at the very centre of political and military activity—but not yet in Achaea, where the climate was unfavourable to returned exiles with close contacts among the Roman aristocracy. On the eve of the Achaean War power had shifted into radical hands, and the effect of Roman policy was to assist the radical cause. Polybius' violent condemnation of those directing Achaean policy at this time confirms the impression that its leaders had no use for him as surely as he had no use for them.[48] However, his services were welcome elsewhere. He had barely reached Arcadia when the consul for 149, M' Manilius, invited the Achaean authorities to send him to Lilybaeum—probably to put his military skill and knowledge of Africa at the service of the Roman government now embarking on the final war with Carthage.[49] At Corcyra he received the news—false, as it proved—that

[44] See below, pp. 74 ff.

[45] xxxv. 6; Paus. vii. 10. 12. Unsuccessful attempts had been made by the Achaeans to secure their release in 164 (xxx. 32), 159 (xxxii. 3. 14–17), 155 (xxxiii. 1. 3–8, 3) and 153 (xxxiii. 14).

[46] Paus. vii. 10. 12, τριακοσίους ἢ καὶ ἐλάσσονας, οἳ μόνοι περὶ 'Ιταλίαν 'Αχαιῶν ἔτι ἐλείποντο, ἀφιᾶσιν.   [47] xxxv. 6 = Plut. *Cato mai.* 9.

[48] xxxviii. 3. 8–13, 10. 8–13, 11. 7–11, 13. 8–9, 16. 11, 18. 8–12; but the whole of Polybius' account of the Achaean War reflects hostility towards those who controlled Achaea at the time. For an analysis of the social background of the war and the policy of the leaders (who seem to have commanded the support of most of the citizens) see A. Fuks, 'The Bellum Achaicum and its social aspect', *JHS*, 90 (1970), 79–89; below, pp. 176–7 n. 122. See too Deininger, 220–38.

[49] xxxvi. 11. 1. Since the invitation (or order?) was conveyed through the Achaean authorities, Polybius must be regarded as in some sense acting as an

Carthage had accepted the Roman ultimatum, and the crisis was over. He returned home, but when hostilities revived went to join his friend Scipio and, as he recounts, shared with him and in his company the mixed emotions aroused by the sight of Carthage in flames.[50] In the following months, when returning to Achaea would have been both difficult and embarrassing, he carried out a voyage of exploration along the African coast and up the coast of Portugal outside the Straits of Gibraltar; we learn from Pliny that his ship was made available by Scipio,[51] whose interest in distant regions is independently attested.[52] Already, in 151, Polybius had accompanied Scipio on official duties to Spain and Africa (where he had met the king of Numidia, Masinissa) and on his return he had crossed the Alps in order to follow in the footsteps of Hannibal.[53] These journeys, together with the voyage on the Atlantic, seem to have convinced Polybius that it was his role to interpret the newly opened up west to the peoples of Greece, and also to have influenced his concept of what his *Histories* should be.[54]

Corinth fell in 146 (the exact month is still uncertain)[55] and

Achaean representative rather than simply as a private individual. Whether the request was repeated officially when the war flared up, or Polybius came the second time in response to a personal invitation from Scipio, is not recorded.

[50] xxxviii. 21. 1–22. 3; on the significance of Scipio's tears on this occasion (their importance has been exaggerated) see now the full and convincing discussion in Astin, *Scipio*, 282–7.

[51] Pliny, *Nat. Hist.* v. 9 = Polyb. xxxiv. 15. 7, 'ab eo (sc. Scipione) accepta classe'.

[52] Cf. xxxiv. 10. 7 for his questioning of Massaliotes and men from Narbo and Corbilo about Britain; they told him nothing.

[53] iii. 48. 12. Cuntz, 58–9, dated Polybius' crossing of the Alps to 132, when he was returning from Numantia. It is not certain (though not improbable) that Polybius was present at the siege of Numantia; but he was about 70 (some would say older than 70) by then, and since there is no evidence that he was confined to Italy during his 'internment', the likelihood is that he made his Alpine crossing after visiting Spain with Scipio Aemilianus in 151/0. See my *Commentary*, i. 382, ad loc. with addendum in vol. ii. 637.

[54] See below, pp. 51–2.

[55] It appears from xxxviii. 1. 1 that that book contained τὴν συντέλειαν τῆς τῶν Ἑλλήνων ἀτυχίας, which must have included the capture of Corinth following the final battle in which Diaeus was defeated (Paus. vii. 16. 3); but although it is likely that book xxxviii was devoted to the events of Ol. 158. 2 = 147/6, given Polybius' normal practice of running an Olympiad year to the end of the campaigning season, the capture of Corinth need not have occurred before mid-summer 146. The destruction of the city (as distinct from its sack) took place later, following a senatorial decision (cf. Livy, *per.* 52, 'Corinthon ex s.c. diruit quia ibi legati violati erant'), and this will have been after the

shortly afterwards Polybius returned to Achaea. The popular leaders had been swept away and the confederacy dissolved, but he could still devote himself to clearing up problems and making the new regime as acceptable as possible within the individual cities.[56] In the course of these negotiations he made one more journey to Rome[57] and after that a curtain descends. Sometime during the rule of Ptolemy Euergetes II, the so-called Physcon or 'Potbelly', he visited Alexandria;[58] and he may have joined Scipio at Numantia since he is said to have enrolled a bodyguard of five hundred friends and clients in response to official obstruction[59]— though indeed Polybius' presence there is not specifically attested.[60] We can assume that he spent these years writing his *Histories*; and though he will no doubt have continued to see Scipio from time to time, in the absence of evidence to the contrary it is reasonable to think that he was normally at home in Megalopolis. The latest date mentioned in his *Histories* occurs in a short sentence, clearly a later insertion in book iii,[61] which states that the road from Emporiae, i.e. the Pyrenees, to the Rhône has now been carefully measured and marked with milestones—which must refer to the

arrival of the commissioners. They are said to have returned to Italy in spring 145, after carrying out their duties over a period of six months (xxxix. 5. 1), which suggests that they came out around October 146. Strachan-Davidson, 43–4, gives a chronology putting the fall of Corinth in September 146, but in fact we have no indication of how long elapsed between that event and the arrival of the commissioners; and indeed only an approximate date is possible for the latter. xxxix. 2 suggests that Polybius was at Corinth shortly after its destruction; but there is no clear evidence that he got there before this took place. See further De Sanctis, iv. 3. 157–60.

[56] xxxix. 5. 1–2; he appears to have acted under the general directives of the Roman commissioners, and describes himself as γράψαντος τοὺς περὶ τῆς κοινῆς δικαιοδοσίας νόμους—probably a code for the regulation of inter-city jurisdiction now that the confederation was no longer there (xxxix. 5. 5).

[57] xxxix. 8. 1. Polybius says that he was able to obtain concessions on the strength of his εὔνοια towards Rome.

[58] Strabo, xvii. 797 = Polyb. xxxiv. 14. 6; see below, p. 48, for the unconvincing hypothesis that Polybius' hostility towards Timaeus arose as a result of this visit to Alexandria.

[59] On Scipio's ἴλη φίλων see App. *Hisp.* 84, cf. 89; and generally on this war Livy, *per.* 57; Cic. *pro rege Deiot.* 19; Schol. Clun. p. 272 Stangl; Vell. ii. 9. 4; Sall. *Iug.* 7. 2; De Sanctis, iv. 3. 260; Astin, *Scipio*, 136.

[60] Polybius wrote an account of the Numantine War (Cic. *fam.* v. 12. 2), and it is possible, given the circumstances in which Scipio marshalled his friends (see previous note), that he was present; but he was seventy at the time (see above, n. 53).

[61] iii. 39. 8.

laying down of the Via Domitia in 118.[62] Its authenticity has been challenged but if it is from Polybius' hand it must be one of the last things he wrote. A report in a not very reliable source attributes his death to a fall from his horse at the age of 82.[63]

3.

He left his *Histories* complete,[64] not his only work, but the only (partially) surviving one, and the one for which he is rightly remembered. About its plan and its revision he has a great deal to say,[65] yet it remains obscure when and in what circumstances he first conceived it. In its final form its purpose is clear; one has only to read the declaration of intention in Chapter 1 of book i and the summary in the epilogue at the end of book xxxix to be in no doubt about that. 'Who', he enquires,[66] 'is so thoughtless and so irresponsible as not to wish to know by what means, and under what kind of constitution, the Romans succeeded in subjecting nearly the whole inhabited world to their sole rule in not quite fifty-three years—an event unique in history?' It is certainly hard to imagine how he could have conceived a work with this object before he came to Rome and became the friend of Scipio. But that is not to say that he had not written history before 168. At one time Gelzer ventured the hypothesis[67] that after his arrival in Rome Polybius began by writing a work on Achaea as part of a campaign to defend and secure the release of the detained Achaeans, and that he incorporated this work in his *Histories* after 146; he has since changed his mind and now believes[68] that Poly-

[62] See my *Commentary*, i. 373 on iii. 39. 8; addendum in vol. ii. 636 for the suggestion that Polybius obtained information about this road from Achaean troops who had served in Gaul under Cn. Domitius Ahenobarbus (*SEG*, xv. 254); against the view that this inscription belongs to 192 (L. Moretti, 'Per la storia della lega achea', *Riv. fil.* 93 (1965), 278–83) see Larsen, *Federal states*, 501 n. 1.   [63] Ps.-Lucian, *Macrobioi*, 23.

[64] For the epilogue see xxxix. 8. 1–8, especially 8. 3, παραγεγονότες ἐπὶ τὸ τέρμα τῆς ὅλης πραγματείας.

[65] See especially iii. 1–3 (original plan), 4–5 (continuation to 146/5).

[66] i. 1. 5; cf. xxxix. 8. 7. See below, p. 130 n. 1.

[67] 'Die hellenische ΠΡΟΚΑΤΑΣΚΕΥΗ im zweiten Buche des Polybios', *Kl. Schr.* iii. 111–22, following Laqueur, 10–11; see my criticisms in *Commentary*, i. 215–16 on ii. 37–70. M. Treu, 'Biographie und Historie bei Polybios', *Historia*, 3 (1954/5), 219–28, thought the Achaean chapters of book ii were derived from Polybius' *Life of Philopoemen*, where they originally formed an excursus; I find this improbable.

[68] 'Über die Arbeitsweise des Polybios', *Kl. Schr.* iii. 178 n. 133 (cf. 206, reviewing my *Commentary*, vol. i). This revised view follows Ziegler, col. 1476.

bius had already completed an Achaean history before he came to Rome, and indeed that it was the composition of his encomiastic biography of Philopoemen[69] that led him on to a larger work taking up the history of Achaea where Aratus' *Memoirs* laid it down in 220.[70] This is not impossible; but it rests entirely on speculation. In fact, although it seems likely that the *Philopoemen* was an early work, perhaps inspired by the emotion of having been chosen to carry the hero's ashes in his funeral cortège, this also cannot be proved[71]—though if Plutarch's *Life of Philopoemen* derives from Polybius' biography, then the absence from it of any passage corresponding to the discussion of Philopoemen's policy and the comparison with that of Aristaenus which we find in book xxiv of the *Histories* could indicate that the biography was an earlier and less mature work. However, other views about its composition can be defended, and it has even been argued that Polybius composed it after arriving at Rome as an educational model for Scipio Aemilianus. This at least seems highly unlikely.[72] One did not

Petzold, *Studien*, 91–128, has argued that the Achaean chapters represent an earlier work inserted in book ii of the *Histories* in the revised edition, where they were to illustrate Polybius' mature conviction that ethical principles were what really mattered in politics. He suggests (p. 95) that they were intended to illuminate the αἱρέσεις of victims and vanquished (though in iii. 4. 6–7 Polybius speaks only of the αἵρεσις τῶν κρατούντων and of the opinions and views of others about them) and to contrast a state based on ἰσότης and φιλανθρωπία— Achaea—with the domination of Rome based on δυνάμεις. This seems to me precisely the sort of contrast Polybius would not have cared to make; see further my comments in *JRS*, 60 (1970), 252.

[69] On this see x. 21. 5–8 (with my *Commentary*, ii. 221–2). H. Homeyer, 'Beobachtungen zu den hellenistischen Quellen der Plutarch-Viten', *Klio*, 45 (1963), 155 n. 5, has argued that Polybius' *Philopoemen* was an encomiastic biography arranged chronologically rather than a formal encomium; so too Petzold, *Studien*, 12 n. 5. Errington, *Philopoemen*, 236–7, queries the view, usual since Nissen, *Untersuchungen*, 280–7, that Polybius' *Philopoemen* was a source for Plutarch's *Life*, but admits that the question cannot be resolved firmly in either direction.

[70] Presumably (on this hypothesis) what are now the Achaean chapters of book ii were included in this Achaean history as an introduction.

[71] Plut. *Philop.* 21. 5. See Errington, *Philopoemen*, 232–6, for a full discussion of Polybius' *Philopoemen*. The view that it was written soon after Philopoemen's death is that of Ziegler, col. 1472, and derives from Nissen, *Untersuchungen*, 280–1.

[72] Pédech's view ('Polybe et l'éloge de Philopoimen', *REG*, 64 (1951), 82–103; cf. Wunderer, *Forschungen*, i. 87) that Polybius wrote the *Life* at Rome as an educational model for Scipio Aemilianus depends largely on an analysis of the supposed structure of the work, which would make it primarily concerned with Philopoemen's education and early years. Against this reconstruction see my *Commentary*, ii. 222 on x. 21. 5–8, Petzold, *Studien*, 12–13 n. 5, and

ask Roman nobles to model themselves on Greek *condottieri*, however distinguished; and if one is looking for an educational model
for Aemilianus, his addiction to the *Cyropaedia* of Xenophon is
doubly attested.[73]

Polybius wrote other minor works, none of them datable with
certainty. His *Numantine War*[74] is necessarily later than 133, an
old man's work, now lost, which need not concern us here. But
his treatise on *Tactics*,[75] referred to in book ix, and later mentioned
in Aelian and Arrian, may belong either to his early years, or to his
time at Rome; unless the passage in book ix which mentions it[76] is
a later insertion—and there is no reason to think this—it preceded
the *Histories*. Still more tenuous and obscure is a monograph mentioned by Geminus—if indeed it was not simply a section of book
xxxiv—on the habitability of the equatorial regions;[77] it may have
been written after his Atlantic voyage, but in fact its date of composition is quite unknown. Thus, none of these minor works is of
much help to us in dating the *Histories*; and the parts of the latter
which deal with Achaea and the unification of the Peloponnese
seem to fit naturally enough into the greater work, where indeed

Errington, *Philopoemen*, 232–4 (though Errington is nonetheless prepared to
entertain the view that the work may have been intended as a model for the
young Scipio).

[73] Cic. *Tusc.* ii. 62; *ad Q. fratr.* i. 1. 23. It is of course true (cf. Errington,
Philopoemen, 236 n. 1) that an addiction to the *Cyropaedia* need not exclude other
reading.

[74] Cic. *fam.* v. 12. 2; see above, p. 12 n. 60. Polybius' monograph may lie
behind part of Appian's account in *Hisp.* 76–98 (cf. A. Schulten, *Numantia, die
Ergebnisse der Ausgrabungen, 1905–1912* (Munich, 1914–1931), i. 284; iii. 7;
'Numantia, eine topographische–historische Untersuchung', *Abhandlung der
göttingischen Gesellschaft der Wissenschaften*, phil.-hist. Kl. N.F. 8. 4 (1905), 77;
RE, 'Numantia', col. 1260); but P. Rutilius Rufus' account was also used
(cf. Norden, *Urgeschichte*, 436 f.).

[75] ix. 20. 4, ἐν τοῖς περὶ τὰς τάξεις ὑπομνήμασιν; this work is also mentioned
by various tactical writers (Arrian, *Tact.* 1. 1; Aelian, *Tact.* 1. 3–4, 19. 10).
Against the view that Polybius' study was the source of Asclepiodotus' *Tactics*
(K. K. Müller, *RE*, 'Asklepiodotos (10)', cols. 1637–41; W. W. Tarn, *OCD*,
'Asclepiodotus') see Pédech, *Polybe i*, p. xiii, who points out that Asclepiodotus'
work was a service manual, dealing only with army structure and formations,
a much narrower field than that which interested Polybius.

[76] ix. 12–20; Pédech, *Polybe i*, p. xiii, thinks it was written at Rome in exile;
and Werner, 15–16, adopts the same date, after Polybius had served as hipparch.
But it can just as easily have been written in Achaea (so Ziegler, col. 1473).

[77] Geminus, 16. 32–8 ed. Manitius, περὶ τῆς ὑπὸ τὸν ἰσημερινὸν οἰκήσεως.
For the view that it was part of book xxxiv see M. C. P. Schmidt, *Jahrbücher*,
125 (1882), 114–22; Pédech, *Méthode*, 590 n. 436; it was first suggested by
Schweighaeuser, v. 25 note f.

they constitute a minor variation on the major theme of oecumenical unity under the guidance of Rome.[78]

If the conception of the *Histories* is hard to date, the stages of its composition and publication are even more controversial. We may, I think, dismiss a recent hypothesis[79] that the work was composed in its entirety after 146 and Polybius' return to Greece. A series of passages in the earlier books down to xv mention Carthage in the present tense as if it still existed, and these can only have been written before its destruction in 146; Erbse's assertion that such present tenses are 'timeless'—'achronistic presents' to use his phrase—seems plausible in one or two cases, but improbable in others, and quite impossible in some.[80] But it is another matter to discover how many books had been written by the end of Polybius' exile—and still yet another to be sure how many had been published by then. The problem is complicated by the fact that book iii contains clear evidence of a change in plan.[81] The first three chapters of this book, which is the first to deal with the main period of his *Histories*—books i and ii being introductory—sketch the contents of the years from 220 to 168; chapters 4 and 5 however outline his intention to extend the account down to the end of the Achaean War in 146, and explain why Polybius feels it necessary to do this. In the final form, books i to xxix of the *Histories* are devoted to Olympiads 140 to 152 inclusive, that is 220/19 to 169/8 B.C., and books xxx to xxxix to Olympiads 153 to 158, that is 168/7 to 145/4 (or in fact more probably 146/5) B.C. (Book xl was devoted to a chronological résumé and some kind of list of contents.)[82] So in effect the revised plan added another third to the

---

[78] Cf. Petzold, *Studien*, 25 ff.

[79] H. Erbse, 'Zur Entstehung des polybianischen Geschichtswerkes', *Rh. Mus.* 94 (1951), 157–79; 'Polybios-Interpretationen', *Phil.* 101 (1957), 269–97. Against Erbse's theory see D. Musti, 'Problemi polibiani', *La parola del passato*, 104 (1965), 383–4; F. W. Walbank, 'Three notes on Polybius xii', *Studi alessandrini*, 203–8.

[80] Cf. i. 73. 4; vi. 52. 1–3, 56. 1–3; ix. 9. 9–10; xiv. 10. 5; xv. 30. 10; xxxi. 12. 12 (of which the last is a special case, since it occurs in what was apparently a memorandum composed at the time of the events described and later incorporated in the revised plan of the *Histories*; see below, p. 18 nn. 84–6). Of these passages, ix. 9. 9–10 in particular resists Erbse's interpretation, since Polybius says there that he is writing to furnish useful *exempla* to the leaders of Rome *and Carthage* and to those who may be in charge of public affairs elsewhere in the future.   [81] iii. 4–5.

[82] Cf. xxxix. 8. 8, λείπεται διασαφῆσαι τοὺς χρόνους περιειλημμένους ὑπὸ τῆς ἱστορίας καὶ τὸ πλῆθος τῶν βύβλων καὶ ⟨τὸν⟩ ἀριθμὸν τῆς ὅλης πραγ-

size of the whole work. It has commonly been assumed that Polybius decided on this extension only after the destruction of Carthage and Corinth in 146; and indeed it is obvious that in the form of an extension down to 146 this must be true. He might of

ματείας. This seems to imply some kind of chronologically arranged résumé, with a contents list of the various books (though the phrase ἀριθμὸν τῆς... πραγματείας is strange). This sentence, which concludes the extract (and apparently the book) is followed in the MS (M) by these words:

ἐν τῶι περὶ τοῦ τίς τί ἐξεῦρε:
τέλος τῆς πολυβίου ἱστορίας λόγου λθ ⲱ τὸν μ̄ λόγον.
περὶ γνωμικῶν ἀποστομισμάτων.

No wholly satisfactory explanation of this subscription has been proposed. The words ⲱ τὸν μ̄ λόγον were transposed by Mai (*Scriptorum veterum nova collatio e Vaticanis codicibus edita*, ii, Rome, Vatican, 1827) to follow ἐξεῦρε, by Struve (reviewing Mai's work in Jahn's *Jahrbücher*, 7 (1828), 374) to the beginning of the extract—on the assumption that ⲱ was a sign of omission, and by de Boor ('Die Excerptsammlungen des Porphyrogennetos', *Hermes* 19 (1884), 140–8) to follow ἀποστομισμάτων (where he takes the meaning to be 'look for book 40—missing in my (the excerptor's) copy'). Both Mai and de Boor understood the words ἐν τῶι περὶ τοῦ τίς τί ἐξεῦρε to refer to another section of the excerpts, entitled *de rerum inventoribus*; and de Boor, who questioned Mai's assumption that book 40 would fall under such a heading, postulated a discussion at the end of xxxix. 8, and within that book, on the character and merits of Polybius' index, which would have some relevance to a set of extracts entitled *de rerum inventoribus*. Such a discussion would, however, be wholly out of place, following on the present xxxix. 8, which as it stands clearly marks the end of the *Histories* proper. Nissen, 'Die Oekonomie der Geschichte des Polybios', *Rh. Mus.* 26 (1871), 278, suggested that τίς τί ἐξεῦρε might well be a Byzantine excerptor's name for an index, on the analogy of τί ποῦ κεῖται, used for the index of basilicas or the *Tipucitus* of the Byzantine jurists. But, as de Boor (art. cit. 143–4) observes, τίς τί ἐξεῦρε needs the addition of ποῦ to enable it to serve as a title for an index, and indeed, even with such an addition, it remains highly implausible, for an index is concerned not with who found what, but with where the reader is to find what he is looking for. Moreover, as de Boor points out, it would be more natural for a reader of the Constantinian excerpts to be directed to another section of the excerpts rather than to be told to look for something in the index volume (of Polybius), which he does not possess; and further, if τίς τί ἐξεῦρε referred to the index of Polybius' *Histories*, one would expect to be told to 'look for the index in book 40' rather than 'look for book 40 in the index'. So on the whole, and with some hesitation, I follow Struve in transposing ⲱ τὸν μ̄ λόγον to precede ἐν τῶι...ἐξεῦρε, and translate: 'For the fortieth book look in the section *de rerum inventoribus*. End of book 39 of Polybius' *History* (for the section) *On didactic lessons*.' The relevance of material contained in book 40 to extracts *de rerum inventoribus* remains a difficulty; but without knowing how the book was organised and just what was included in it, one is not entitled to dismiss what on all other counts remains the most likely interpretation of this passage. (Nissen may be right, following Dindorf, in correcting ἀποστομισμάτων to ἀποστοματισμάτων.)

course have decided to write an extension[83] down to some earlier
date and then, after 146, have fixed on that as the most appropriate point at which to finish; and this view gains some superficial support from a passage in book xxxi,[84] dealing with events
of Ol. 154. 3, that is 163/2 B.C., in which Carthage is clearly referred
to as still existing, and which might therefore be supposed to have
been written before its destruction in 146. But here appearances
are misleading. The reference to Carthage in book xxxi comes in the
passage already mentioned which tells how Polybius engineered
the escape of the Seleucid prince Demetrius from Rome. De Sanctis
suggested, with great plausibility,[85] that Polybius wrote a memorandum on the affair immediately after its occurrence, and later
incorporated this in the extension of his *Histories*. If so, this passage
clearly cannot be used as evidence that Polybius had already
carried his *Histories* beyond 168 before 146—though it does show
that in preparing such a personal ὑπόμνημα or 'memorandum',
and no doubt other similar ones, he was at any rate envisaging
the possibility of writing about this later period. Whether he already
saw this as an extension of his main work or as a separate treatise
we cannot tell. Indeed there is no way of knowing whether Polybius had yet taken any decision about this; he may simply have gone
on making notes and collecting material out of ingrained habit.[86]

If, however, the mention of Carthage in book xxxi throws no
light on the composition of the *Histories*, there is no evidence that
Polybius had written beyond book xv by 146, since the last previous
reference to Carthage as being still in existence occurs in that
book,[87] which deals with the events of 203/2. Therefore it may
fairly be assumed that Polybius' decision to extend his *Histories* to
cover the twenty-two years from 168 to 146 was taken after the
catastrophic events of the latter year. But how much was actually
written by 146—or should we say, by 150, since it is unlikely that
the events of 150 to 145 left Polybius much time for composition?
Ziegler[88] has argued that by that year he had already got down
to Pydna and the embassy of Popillius Laenas to Antiochus in

---

[83] So Svoboda, 'Die Abfassungszeit des Geschichtswerkes des Polybios',
Phil. 72 (1913), 465–83.   [84] xxxi. 12. 12.

[85] iii. 1. 202 f.; see Gelzer, 'Über die Arbeitsweise des Polybios', *Kl. Schr.*
iii. 161–4, on the importance of this passage on the escape of Demetrius as an
indication of Polybius' method of composition. See below, p. 75.

[86] See below, pp. 182–3.

[87] xv. 30. 10.   [88] Col. 1477.

Egypt—in short that his original plan had been completed—and that he wrote books xxx–xl afterwards in Greece or elsewhere. As far as I can see, this proposition can be neither proved nor disproved. Aymard argued that a reference in book xviii to Aristaenus' success in preserving Achaea by securing the transfer of Achaean support to Rome in 198 could hardly have been written after the dissolution of the confederacy in 146;[89] but Aristaenus' policy could be justified from the territorial expansion of Achaea in the half-century following 198 quite irrespective of what happened in 146, and Aymard's conclusion seems unwarranted. On the other hand, a reference in the same book[90] to the destruction of Carthage cannot be used to prove incontrovertibly that book xviii as a whole must have been written after 146, since it occurs in a discussion of Roman integrity in which mention is made of a later passage in book xxxi[91] on the character of Aemilius Paullus and that of Scipio Aemilianus, which clearly hints at Scipio's death.[92] It seems virtually certain that this later passage was written after 129; and on balance it is likely that the passage in book xviii which refers forward to it was composed at the same time and is consequently to be regarded as a later insertion in the text of that book. Summarising then, one can only say that there is no certain proof that Polybius had written beyond book xv by 150, when his exile ended, but that it is equally impossible to disprove the view that he had completed his *Histories* down to Pydna by that date.

4.

There is another, related, problem: how much of the work had been presented to the public by 146? It has been observed[93] that

[89] Aymard, 'Le fragment de Polybe "sur les traîtres" (xviii. 13–15)', *Études*, 356 n. 8. But this view rests partly on the belief that νῦν δέ in 13. 9 is contrasted with τότε in 13. 8, whereas in fact τότε refers back to ἐξ αὐτῶν τῶν ἐνεστώτων in 13. 7, and νῦν δέ means 'as it was'. More important, the rightness or wrongness of Aristaenus' decision was to be judged in the light of the situation when it was taken (τῆς παρ' αὐτὸν τὸν καιρὸν ἀσφαλείας (13. 9)), not of developments fifty years later. On this fragment of Polybius see below, pp. 84–6.

[90] xviii. 35. 9.

[91] xxxi. 22–30 (see especially 22. 4 and 23. 1 for references back and xviii. 36. 1 for a reference forward).

[92] xxxi. 28. 13; another passage which seems to imply the death of Scipio is xxxviii. 21. 3, ἀνδρός ἐστι μεγάλου καὶ τελείου καὶ συλλήβδην ἀξίου μνήμης.

[93] Cf. my *Commentary*, i. 293–4.

several passages in books iii and iv seem to have some bearing on
the political situation in Rome or Achaea just before 150, and
would be consistent with publication about then. The topicality of
the Punic treaties[94] about this time was first pointed out by
Mommsen;[95] and the earnest recommendation of the Acarnanians
as allies,[96] the exhortation to Arcadia and Messenia to unite
against Sparta,[97] and to Elis to resume her ancient (and in reality
imaginary) *asylia*,[98] all read somewhat oddly in their context yet
would not be out of place in the situation just before 150, when
events were working up towards a new Achaean confrontation
with Sparta, and would have little point after 146. Such parochial
references may seem out of place in a universal history;[99] but
there they are, and clearly intended to be of relevance, and it is
entirely in accordance with Polybius' views about the utility of
his *Histories* that he should have included them.[100] They suggest
publication of books i to iv—together with v, which connects
closely with iv—by about 150; and book vi, discussing the Roman
constitution, may well have come out at about the same time.[101]
Indeed it has been argued that books i to vi appeared together as
a first edition,[102] since in his introduction to book xi Polybius
states[103] that books i to vi were originally equipped with προγραφαί,
lists of contents attached to the outside of the scroll or preceding
the text inside, but that this was not true of the later books. Such
προγραφαί have not survived: but it need not be assumed that
they were lost in a second edition, for Polybius refers to their

[94] iii. 21. 9 f.
[95] Mommsen, *Chronologie*, 320 ff.   [96] iv. 30. 5.
[97] iv. 31. 3–33. 12.   [98] iv. 73. 6–74. 3.
[99] Cf. Gelzer, *Kl. Schr.* iii. 209, 'Der Gedanke, dass an so versteckter Stelle in
einer Universalgeschichte vorgebrachte Meinungen gerade i. J. 150 auf
Messenier und Elier Eindruck machen würden, scheint mir wunderlich'.
[100] Cf. A. H. McDonald, *JRS*, 48 (1958), 180, 'The issue is not whether
a universal history may or may not be influenced by pamphleteering purposes.
It simply means that Polybius had brought a substantial part of his draft to
a stage at which he could begin publishing it, about 150, and in doing so
pointed its topical significance.'
[101] Cf. Brink and Walbank, 'The construction of the sixth book of Polybius',
CQ, 4 (1954), 100–1. It is of course theoretically possible that Polybius wrote his
work including these topical passages without taking the necessary steps to
ensure that they were read—by publishing them; but I find this alternative
unlikely.
[102] See De Sanctis, iii. 1. 205, following Leo, i. 326 n. 1.
[103] xi. 1 a. 5: the reading of the MS (M), ϛ, was emended to ε′ by Mai and
to ι′ by Cobet. Against any change see my *Commentary*, ii. 267 ad loc.

vulnerability, and they could have got detached and lost at any time in the history of the text. Polybius in fact explains that he has included προγραφαί in the first six books and omitted them from the rest of his work because he thought it more appropriate to write prefaces (προεκθέσεις) to each separate Olympiad, once he had reached the period—roughly from 216 onwards—when the interconnection of events justified the full use of the Olympiad-year arrangement. This being so, the original use of προγραφαί for books i to vi is not to be taken as evidence that their publication in a first edition came all at once, and distinct from the rest of the *Histories*. Indeed, there is some evidence that these books were published in succession, rather than in a single batch. In book v there is a reference[104] to the famous Rhodian earthquake of about 227 which is so ill-adapted to its present position and would have been so entirely appropriate to the discussion of Rhodian affairs in book iv,[105] that Holleaux suggested[106] with some plausibility that Polybius had already published book iv when he decided to include this digression. If this is so, it indicates piecemeal publication of books i to v before 150; but it does not of course tell us anything about how far the publication went.

Polybius' purpose in writing was to awaken his fellow-countrymen to the significance of Rome and to explain the character of the Roman constitution and the growth of Roman power to men who were increasingly having to deal with Roman envoys and generals. This purpose could only be achieved by publication; and since between 168 and 150 Polybius had written at least the first fifteen books (if not more) there seems to have been every reason why he should have gone ahead and published them. This cannot be proved; but there is no valid reason against it,[107] and it is a plausible hypothesis that by 147 or thereabouts books i to xv had been not only written but also published. Indeed, if Polybius' purpose was to publish his account of the events down to the end of the Hannibalic War, he may also have included book xvi, which contained Scipio's triumph; on the other hand, this book opens up a set of new events in the Aegean which lead on directly to the Second Macedonian War, and if Polybius *did* pause in his

[104] v. 88–90.   [105] iv. 47–56.
[106] Holleaux, *Études*, i. 445–62.
[107] So A. H. McDonald, *JRS*, 48 (1958), 180; Gelzer, *Kl. Schr.* iii. 209; Mioni, 33–48. This modifies the view expressed in my *Commentary*, i. 295, that only books i–vi were published before 150–145.

writing and publication at this point, book xv was on the whole the more appropriate place to do so.[108]

Where Polybius published is unknown; and equally unknown is the size of the edition. Indeed both questions may be anachronistic, for once the original manuscript, the αὐτόγραφον, had been copied, and a copy or copies distributed—whether privately or through bookshops—the book may be said to have been published; and the multiplication of copies was something that could go on over the years to meet the demand,[109] for there were no laws of copyright. Rome will have had plenty of facilities for copying Greek works, and the early books may well have come out there—though if so, Polybius must have taken steps to get copies to his intended public in Greece. Whether the later books were copied in Greece or Rome is unknown.

For after 146, as we have seen,[110] Polybius decided to extend his *Histories* to cover the events down to that date. The final work comprising all 40 books appeared in his lifetime: at any rate his epilogue has survived.[111] A reference to his death in a passage in book xxxix,[112] describing the honours paid to him in Achaea after 146, must imply a posthumous edition; but this is no proof that it was the first one. Indeed it seems unlikely that Polybius, when already an old man of over 70, would turn aside to write a monograph on the Numantine War, unless his main work was already finished and either already published or at least in the publisher's hands.[113]

---

[108] Despite the statement to the contrary in *Commentary*, ii. 540 on xvi. 29. 12.

[109] On this see Birt, *Buchwesen*, 342–70.

[110] See above, p. 18.

[111] xxxix. 8; and see below, p. 23 n. 115. A. Philippson. *Phil. Woch.* 1930, 1181–2, argued that Cicero, *rep.* ii, drew largely on Polybius vi and that when in ii. 21 Laelius describes Scipio's argument as one 'quae nusquam est in Graecorum libris', this is meant to indicate that in 129 B.C., the dramatic date of the dialogue, Polybius vi was not yet published. But this is to press Cicero altogether too hard; and moreover the *ratio ad disputandum nova* there mentioned is probably not derived from Polybius at all (cf. Laqueur, *Phil. Woch.* 1924, 334); hence no conclusions follow for the date of publication of Polybius vi.   [112] xxxix. 5. 4.

[113] This does not of course exclude such later additions as the passages which imply Scipio's death (see above, p. 19 n. 92) or the reference to the laying down of the via Domitia (see above, pp. 12–13 nn. 61–2); cf. Gelzer, *Kl. Schr.* iii. 209, 'Die genannten Einschübe waren danach für eine "Ausgabe letzter Hand" bestimmt'. I assume it to be likely (though obviously it cannot be proved) that Polybius wrote his monograph on the Numantine War shortly after its conclusion; it must have been a project in which Scipio was deeply interested.

It is clear that in the edition of the whole work some changes were made in the earlier books to conform to the extended plan and to take account of later events. A good many of these occur in book iii which, as I have already mentioned, contains an addition to the introduction[114] explaining why Polybius now proposes to carry his narrative down to 146 and sketching the events to be contained in books xxx–xxxix. A few chapters later there is a reference[115] to the fall of Carthage and the ease with which one can read the forty books of the *Histories*—thanks to the careful principles governing their composition—evidently a reply to criticism that the work was hard to come by and difficult to read (δύσκτητον...καὶ δυσ⟨ανά⟩γνωστον) because of its scope and length.[116] But many of the additions seem to concern the geography of the west and to be inserted in book iii because its subject matter included Hannibal's march from Spain and so lent itself to comments of this kind. For example, the remark[117] that the part of Europe bounded by the Outer Sea—the Atlantic—has no common name because it has only recently come under Roman observation is probably a late insertion following the campaign of D. Iunius Brutus Callaicus in north-west Spain in 138/7 B.C.[118] The reference to the laying down of the Via Domitia has already been mentioned:[119] that it falls into place as one of a number

[114] iii. 4–5.

[115] iii. 32. 2. This passage does not necessarily imply that when Polybius wrote it all the forty books of his work were already available to the public, only that they were planned and perhaps mostly if not all written. It could be argued from the passage in which Polybius tells how he sent corrections to Zeno (xvi. 20. 5 f.), but how the unfortunate man, knowing that it was impossible to make any change διὰ τὸ προεκδεδωκέναι τὰς συντάξεις, ἐλυπήθη μὲν ὡς ἔνι μάλιστα, ποιεῖν δ' οὐδὲν εἶχε, that once a book was 'published' no changes were possible; and clearly under ancient conditions there was nothing like a 'revised edition' in the modern sense (cf. p. 22 n. 109). But Polybius may simply mean that Zeno could not eliminate errors from the copies that had gone out, not that there was no possibility of a revised text in copies to be made in the future. That such changes could be made after 'publication' is not merely inherently likely in itself, but is proved by a comparison of iii. 32. 1 (previous publication implied) and xxxix. 5. 4 (implying Polybius' death; there seem no good reasons for extruding the words καὶ ζῶντα καὶ μεταλλάξαντα as a gloss).

[116] Cf. Birt, *Buchwesen*, 312–15, who points out that Polybius' books, compared with those of other writers, were in fact large and clumsy.

[117] iii. 37. 11.

[118] The reference (xvi. 29. 12) to τὴν ἀγνωσίαν τῆς ἐκτὸς θαλάσσης seems more naturally to apply to a time before the coast of north-west Spain was known.   [119] See above, pp. 12–13.

of geographical insertions in this book is perhaps an additional argument for its authenticity—though indeed it must have been inserted as an addendum after 118. Another late passage is the geographical digression which stands immediately after the description of Hannibal's arrival in the Po valley,[120] for this not only refers forward to book xxxiv, which is devoted to geographical matters, but also mentions Polybius' own voyages on the Atlantic,[121] and the new opportunities for study now enjoyed by Greeks, who are relieved from the ambitions of a military or political career[122]—a wry comment on the enforced leisure of the years after 146. There are also two passages which seem to imply that the frontier of Italy was at the Rubicon,[123] and will therefore have been written or adapted after 133, if indeed it was Tiberius Gracchus who made the change from the River Aesis.

One of the more striking passages in the *Histories* is Polybius' account in book x of the capture of New Carthage by the elder Scipio. If, as seems likely,[124] Polybius' visit to that city was in 151 in the company of Scipio Aemilianus, his reference to autopsy[125] may well have been inserted into an account already written (but perhaps not yet published) and need not be taken as evidence for the composition of book x after 150; for the impression here is of a superficial adjustment to a narrative already worked out in detail on the basis of several sources, written and oral.[126] Finally,

[120] iii. 57–9.   [121] iii. 59. 7.

[122] iii. 59. 4; it can hardly refer to the internment of the Achaean leaders in Italy between 167 and 150 (so R. Thommen, 'Über die Abfassungszeit der Geschichten des Polybios', *Hermes*, 20 (1885), 215).

[123] iii. 61. 11, 86. 2; it was argued by Cuntz, 27–34, that these two passages must have been written after the frontier of Italy had been moved northward (for the change see Strabo, v. 217), and he showed convincingly that the figures for the distances between Iapygia (S. Maria di Leuca) and Aquileia given in Strabo, vi. 285 (Polyb. xxxiv. 11. 8), imply the Rubicon frontier; this is also to be assumed in *CIL*, i². 2. 719, where the Gracchan *tresviri* of 132 are active near Fanum and Pisaurum in the *ager Gallicus*, i.e. between the Aesis and the Rubicon. This evidence is against the assumption of Mommsen, *RG*, ii. 355 n. 1 (cf. E. G. Hardy, 'The transpadane question and the alien act of 65 or 64 B.C.', *JRS*, 6 (1916), 65 ff.; U. Ewins, 'The enfranchisement of Cisalpine Gaul', *BSR*, 23 (1955), 75–6), that the extension did not take place until Sulla.   [124] See above, p. 11.

[125] x. 11. 4, οὐ γὰρ ἐξ ἀκοῆς ἡμεῖς, ἀλλ' αὐτόπται γεγονότες μετ' ἐπιστάσεως ἀποφαινόμεθα.

[126] On the sources used by Polybius for his account of Scipio's capture of New Carthage (x. 6. 1–20. 8) see Walbank, 'The Scipionic legend', *Proc. Camb. Phil. Soc.* 13 (1967), 54–69, especially 59 ff. It is only for the length of the walls that he supports his statement with a claim that he has actually seen them.

it is at least a possibility that book xii, in the form in which we partially possess it now, was composed after 146, and perhaps first appeared as part of the final edition. A Herodotean-like excursus on the fruit of the lotus,[127] which has survived only because Athenaeus compared it with Herodotus' account of date-palms in Babylon, and an assertion[128] that the real historian must be a man capable of sustaining the labours and hardships of the much-travelled Odysseus—he is even inspired to quote three passages of Homer to underline this point—seem both to have been written after Polybius' journey to Africa and his voyage on the outer ocean. This does not of course in itself prove that the whole book was late, since an original draft can have been planned, sketched in and even published by 147 or 146; on the other hand, the central theme of the book—the shortcomings of the historian Timaeus—develops out of a criticism of his misstatements concerning Africa,[129] and this is something about which Polybius is more likely to have been sensitive after he had become an authority on that continent, than before 151/0 when he visited it for the first time. However, I propose to say rather more about book xii in the next chapter.[130]

5.

I have been discussing the composition of a history which in its final form probably extended to about five times the length of Thucydides, and on which Polybius will have been working, with interruptions, for something like fifty years. Given this situation, it is not surprising that attempts have been made to trace some development in Polybius' ideas, and even to dissect his work into a series of chronological layers and phases. The enterprise is notably dangerous and so far the results achieved have been meagre. The most famous example of this kind of approach is the disastrous experiment of Laqueur in which he claimed to identify five successive stages in Polybius' historical thought,[131] but failed to

---

[127] xii. 2 = Athen. xiv. 651 d. Pédech, *Polybe i*, p. xli, sees the influence of Callisthenes in this kind of digression.

[128] xii. 28. 1; the quotations from the *Odyssey* (i. 1–2, 3–4, viii. 183 = *Iliad*, xxiv. 8) are in 27. 10–11. See further below, pp. 51–2.

[129] Cf. Schweighaeuser, vii. 71–2, following Reiske; Africa comes to the fore at the point where Scipio Africanus is about to carry the war over into that continent (in 204). See my *Commentary*, ii. 317.

[130] See below, pp. 51 ff.   [131] See his *Polybius*, passim.

produce results which have seemed convincing to anyone else. This is indeed a warning to others. Nevertheless it remains true that no man can remain entirely the same for fifty years; and Polybius has given us some indications of his change of mind, especially in the passage in which he discusses the extension of the *Histories* to cover the years from 168 to 146.

As I have already indicated,[132] his fundamental purpose remained unchanged from his first chapter to his epilogue. It was one which grew out of his own political experience and was directly related to what he knew were the needs of his own people living under the shadow of the cloud from the west. But of course those needs themselves changed, with changes in the situation of the Greek states. After 146, as we have seen, any dream of an independent political and military career for the Greeks of the mainland had faded—as it had faded for the Greeks of Italy after 270 and for the Greeks of Sicily after 241, or at the latest 211. Twenty years earlier, in 168, the picture was very different. Roman power was already supreme in the Mediterranean; but this was not in itself necessarily disastrous to Greece, nor had it removed all independence. Indeed, the Roman alliance had enabled Achaea to incorporate the whole Peloponnese. After Pydna there had been problems and for many, including Polybius, personal disaster; but Achaea and Greece generally might still hope to prosper, if only Greeks could be made to understand Roman aims and methods. In trying to interpret Rome and its constitution to his Greek readers between 168 and 146, Polybius was writing with a very specific political purpose in mind, and this purpose sprang directly out of his Peloponnesian background. The same is true of much else in his *Histories* which at first sight seems part of his universal theme.

For example, his account of the rise of Rome naturally involved describing the fall of Macedonia; but the importance he attributes to this in the context of what is nominally a universal history clearly reflects the perspectives of a Peloponnesian Greek. Polybius describes with amazement Demetrius of Phalerum's prophecy[133] of the future downfall of Macedon, and he sees the counterpart of this in the rise of Rome, and believes that he has in his own lifetime seen this prophecy fulfilled. But this is a distortion of history. Antigonid Macedonia was in reality only one of several

---

[132] See above, p. 13.   [133] xxix. 21.

Hellenistic states which shared Alexander's heritage, and it was only to an Achaean like Polybius—or of course a Macedonian like Perseus[134]—that Pydna, rather than Magnesia for instance, could appear as the direct counterpart of Issus and Gaugamela. This Peloponnesian bias shows in other ways too; for example, Polybius accompanies his main theme with a variation[135]—the rise of Achaea to include the whole of the Peloponnese. It was a convenient coincidence that here too Macedonia played a dominant role; and just as the rise of Rome brought up the issue of Demetrius' prophecy and Alexander's conquest of Persia, so the relations between Achaea and Macedon in the third century recalled the problems arising out of the relations between Philip II and the Greeks in the fourth. This is a point to which I shall return later.[136]

6.

During the period down to 150 Polybius regarded his *Histories* as furnishing practical help to Greeks—politicians and others—who still had room for political manoeuvre, but who must learn to understand the nature of Roman power and how to deal with it if their political actions were not to lead to disaster. The events of 146 changed this situation, and in extending the scope of his *Histories* to cover the years 168 to 146 Polybius also indicates a new purpose. It is still essential for his contemporaries to understand Rome, for practical reasons; but in his programme we also find him looking ahead to posterity. From 168 onwards, he writes,[137] Roman power was complete: it was universally accepted that henceforth everyone must submit to Rome and obey her orders. But judgements regarding either conquerors or conquered which rest solely on the actual struggle cannot be final;[138] for a full assessment it is necessary to show how the victors used their power and how the rest reacted to them. Such an assessment will enable his contemporaries to decide whether Roman rule is a thing to be avoided or welcomed (φευκτὴν ἢ αἱρετήν);[139] and since he has just explained

---

[134] Polybius attributes his reflections on Fortune at this point to some person whom the excerptor has not named, but who appears to be Perseus; but in fact they are Polybius' own thoughts (see above, p. 2 n. 10).

[135] ii. 37. 7–11; for the αὔξησις καὶ προκοπή of the Achaean confederation (ii. 45. 1) as a parallel to the αὔξησις καὶ κατασκευή of Rome (ii. 2. 2) see Petzold, *Studien*, 25 ff.

[136] See below, pp. 85 ff.   [137] iii. 4. 2–3.

[138] iii. 4. 4–6.   [139] iii. 4. 7.

that it has to be accepted as a necessary fact, he can only mean that his history will provide the evidence on which men can decide whether to resist the Romans or embrace their domination willingly as an act of choice.

That is half the story. There is however a second object, to enable future generations to decide whether Roman rule was deserving of praise and admiration or of blame (ἐπαινετὴν καὶ ȝηλωτὴν ἢ ψεκτήν) and Polybius emphasises the fact that this no less than the former purpose is utilitarian. 'Neither the rulers themselves', he writes,[140] 'nor their critics should regard the end of action as being merely conquest and the subjection of all to their rule; since no one who is in his right mind goes to war with his neighbours simply for the sake of crushing an adversary, just as no one sails on the open sea just so as to cross it. Indeed no one even takes up the study of arts and crafts merely for the sake of knowledge, but in all their activities men are universally moved by pleasure, honour or interest.' The utilitarian ideas implicit in this passage are somewhat crude; but they are of a piece with Polybius' views generally. His history is pervaded by a spirit of utilitarianism which embraces all aspects of life;[141] for example music,[142] religion[143] and even the notion of justice[144] are all explained at various times as both coming into existence and continuing to function because they are of practical utility to men. It is not made entirely clear what precise advantage Polybius' future readers[145] are to gain from passing a moral judgement on Roman rule, other than the general advantages that accrue from the study of history; but that they are envisaged as practical— οὐδὲ... αὐτῆς ἕνεκα τῆς ἐπιστήμης—'not merely for the sake of

[140] iii. 4. 9–10.
[141] Cf. Roveri, *Studi*, 106.
[142] iv. 21. 1, on the Arcadian practice of music in order to combat the brutalising effects of the climate.
[143] vi. 56. 6–12, on the use of religion to discipline the plebs at Rome; xvi. 12. 9–11, on the justifiable use of pious fictions among the populace. For Polybius' favourable attitude towards Scipio Africanus' supposed cynical pretence that Neptune had undertaken to help him capture New Carthage see my *Commentary*, ii. 191–6 on x. 2. 1–20. 8.
[144] vi. 6; the concept of justice arises when men see children behaving with ingratitude towards their parents, and envisage the same thing happening to themselves, to their own disadvantage; see my *Commentary*, i. 653–5 for the background of this idea.
[145] iii. 4. 7, τοῖς ἐπιγενομένοις, who are the same as τοῖς ἀποφαινομένοις ὑπὲρ τούτων (i.e. about οἱ ἡγούμενοι) in 4. 9.

knowledge', is made abundantly clear.[146] How in fact he judges Rome and her subjects is a question to which I shall return later when I shall be discussing Polybius' views about Rome generally in more detail.

The period after 168 which is to facilitate these judgements terminates somewhat oddly: it extends, Polybius says,[147] 'until the disturbed and troubled time that followed'. This time of ταραχὴ καὶ κίνησις is not clearly defined chronologically but he says that it is a period of important actions with unexpected events and that he witnessed some of these and took part in and even directed others. The events which he appears to associate with this time of ταραχὴ καὶ κίνησις in his next chapter[148] are in fact a mixed lot, some like the expulsion of Ariarathes from Cappadocia or the war between Prusias and Attalus going back to as early as 158 or 156–154; and since he gives no list of any events between 168 and the onset of the period of disturbance, it looks as if he has not entirely sorted out his ideas on this, or else he has expressed himself very carelessly. There is some reason to think that book xxxiv—his geographical book—which falls between Olympiads 156 and 157 (i.e. between 153/2 and 152/1) gives some indication of the point at which Polybius regards the 'disturbed and confused time' as really beginning.[149] But—as one might perhaps expect in a period of ταραχὴ καὶ κίνησις—the onset is not clearly marked; and the start of the Second Celtiberian War which our texts of Polybius put in book xxxv in fact belongs to book xxxiii.[150] However, the war itself fell within the years of confusion, which also embrace the Third Punic War, the Fourth Macedonian War and the Achaean War, followed by the settlement of Achaea in which Polybius could fairly claim to have played a leading role as χειριστής.

In all these wars the Roman forces, though not uniformly successful, were raised and commanded in the normal manner

---

[146] Cf. iii. 4. 8, τὸ...ὠφέλιμον τῆς ἡμετέρας ἱστορίας.

[147] iii. 4. 12.   [148] iii. 5. 1 ff.

[149] Book xxxiv thus provides a climax to books vii–xxxiii and, as it were, insulates them from books xxxv–xxxix, in which Polybius plays a more personal role; its position in the scheme of Polybius' *History* can therefore be compared with that of book vi, which separates the period down to Cannae and the Peace of Naupactus from the period afterwards, during which events throughout the whole *oecumene* become intermingled.

[150] See below, p. 124.

and did eventually carry through operations to a successful conclusion. It is not therefore at first sight apparent why Polybius
describes these years as a time of ταραχὴ καὶ κίνησις. The words
are used in other historians, κίνησις at the very beginning of book i
of Thucydides,[151] ταραχή in the famous passage in which Xenophon describes the state of Greece after Mantinea at the end of the
Hellenica;[152] but these passages are not of great help here. I am
inclined to think that Polybius uses these words, with their suggestion of confusion, to describe these years because he saw them
as dominated by inexplicable and irrational military risings in
Greece, Macedonia and Carthage. Not only does he feel no
sympathy for the men directing events in those lands but he cannot understand why the events took place at all; this is clear from
his account of the Macedonian revolt[153] as 'heaven-sent infatuation' (δαιμονοβλάβεια), his reference to the shame which their
own folly brought upon the Greeks,[154] and his contemptuous
account of the Carthaginian general Hasdrubal,[155] whose behaviour he describes at some length in order to prove that 'it
would not be easy to find men more like each other than those
who controlled the destinies of Greece and Carthage at this time'.[156]

Thus the closing stage of Polybius' *Histories* is one which covers
events in which more than ever before the historian felt himself
identified with the Roman point of view; for it was also, as he says,
a period in which he was personally involved and in which a major
part was played—at Carthage at least—by his close friend
Aemilianus. The effect of all this on his *Histories* is a subject to
which I shall return in my final chapter. But it is at least clear that
what he wrote after 146—and, as I have explained, we are quite
uncertain how far he had gone beyond book xv by that date—was
bound to bear the imprint of the events he had lived through
during those 'years of trouble'. It was also influenced by his
widening experiences in the west—his journey to Spain, his

---

[151] Thuc. i. 1. 2, where it is usually taken to refer to the Peloponnesian War;
see, however, N. G. L. Hammond, 'The arrangement of thought in the proem
and in other parts of Thucydides i', *CQ*, 2 (1952), 133 n. 1, who takes it to
mean the emergence of two hostile coalitions in the period before it broke out.

[152] Xen. *Hell.* vii. 5. 27.

[153] xxxvi. 17. 15, δαιμονοβλάβειαν...καὶ μῆνιν ἐκ θεῶν; cf. 10. 1–7 for a more
detailed account.

[154] xxxviii. 3. 7–13; cf. 12. 5, 16. 7–8.

[155] xxxviii. 7–8, 20.

[156] xxxviii. 8. 14–15; see below, pp. 176–7.

crossing of the Alps, his visits to Africa and his voyage of exploration beyond the Pillars of Hercules. His impatience towards
Timaeus, the armchair exile at Athens, grows alongside his resentment that any predecessor should claim his laurels as the historian
of the barbarian west and of Rome. The geographical aspects of
his work receive fresh emphasis:[157] there are additions, as we saw,
book xii is amplified if not newly conceived to deal with these
matters,[158] and he writes book xxxiv as a further digression to
expound the geography of a wide section of the world.[159] In doing
this, however, he is not simply bringing a new dimension to the
writing of history: he is also taking up an old tradition which from
the outset emphasised the close links existing between history and
geography.[160] In this, as in much else in Polybius' *Histories*, innovation and tradition march side by side.

[157] See above, pp. 23–4.
[158] See above, p. 25.   [159] See below, pp. 122–4.
[160] Cf. Walbank, 'The geography of Polybius', *Class. et med.* 9 (1948), 155 ff.;
for emphasis on the importance of geography for statesmen see also Aristotle,
Rhet. i. 4. 13, 1360a 25 ff. (cf. M. A. Levi, 'La critica di Polibio a Timeo',
Studi alessandrini, 196 n. 3).

II

Historical Traditions

1.

In the previous chapter I pointed out that, in devoting special attention to the geography of the western Mediterranean in the parts of his *Histories* which he composed after 146, Polybius was reverting to an earlier tradition which had associated the study of lands with the study of peoples. This coincidence is a good illustration of how novelty and tradition are frequently combined in Polybius' work. There are of course many ways in which traditions are absorbed. One is through education, and though no direct information survives about Polybius' education, it is clear from the way he writes that it took the usual Hellenistic form of a training in literature and rhetoric. He quotes Homer fairly often, and occasionally other writers too; but he displays no deep knowledge of literature.[1] His quotations suggest the use of a commonplace-book as often as they do a first-hand acquaintance with the work he quotes. Philosophy receives lip-service. Both the historian Timaeus and Prusias II, the king of Bithynia, are accused of being unphilosophical,[2] and he mentions several philosophers by name—Heracleitus, Plato, Aristotle, Demetrius of Phalerum and Strato of Lampsacus;[3] but here again his knowledge is somewhat

[1] This point is made by Ziegler, cols. 1464–71, against the exaggerated picture of Polybius' knowledge of literature painted by von Scala, 63 ff.; see further D. Musti, 'Problemi polibiani', *La parola del passato*, 104 (1965), 392–3. For Polybius' acquaintance with Homer see Wunderer, *Forschungen*, ii. 16 ff., who perhaps underestimates his knowledge of the standard school authors; but he makes a good case for thinking that Polybius made some use of a common-place book or florilegium.

[2] xii. 25. 6 (Timaeus); xxxvi. 15. 5 (Prusias II).

[3] Cf. iv. 40. 3; xii. 27. 1 (Heracleitus); vi. 5. 1, 45 (Plato mentioned along with Ephorus, Xenophon and Callisthenes); vii. 13. 7; xii. 28. 2 (Plato); xxix. 21. 1 f.; xxxvi. 2. 3 (Demetrius); xii. 25c. 3 (Strato; but the arguments about the silting-up of the Black Sea in iv. 39–42 probably go back to him; see my

superficial.[4] For Polybius was not by temperament a scholar. As I have already said, his upbringing in Achaea was in a political and military ambient, and his genuine interest in the techniques of warfare is reflected in his writings,[5] where he describes such things in meticulous detail and with passion. His predilection for hunting,[6] which endeared him to Ortega y Gasset,[7] as it had helped to endear him to the younger Scipio,[8] stamps him as a man fond of an out-of-doors life. In short, he came to the writing of history, not as a scholar, but rather in the spirit of the Roman senatorial writers, who saw this activity as a complement to their public careers, and also as a man who believed fervently and often repeated that the study of history was the best way of acquiring experience in war and politics. That, rather than mere bookishness, is why he was widely read in the Greek historians, especially those of the fourth and third centuries.

Commentary, i. 490–5; 'Polybius on the Pontus and the Bosphorus (iv. 39–42)', *Studies presented to D. M. Robinson* (St Louis, 1951), i. 470–4). For the view that Polybius' account of his relations with Scipio Aemilianus owes something to Plato's account of the relations between Socrates and Alcibiades in the *Greater Alcibiades* see P. Friedländer, 'Socrates enters Rome', *AJP*, 66 (1945), 337–51; it seems just possible (cf. Ziegler, col. 1459 n. 1). Von Scala, 127 ff., argues that Polybius was acquainted with Aristotle's works, but it seems unlikely that he knew the *Poetics*, the *Politics* or the *Nicomachean Ethics* (cf. Susemihl, ii. 81 n. 4; B. Niese, *Göttingische gelehrte Anzeigen* (1890), 892; Ziegler, col. 1470). Aristotle is mentioned at length in xii. 5. 4 ff.; 6a. 1 ff.; 6b. 3 ff.; 7. 2; 7. 4; 8 ff.; 11. 5; 23. 8 (where Polybius defends him against Timaeus' attacks), and in one place (xxxi. 16. 3) Polybius quotes anonymously a saying which Diogenes Laertius (v. 1. 18) attributes to Aristotle.

⁴ One can perhaps neglect Diod. xxxi. 26. 5 on Scipio Aemilianus: γεγονὼς ...ὀκτωκαίδεκα ἐτῶν, ἔδωκεν ἑαυτὸν πρὸς τοὺς ἐν φιλοσοφίᾳ λόγους, λαβὼν ἐπιστάτην Πολύβιον τὸν Μεγαλοπολίτην τὸν τὰς ἱστορίας συντεταγμένον. Polybius himself (xxxi. 23 ff.) makes no mention of philosophy, which must then be taken to be Diodorus' term for the practical training Polybius gave the young Roman.

⁵ See above, p. 15 n. 75, for his *Tactics*; see also the many military digressions in his *Histories*, e.g. iii. 81. 10, 105); v. 98; x. 16. 1–17. 5, 22–4, 32. 7–33, 43–7; xi. 25. 6; xviii. 28–32 (legion and phalanx compared); and of course his careful account of the Roman army and Roman method of making a camp, in vi. 19–42.

⁶ Cf. xxxi. 14. 3 (Demetrius of Syria makes Polybius' acquaintance boar-hunting); 29. 3–9 (Polybius approves Scipio Aemilianus' hunting activities; cf. 29. 8 for his own enthusiasm); x. 41. 7 (a comparison taken from hunting; cf. Plut. *Philop.* 10. 9). Arcadia was of course hunting country (cf. Paus. viii. 4. 7, 4. 10, 38. 6). See further von Scala, 24–5 (not all of whose examples are strictly relevant).

⁷ J. Ortega y Gasset, *Obras completas*, vi (Madrid, 1953, ed. 2), 429–33, 'Polibio y Escipión Emiliano'.   ⁸ See above, n. 6.

2.

By and large he appears to have disliked what he read. Indeed, to the reasons already mentioned for his decision to write history, we must add yet another—to assert his own view of what history should be against the sort of history which was widely written and read in the Hellenistic age.[9] The historian Phylarchus, whom he also found uncongenial because of his sympathy for revolutionary Sparta, is criticised in harsh terms[10] for meretricious and emotional writing, for emphasising the sufferings of the Mantineans—rebels from Achaea who deserved all they got—and for depicting women clinging together with dishevelled hair and naked breasts, and crowds of children and old people, men and women, led off weeping into slavery. But Phylarchus by no means stands alone. Polybius has no good to say of the historians who told fantastic tales about Hannibal's crossing of the Alps,[11] or of others who retailed fabulous stories about Phaethon's chariot and how his sisters were turned into Lombardy poplars,[12] to mention only two examples out of many.[13] History-writing was riddled with the tragic and the monstrous; and in this way trivialities ousted serious topics.[14]

There has been a long debate on the origins of what has sometimes been termed 'tragic history'.[15] The most popular theory has linked it with the teachings of the Aristotelian school, which is supposed to have blurred Aristotle's own clear distinction between poetry and history and to have taken the criteria and characteristics of the former and applied them to the composition of the latter.[16] A name much mentioned in this context is that of a pre-

[9] For this section see Walbank, 'History and tragedy', *Historia*, 9 (1960), 216–34.   [10] ii. 56. 10–13.   [11] iii. 48. 8.

[12] ii. 16. 13–15; perhaps Timaeus is indicated.

[13] Other examples are vii. 7. 1–2 (writers on Hieronymus of Syracuse); xv. 34. 1–36. 11 (writers on Agathocles of Alexandria—perhaps especially Ptolemy of Megalopolis); x. 27. 8 (the wonders of Ecbatana); xvi. 12. 3 (the marvels of Iasus), 18. 2 (the sensational writing of Zeno of Rhodes).

[14] iii. 20. 5: Sosylus and Chaereas retail trivialities comparable to the gossip heard in a barber's shop.

[15] See most recently Walbank, 'Tragic history', *Bull. Inst. Class. Stud.* 2 (1955), 4–14; 'History and tragedy', *Historia*, 9 (1960), 216–34; C. O. Brink, 'Tragic history and Aristotle's school', *Proc. Camb. Phil. Soc.* 6 (1960), 14–19; Zegers, *Wesen*, passim, and works there quoted.

[16] First proposed by Ed. Schwartz, *Fünf Vorträge über den griechischen Roman* (Berlin, 1896; ed. 2, Berlin, 1943), 123–5 (of ed. 2); cf. 'Die Berichte über die

decessor of Phylarchus, Duris of Samos,[17] who is known to have regarded *mimesis*, 'imitation', as an essential part of the historian's task and to have criticised Ephorus and Theopompus for neglecting this side of history and concerning themselves only with the formal aspects of writing. Duris was a pupil of Theophrastus, and it seems very likely that he used the word *mimesis* because it was familiar to him from the vocabulary of the Peripatetic school. But Aristotle believed the distinguishing mark of tragedy to be the representation of the universal, and it is not easy to see any connection between this and *mimesis* in the sense in which Duris uses it; for as far as we can tell, *mimesis*, to Duris, means simply a vivid and emotional representation of events, such as is constantly to be found in the fragments of his history.[18] Whether in

catilinarische Verschwörung', *Hermes*, 32 (1897), 560 ff.; 'Kallisthenes' *Hellenika*', ibid. 35 (1900), 106 ff.; 'Die Zeit des Ephoros', ibid. 44 (1909), 491 ff.; P. Scheller, *De hellenistica historiae conscribendae arte* (Diss. Leipzig, 1911). For Aristotle's distinction between history and poetry see *Poet.* 9. 2–9, 1451 b 1–32. The view mentioned in the text has been encouraged by the fact that in criticising Phylarchus Polybius uses expressions familiar from the *Poetics*, such words and phrases as ἔλεος, συμπαθεῖς ποιεῖν, πρὸ ὀφθαλμῶν τιθέναι, δεινά, τερατεύεσθαι, πιθανόν, ἔκπληξις, ψυχαγωγεῖν, περιπέτεια and ὀργίζεσθαι (see the comparative table in Zegers, *Wesen*, 5–6). These parallels show clearly that Aristotle had formulated a set of concepts applicable to tragedy, and it is not surprising that when he accuses Phylarchus of writing history in a manner appropriate to tragedy, Polybius makes use of them. But it is a large and obviously unwarranted step to go on to assume that this use of Aristotelian vocabulary by Polybius proves that the Peripatetic school had itself already taken over and applied in a formal manner to the writing of 'tragic history' Aristotle's theory of tragedy. As I point out below, 'tragic history' has origins that go back well beyond Aristotle.

[17] *FGH* 76; see T 12, F 5, 7, 14, 18, 52 for examples of his liking for sensational and emotional situations, and F 1 (= Phot. *Bibl.* 176, p. 121 a 41) for his criticism of Ephorus and Theopompus, who, he says, proved for the most part unequal to the events they described (τῶν γενομένων ἀπελείφθησαν); for in their presentation they made no attempt at dramatic *mimesis* with its associated pleasure in the narrative, and concerned themselves only with the formal aspects of writing: οὔτε γὰρ μιμήσεως μετέλαβον οὐδεμιᾶς οὔτε ἡδονῆς ἐν τῷ φράσαι, αὐτοῦ δὲ τοῦ γράφειν μόνον ἐπεμελήθησαν. Cf. Strasburger, *Wesensbestimmung*, 41 n. 2 and 43–4, where he argues that by ἡδονή Duris meant no mere titillation but something nearer to the κάθαρσις, 'die Seelenreinigung bzw. -befreiung', of Aristotle's *Poetics*. But he admits that in practice Duris did not reach these heights, and one may doubt whether they are in fact implied in his use of ἡδονή.

[18] The word μίμησις is also implied in Diod. xx. 43. 7, a criticism of 'history' because in contrast to 'reality' (ἀλήθεια), in which events are occurring simultaneously in different places, she is obliged to divide them up unnaturally and relate them in sequence; consequently the real events exhibit πάθος, but the

fact Aristotle would have accepted the view that history was a kind of *mimesis*—a representation of the particular, of course, not of the universal, of what happened, οἶα ἐγένετο, not of what would happen, οἶα ἂν γένοιτο, to use Aristotle's vocabulary—we cannot be sure, for he has virtually nothing to say on the subject. That he would is not, I think, to be excluded, since the list of art-forms which he gives in the first chapters of the *Poetics* is certainly not comprehensive: for example, it includes epic, tragedy, comedy, dithyramb and most forms of flute and lyre music, but omits sculpture and painting, and so perhaps history too.[19] But since Duris seems to be using *mimesis* in quite a different sense the question is only marginally relevant.

The view has also been put forward that 'tragic history' was composed according to a theory formulated in such manuals as Theophrastus and Praxiphanes wrote *On History*.[20] It seems in fact highly probable that the two Peripatetic works bearing this title were concerned with the theory of historiography; Praxiphanes, we know, dealt with Thucydides.[21] Unfortunately there is complete

narration of them (ἀναγραφή) μιμεῖσθαι μὲν τὰ γεγενημένα, πολὺ δὲ λείπεσθαι τῆς ἀληθοῦς διαθέσεως. Diodorus' source here is probably Duris; cf. Strasburger, *Wesensbestimmung*, 47 n. 4. There appears to be no evidence for the use of the word as a technical term in historical theory in any other author but Duris.

[19] C. O. Brink, 'Tragic history and Aristotle's school', *Proc. Camb. Phil. Soc.* 6 (1960), 14–19, argues that Aristotle's *mimesis* is inextricably attached to the concept of universality in poetry (τὰ καθ' ὅλου); where we disagree is that I see no evidence that *mimesis* is so linked in all fields (e.g. in music), and therefore do not think that the absence of universality (or its *comparative* absence—for in *Poet.* 9. 3, 1451 b 5–7, ἡ μὲν γὰρ ποίησις μᾶλλον τὰ καθ' ὅλου, ἡ δ' ἱστορία τὰ καθ' ἕκαστον λέγει, the word μᾶλλον goes with both wings of the sentence) necessarily excludes the process which Aristotle calls *mimesis*.

[20] For Theophrastus' Περὶ ἱστορίας cf. Diog. Laert. v. 47; Cic. *orat.* 39; for Praxiphanes' work with the same title see Marcellinus, *Vit. Thuc.* 29. There is no reason to doubt that these works dealt with the theory of history: for when Cicero, *de orat.* ii. 62, makes M. Antonius remark that 'neque eam (sc. historiam) reperio usquam separatim instructam rhetorum praeceptis', this means simply that in rhetorical handbooks history is not given special treatment distinct from general precepts, not that no treatises on the writing of history existed (cf. Walbank, *Gnomon*, 29 (1957), 418–19). For the view that they contained the theoretical justification of 'tragic history' see most recently Zegers, *Wesen*, and Strasburger, *Wesensbestimmung*, 43 n. 5; contra, Walbank, 'History and tragedy', *Historia*, 9 (1960), 219–20. See further Brink, 'Tragic history and Aristotle's school', *Proc. Camb. Phil. Soc.* 6 (1960), 18; M. I. Finley, 'Myth, memory and history', *History and theory*, 4 (1965), 282.

[21] Brink, 'Callimachus and Aristotle: an inquiry into Callimachus' ΠΡΟΣ ΠΡΑΞΙΦΑΝΗΝ', *CQ*, 40 (1946), 24, suggests that Praxiphanes' work took the form of a dialogue at the court of Archelaus of Macedonia between Thucydides

uncertainty about their contents and any doctrines they may have expounded. One of the few things we do know about Theophrastus' views on historians is that he praised Herodotus and Thucydides for a rich and ornate diction,[22] and this is perhaps hard to reconcile with any theory which could be exemplified in Duris of Samos, whose lack of interest in style is pilloried by Dionysius of Halicarnassus.[23]

However these problems vanish once it is realised that the kind of sensationalism which Polybius deplores in Phylarchus is not a recent innovation based on rules laid down in any Hellenistic school, Peripatetic or any other. It is a characteristic which undoubtedly grew more pronounced in certain Hellenistic writers, but as Laistner pointed out in the first of his Sather Lectures[24] on the Roman historians, it is one to be found in Greek historical writing from an early date, and certainly long before the time of Aristotle. In an important study of Thucydides' role as the inventor of political history,[25] Strasburger has shown how the reaction against him took the form of a return to the principles of Herodotus, with his bolder colouring and variety of material, his appeal to the feelings rather than the intellect and a didacticism more moral than political. To Aristotle[26] Herodotus was μυθολόγος—a story teller. Diodorus was later to accuse him of making up wonder-stories and myths regardless of the truth, provided they were entertaining;[27] and in a neglected but very characteristic prolusion

and the five poets mentioned in Marcellinus, *Vit. Thuc.* 29; but we have really nothing to go on.

[22] Cicero, *orator*, 39, 'primisque ab his, ut ait Theophrastus, historia commota est, ut auderet uberius quam superiores et ornatius dicere'.

[23] Dion. Hal. *de comp. verb.* 4 (= *FGH* 76 T 10), παντάπασιν ἠμελήθη (sc. τὸ συντιθέναι δεξιῶς τὰ ὀνόματα) καὶ οὐδεὶς ᾤετο δεῖν ἀναγκαῖον αὐτὸ εἶναι οὐδὲ συμβάλλεσθαί τι τῷ κάλλει τῶν λόγων· τοιγάρτοι τοιαύτας συντάξεις κατέλιπον οἵας οὐδεὶς ὑπομένει μέχρι κορωνίδος διελθεῖν.

[24] Laistner, 12 ff.

[25] H. Strasburger, 'Die Entdeckung der politischen Geschichte durch Thukydides', *Saeculum*, 5 (1954), 395–428 (reprinted with additions in *Thukydides*, 412–76, from which I quote). See also his *Wesensbestimmung*, 24 ff., where he observes that Thucydides too drew on the epic tradition for his concept of war and suffering as the subject of his work and for his conviction (p. 25) 'dass ein ἔργον, ein "Werk" schlechthin, welches durch seine "Redenswürdigkeit" seinen Historiker fordert, re ipsa nur ein grosser *Krieg* (theoretisch ausgedrückt: eine κίνησις) sein kann'.

[26] Aristotle, *de gen. anim.* 3, 75 b 5.

[27] Diod. i. 69. 7; cf. Momigliano, 'Storiografia su tradizione scritta e storiografia su tradizione orale', *Terzo contributo*, i. 16–17.

published over fifty years ago, entitled 'Herodotus the Tragedian', J. L. Myres[28] reconstructed the *Taking of Sardis* or Σάρδεων ἅλωσις from book i, and the *Cleomenes Raving* or Κλεομένης μαινόμενος from books v and vi.

However, the reaction against Thucydides took yet more violent forms. Ctesias of Cnidus wrote Persian and Indian histories which are described by Photius as 'arousing emotion and providing many examples of the unexpected and of various embellishments which bring them close to the confines of the mythical'. These works are in some ways forerunners of Callisthenes, who furnished many incidents of precisely this kind—the marvellous ravens which rounded up Alexander's stragglers, the sea that offered *proskynesis* to the king.[29] To such historians the word τραγικός could be loosely but not inappropriately applied; and despite the clear distinction drawn by Aristotle between history and tragedy and despite the protests familiar to us from Polybius, the temptation so to apply it was very strong. This was because there existed in reality a long-standing affinity between the two art-forms of history and tragedy, based on a common subject matter in the panhellenic legends (which were universally regarded as true), on the fact that both make their appeal to easily aroused emotions— for history like poetry was normally read aloud, on a common emphasis on moral purpose shared by both, and on an identical background in the schools of rhetoric, which exploited both historical and tragic *exempla* for their own ends.

Polybius then is not attacking a closely and narrowly defined peripatetic school of tragic history, but a way of writing history both more widespread and more persistent[30]—and incidentally,

[28] *A miscellany presented to John MacDonald Mackay, LL.D., July 1914*, ed. Oliver Elton (Liverpool–London, 1914), 88–96.

[29] On Ctesias cf. F. Wehrli, *Eumusia: Festgabe für Ernst Howald zum 60. Geburtstag* (Zürich, 1947), 68; see Photius, *Bibl.* 72, p. 45 a 5 ff. (*FGH* 688 T 13). See further Walbank, 'History and tragedy', *Historia*, 9 (1960), 232. Gorgias too developed a theory and style which confused poetry and prose (cf. Aristotle, *Rhet.* iii. 1, 1404 a 29) and probably made ψυχαγωγία a goal common to works of art, literature and oratory (cf. Avenarius, 140); but there is no evidence that he either concerned himself with the writing of history or had any influence on views about its purpose. For the passages of Callisthenes mentioned in the text see Plutarch, *Alex.* 27. 1–3 (*FGH* 124 F 14 (b)) on the ravens, and *FGH* 124 F 31 (a Homeric scholion) on the *proskynesis* of the sea.

[30] I am not of course suggesting that Polybius was acquainted with all these earlier authors; indeed there is no firm evidence that he was acquainted with

as Strasburger has shown, a way which was to prove by no means sterile.[31] The emphasis which Duris laid on personalities and on the emotional aspect of human affairs, and the interest which his successors showed in ethnographical differences and social and economic factors represent a widening of the scope of history with positive gains. But Polybius was aware of the danger that sensational writing represented to what he regarded as the political and moral purpose of history, and the appeal it made to the frivolity of the reader. This is one reason for his angry attack on Phylarchus and on those who wrote like him.

Another reason must be that he felt the temptation to write emotionally himself—and occasionally succumbed to it. Such passages as his description of the mutiny at Alexandria which followed the accession of the boy-king Ptolemy V or of Philip V's capture of Abydus[32] clearly owed much to Hellenistic techniques of writing. Moreover the principle of adducing the περιπέτειαι which have befallen others so as to fortify the reader against the vicissitudes of fortune, τύχης μεταβολάς, easily led the historian to elaborate such events. One example is the pathetic account of Hasdrubal's surrender, reproached by his wife and cursed by his fellow citizens, at the fall of Carthage;[33] another is the final downfall of the house of Philip,[34] which we can reconstruct from the fragmentary text and from Livy's version, and yet another is the

Herodotus (for there are no good reasons for changing 'Ηράκλειτον to 'Ηρόδοτον in xii. 27. 1; cf. von Scala, 88 n. 1).

[31] Strasburger, 'Die Entdeckung der politischen Geschichte durch Thukydides', Thukydides, 469–70, mentions Agatharchides (FGH 86) and Poseidonius (FGH 87) as examples of the positive side of this legacy; see too Wesensbestimmung, 45 ff. But Strasburger perhaps exaggerates both the originality and the merits of the sort of history written by Duris (cf. O. Murray, CR, 18 (1968), 219, for 'over-valuation of the mimetic theory' in which he detects 'shades of Croce and Collingwood').

[32] xv. 25–33 (Alexandria); xvi. 30–4 (Abydus).

[33] xxxviii. 20; Pédech, Polybe i, p. xliii, quotes Chateaubriand, Itinéraire de Paris à Jérusalem, part 7, for a page borrowed from this scene in Polybius. See also xxxix. 2 for Polybius' account of the capture of Corinth, in which he mentions the soldiers' contempt for art objects and votive offerings ἐν οἴκτου μέρει. The capture of cities was a favourite theme for emotional writing, naturally; see above, p. 34 n. 10, for Phylarchus' description of the fall of Mantinea, and cf. Strasburger, Wesensbestimmung, 29 ff.

[34] xxiii. 10–11; cf. Livy, xl. 3. 3 ff. (drawing on Polybius and elaborating the dramatic aspects already in his original). See C. F. Edson, 'Perseus and Demetrius', Harv. Stud. 46 (1935), 191–202; Walbank, 'Φίλιππος τραγῳδούμενος', JHS, 58 (1938), 55–68; Meloni, Perseo, 41–7.

long passage in book xxxviii,[35] in which he seems determined to show that of all the ruin that ever befell Greece no ruin was comparable to that which he, Polybius, had witnessed in 146 B.C. Indeed he has to pull himself up short with the remark that 'no-one should be surprised if I go beyond the style suited to history and here express myself on these matters in a more ambitious and declamatory style'—his defence being the moral purpose which his remarks were intended to promote.

Polybius admits that the historian is entitled to entertain. Both aims, the useful and the enjoyable, τὸ χρήσιμον and τὸ τερπνόν, have their proper place in history. But in practice, as we have seen,[36] the scales should come down decidedly on the side of utility. If at times Polybius' criticism seems over-strident, the reason lies at least in part in the literary situation in which he was writing and in the importance of the values which were threatened. There had been honourable exceptions: one thinks of Ptolemy and Hieronymus. But the historians of the last two centuries had mostly chosen the sensational incidents and emotional situations typical of Duris or had emulated the rhetorical colouring of Theopompus, whom Polybius censures[37] violently for his unacceptable criticism of Philip II, his bad taste and his failure to maintain the standards of decent controversy.

3.

So, for all his own occasional lapses, Polybius stands for a return to the aims and methods of Thucydides; and this means that his work is in many ways somewhat traditional and even old-fashioned. His relationship with Thucydides is never explicitly stated. Indeed Thucydides' name is mentioned only once, and that casually, in the surviving parts of Polybius' *Histories*;[38] and it has been argued[39] that Polybius knew little of him and was indifferent to that. But there are verbal echoes of his predecessor which, I think, leave us in no doubt that Polybius was familiar with his work;[40] for instance,

---

[35] xxxviii. 1–4, 16. 7 (people throwing themselves into wells).

[36] See above, pp. 6 ff.

[37] viii. 9–11; see my *Commentary*, ii. 79–80; 'Polemic in Polybius', *JRS*, 52 (1962), 1–2.

[38] viii. 11. 3.

[39] Cf. Pédech, *Polybe i*, pp. xli–xlii.

[40] Cf. Walbank, *Speeches*, 8; Gelzer, 'Die pragmatische Geschichtsschreibung des Polybios', *Kl. Schr.* iii. 160, argues that Polybius derived his ideas only

his remark[41] that while tragedy charms its audience for the moment, history brings them profit for all time, is surely intended to recall Thucydides' famous claim to be writing 'a possession for all time rather than an essay to win the applause of the moment'.[42] Thucydides' word is ἀγώνισμα and a book later Polybius observes[43] that without a proper study of causes history furnishes only 'a show-piece' (ἀγώνισμα) but no real lesson. The historians who have introduced an element of the miraculous and the colouring of tragedy into their account of the downfall of Hieronymus of Syracuse are referred to[44] as λογογράφοι, an unusual word which assumes a critical overtone here precisely because Thucydides had used it of his own predecessors. These and other examples confirm that Polybius was conscious of his relationship to a predecessor like himself in theme, temperament and personal vicissitudes. For each of the two had had his political career cut short by exile, and in exile had learnt to widen his horizon as a historian. Both wrote contemporary history[45] and either by chance or design Polybius followed Thucydides in prefacing his main narrative with an introductory period of roughly fifty years.[46] Both were politicians and generals, both—though not perhaps to an equal degree[47]—were convinced of the importance of the constitution for the welfare of a state, and both wrote to instruct statesmen in the art of government. In these circumstances Polybius' virtual silence about Thucydides may seem odd. I have suggested elsewhere that though he did not agree in all things with Thucydides, he regarded him as an ally on the main issue of what history should be about. He

indirectly from Thucydides, but Thucydides was regularly read in the Hellenistic period, and I have explained in the text why a direct legacy seems to me more likely.

[41] ii. 56. 11.   [42] Thucyd. i. 22. 4.
[43] iii. 31. 12; see Walbank, *Speeches*, 8 n. 56.
[44] vii. 7. 1; cf. Thuc. i. 21. 1; Walbank, *Speeches*, 9 n. 58; von Fritz, *Geschichtsschreibung*, i, 'Anmerkungen', Excurs i, 337–47, 'Die sogenannten Logographen'.   [45] iv. 2. 2.
[46] Walbank, *Speeches*, 9 n. 64. Thucydides wrote on the Pentekontaetia and Polybius on the years between the 129th and 140th Olympiads, 264–260 and 220–216 (together with the rise of Hiero: i. 7 ff.).
[47] Cf. Bury, *Historians*, 219: 'he (sc. Thucydides) was not imposed upon by constitutional forms and never ascribed to them the significance which they possessed for Polybius'; but Thucydides' interest in Theramenes' constitution (Thuc. viii. 97. 2: cf. G. E. M. de Ste. Croix, 'The constitution of the five thousand', *Historia*, 5 (1956), 1–23) is evidence that he did not underestimate their importance.

had no immediate occasion to refer to him with praise (and in any case did not find praising a very congenial activity); but significantly he nowhere speaks against him, but devotes his polemic to those who regarded historical composition as a rhetorical exercise or as an occasion for emotional indulgence.[48]

Like Thucydides, Polybius also wrote contemporary history, rejecting Timaeus' preoccupation with early myths and legends and Ephorus' concern with the whole of the past since the return of the Heracleidae. To both Polybius and Thucydides the distant past was not merely obscure, it was unimportant. Thucydides' enthusiasm for the Peloponnesian War, 'more worthy of relation than any that had preceded it',[49] is paralleled by Polybius' claim that the rise of Rome to world power is a thing unique in history;[50] both were contemporary, the facts could be ascertained. Whereas of the distant past all one could know was myth[51] or, when one reached 'historical' times, what predecessors had discovered and written down—so what was the point of doing the work again?[52] Polybius, it is true, claims to be writing a universal history; but it is universal not in Ephorus' sense of covering the whole of the past,[53] but simply in embracing the whole of the *oecumene* at a time —the present—when its history has coalesced to form a single whole. He chooses 220 B.C., the date at which Aratus' *Memoirs* terminate,[54] as his starting-point, not only because he conceives his work as continuing that of Aratus, but also because, he says, the period following on this year coincides with his own generation and the previous one, so that he has either his own personal experience or the evidence of eye-witnesses to draw on. This statement lines him up clearly beside Thucydides; indeed, Momigliano regards[55] his successful assertion of these principles as marking the

---

[48] Cf. Walbank, *Speeches*, 10–11.

[49] Thucyd. i. 1. 1.   [50] i. 1. 5.

[51] Cf. Finley, 'Myth, memory and history', *History and theory*, 4 (1965), 283 ff.

[52] ix. 2. 1–3; cf. Collingwood, *Idea*, 25 ff.

[53] v. 33. 2 for Polybius' praise of Ephorus' work as the first attempt to write a universal history.

[54] iv. 2. 1–2; see below, p. 79 n. 73.

[55] 'Atene nel iii secolo A.C. e la scoperta di Roma nelle storie di Timeo di Tauromenio', *Terzo contributo*, i. 18. For Polybius' role as a populariser of the Thucydidean form of history at Rome see Strasburger, 'Die Entdeckung der politischen Geschichte durch Thukydides', *Thukydides*, 471, who notes the continuation of this tradition throughout a thousand years of Byzantine historiography.

triumph of the Thucydidean school at Rome and he has pointed out that this stress on oral testimony is characteristic of a pre-occupation with current political events and a political purpose, whereas written sources are much more the preserve of the local historian and the antiquarian.[56] This does not of course mean that Polybius makes no use of written sources. For his introductory books dealing with the period before 200 this was inevitable;[57] and for the main period of his work he undoubtedly used a wide range of written histories, about which I shall say something in the next chapter. But he asserts very firmly that the questioning of eye-witnesses comes first—κυριώτατον τῆς ἱστορίας.[58]

4.

Polybius' object was to discover the truth—but for utilitarian reasons. It was only from the truth that the reader could derive profit; without it nothing remained but an empty story, ἀνωφελὲς ...διήγημα.[59] 'Truth is to history', he writes,[60] 'what eyesight is to a living creature.' And here there is a problem. Among the traditional features of history-writing, which Polybius took over from his predecessors, was the inclusion of speeches. Thucydides[61]

[56] But one cannot always draw a clear distinction (cf. Momigliano, art. cit. (n. 55), i. 18–19.

[57] For his use of written sources cf. i. 14–15 (Fabius and Philinus); iii. 26. 3–4 (criticism of Philinus); ii. 56. 2 (Aratus and Phylarchus). See further below, p. 78 n. 61.   [58] xii. 4 c. 3.

[59] i. 14. 6. Polybius' own reliability and regard for truth are generally (and justly) accounted high, and they have been defended, sometimes over-zealously, by Lehmann, *Untersuchungen*, passim. The discovery at Thyrrheum in Acarnania of an inscription containing fragments of the Romano-Aetolian treaty of 211 (*SEG* xiii. 382) has raised this issue in an acute form, since the treaty, as inscribed, apparently provides for a situation in which towns sur-rendering voluntarily to the Romans or the Aetolians were to be allowed to join the Aetolian confederacy. This seems to be in direct contradiction to Flamininus' interpretation of the treaty in his reply to the Aetolian demand for certain Thessalian towns after Cynoscephalae (xviii. 38. 8–9). Scholars have drawn the conclusion that Flamininus or Polybius (or both) should be con-victed of dishonesty; but this seems scarcely justified so long as the fragmentary character of the inscription leaves open the possibility of an additional clause further qualifying the conditions under which voluntary surrender might be made. For the relevant texts, discussion and full bibliography see now H. H. Schmitt, *Die Staatsverträge des Altertums*, iii. *Die Verträge der griechisch-römischen Welt von 338 bis 200 v. Chr.* (Munich, 1969), no. 536.

[60] See also xii. 12. 3; xxxiv. 4. 2 (if this remark of Strabo comes from Polybius).

[61] Thucyd. i. 22. 1–2, τὰ λεχθέντα and τὰ πραχθέντα; see Strasburger,

regarded history as consisting of action and speeches—πράξεις καὶ λόγοι—and the distinction is commonly made both in theory and by historians themselves.[62] To Polybius too such speeches were an integral part of the historian's business: 'the peculiar function of history', he says,[63] is to discover in the first place the words actually spoken, and next to ascertain the reason why what was done or spoken led to failure or success. Policy can only spring from discussion: consequently speech is at the roots of political life. However, the recording of speeches is an operation fraught with difficulties, and their role in Thucydides' history is a subject of long debate, not yet satisfactorily resolved. This is not the occasion to take it up again and I will merely say that when Thucydides announces his intention[64] of making the speakers say what in his opinion was demanded of them by the various occasions, of course adhering as far as possible to the general sense (τῆς ξυμπάσης γνώμης) of what was really said, he enunciates a formula which allows for a good deal of elasticity in interpretation. The phrasing of the speeches is of course that of the historian: no speakers of the fifth century ever talked as Thucydides wrote.[65] But the statement of intent remains, and unless one is prepared to regard Thucydides as blind or dishonest, then his speeches must presumably have borne some relation to 'the overall purpose of what was said', and remain anchored, however loosely, to τὰ ἀληθῶς λεχθέντα.

However, since Thucydides the whole situation had changed and the ambiguity had dissolved. During the fourth and third centuries speeches in history had dropped all pretence of giving the real words and had become mere occasions for rhetorical display or useful devices for bringing out the character and personality of the orator.[66] For all this Polybius shows a great contempt; Timaeus' speeches he regards as plumbing the depths of puerility,[67] while those which Chaereas and Sosylus record as delivered in the Roman Senate on the eve of the Hannibalic War are dismissed as

'Thukydides und die politische Selbstdarstellung der Athener', *Thukydides*, 498 ff., on Thucydides' speeches.

[62] See Walbank, *Speeches*, 1 nn. 4–5, for a similar distinction in Plato, Ephorus, Dionysius of Halicarnassus and Quintilian.

[63] xii. 25 b. 1; cf. xiv. 1 a. 3, ἔργα καὶ λόγους.

[64] Thucyd. i. 22. 1.

[65] Cf. Jones, 'The Athenian democracy and its critics', *Democracy*, 66–7.

[66] Cf. Walbank, *Speeches*, 4–6.

[67] xii. 25 k, 26 a.

nothing more than barber's shop gossip.[68] He states his own attitude very clearly. 'The historian should simply record...what
was really said, however commonplace';[69] or, as he remarks
elsewhere, 'it is not the business of a historian to show off his
ability to his readers, but rather to devote the whole of his energy
to discovering and recording what was really and truly said, and
even of this only the most vital and effective parts (τὰ καιριώτατα
καὶ πραγματικώτατα).[70] In practice, this programme suffers some
modification. Clearly, as he admits, there has to be some selection;
and in the consequent reshaping of material a personal colouring
appears, as it had done in Thucydides.[71] Sometimes, too, especially where troops are being harangued before battle, one is forced
to choose between the hypothesis that Polybius has in fact had
recourse to his imagination or that he has drawn somewhat uncritically on sources that have themselves done just that.[72] But
taken together the speeches recorded in Polybius were delivered on
occasions such that Polybius can have had authentic sources of
information about them and it is noteworthy that many of them
have been selected for reproduction because they illuminate critical
moments in the history of Greece.[73] When dealing with Rome, as
we shall see, Polybius is inclined to be schematic and a little

---

[68] iii. 20. 5.

[69] ii. 56. 10, in a passage criticising Phylarchus.

[70] xxxvi. 1. 6–7. Another passage, xii. 25 i. 4 ff., has frequently been misunderstood as saying that the historian's duty is to choose arguments suitable
to the speaker and the occasion (cf. Gomme, *Thucydides*, iii. 522). In fact
Polybius is here saying that statesmen, not historians, should choose the right
arguments; and studying the speeches recorded by historians is one way of
gaining the experience necessary to do this. See my analysis of the passage in my
Commentary, ii. 397 (cf. 'Three notes on Polybius xii', *Studi alessandrini*, 211–13).

[71] For an admission that the material was cast into a Polybian form see xxix.
12. 10, where Polybius remarks that the elaboration of sieges and battles and
the reports of speeches and other parts of history is common in the writers of
monographs, and goes on to say that 'in all these...I may justly be excused if
I am found to be using the same style or the same disposition and treatment,
or even actually the same words as on a previous occasion...for in all such
matters the large scale of my work is sufficient excuse'. Clearly this implies that
though he reports what is actually said, a historian may use his own words
and these may in fact be identical for different occasions.

[72] Cf. Walbank, *Speeches*, 18.

[73] For a noteworthy example see the speeches of the Aetolian Chlaeneas and
the Acarnanian Lyciscus delivered at Sparta in 210, and illuminating the crisis
in Greek political life during the early years of Roman intervention in Greece.
See Walbank, *Speeches*, 16–17; Polyb. ix. 28–39 and my *Commentary*, ii. 162–82.
On the speech of Agelaus of Naupactus see below, p. 69 n. 11.

unresponsive to the various currents of internal policy: he sees this as more monolithic than it really was.[74] But in speeches made at gatherings in Greece or by Greek envoys addressing the Senate at Rome he allows us to hear the genuine tones of Greek statesmen in dispute and to share in their dilemmas and their clashes of policy. In this way a traditional device is employed to reinforce the purpose of his *Histories* as a handbook of political and moral instruction for his Greek readers.

5.

Another traditional feature of Greek historiography which went back to Herodotus and Thucydides was the digression; and this too Polybius adapted to serve his own ends. He has some comments on this. The human senses, he points out,[75] are incapable of lengthy concentration on a single object. This is true of taste and sight, and it is true of the prolonged effort involved in reading a history; hence there arose the practice of the most learned authors of the past, who were in the habit of providing myths and stories to serve as digressions (παρεκβάσεις), and so give their readers a rest. However, this device is unnecessary for Polybius himself, since the fact that he moves from one field to another within each Olympiad year automatically and regularly secures the variety required, and that without any interruption to the development of the main theme. This leaves him free to use the excursus as a means of instruction,[76] in which he can develop the exemplary aspects of his history. 'In this way', it has been observed,[77] 'the event sanctions a truth, demonstrates a theoretical proposition, or provides the pretext for an exhortation.' If one quickly turns the pages of our surviving text one soon becomes aware of the richness

[74] For a discussion of the clear discrepancy existing between Polybius' analysis of Roman policy and the evidence he himself furnishes for its evaluation see Walbank, 'Polybius and Rome's eastern policy', *JRS*, 53 (1963), 1–13. The ideological conflicts and clashes recorded in his *Histories* are all Greek and it is significant that he sneers at Chaereas and Sosylus for suggesting that Roman policy was split on the eve of the Hannibalic War and that he ostentatiously refuses to record speeches on the eve of the Third Punic War on the grounds that the Romans 'had long made up their minds to act thus, but were looking for a suitable opportunity and pretext that would appeal to foreign nations' (cf. iii. 20. 5; xxxvi. 1. 1–2. 1).

[75] xxxviii. 5–6; cf. K. Meister, *Hermes*, 99 (1971), 506–8.

[76] For conscious use of the παρέκβασις cf. i. 15. 13; ii. 36. 1; iii. 2. 7, 9. 6, 33. 1; iv. 9. 1; v. 13. 1; vi. 50. 1; xii. 28. 10 (Ephorus).

[77] Roveri, *Studi*, 136–7.

and variety of subjects covered in this way. The *Histories* contain countless passages discussing the character of history itself, how it should be treated, and the merits of universal history as compared with separate monographs;[78] and along with these there are specific criticisms of earlier writers such as Philinus and Fabius,[79] Phylarchus,[80] Theopompus,[81] Zeno and Antisthenes.[82] Also many digressions derive directly from Polybius' own experience and interests—for instance those concerned with military matters, on which I propose to say more later.[83] There are also many character-sketches of individuals which spring naturally out of certain contexts and should not, I suppose, strictly speaking be regarded as digressions.[84] Another category to which I shall also return later is represented by the frequent geographical excursuses, with a didactic purpose, which do not always seem particularly at home at the points where they now stand.[85] Other digressions are used to draw moral and political lessons, for example to discuss the merits of choosing to be neutral or (depending on the context) of putting freedom before peace,[86] to condemn the plundering of temples,[87] to caution his readers against over-readiness to entrust themselves to their enemies,[88] to sketch the causes of Greek social and political decline[89]—a phenomenon which ought not to be attributed to Fortune—or to define the nature of treason.[90] In this way a feature traditional in history writing which can be traced back to Herodotus or, to the extent that it shows rhetorical features, to Isocrates, is converted by Polybius to his own special didactic ends; and this use of the digression culminates in three books, each of which can be regarded as in some degree an interruption in the narrative. Like the shorter digressions, these books are however in no way irrelevancies. All three play a part in the overall plan of Polybius' *Histories*. They are book vi, which is

---

[78] Cf. xxix. 12, for the superiority of universal history over monographs; see also i. 4. 2, ii. 37. 4, and other passages quoted in my *Commentary*, i. 9.

[79] i. 14–15; iii. 26. 3–4.   [80] ii. 56–63.

[81] viii. 9–11.   [82] xvi. 14–20.

[83] See below, pp. 88–91.

[84] E.g. ix. 22–6 (Hannibal); x. 2–5 (Scipio Africanus); xxxi. 22–30 (Aemilius Paullus and Scipio Aemilianus).

[85] E.g. i. 42 (Sicily); iii. 36–8 (division of the earth), 57–9 (general observations); iv. 39–45 (the Black Sea and the Bosphorus).

[86] iv. 31, 74.   [87] v. 9–12.

[88] viii. 35–6.   [89] xxxvi. 17; xxxviii. 1–4.

[90] xviii. 13–15.

devoted to a detailed examination of the Roman constitution and the Roman army; book xii which, arising out of a specific criticism of a point in Timaeus, has grown into a full-scale critique both of him and of many others of Polybius' predecessors; and finally book xxxiv, which is devoted to geography. I shall have something to say about books vi and xxxiv in later chapters; but now I want to turn to book xii.

6.

As we saw earlier,[91] this book was probably written after 146 in the form in which it eventually appeared, though it could have been planned before then. Polybius recognises that it constitutes a digression, but remarks[92] that 'I referred my discussion of Timaeus to one place just because I do not want to be frequently compelled to neglect my main task'. In fact, though it develops into a general criticism of several historians and earlier writers—including Aristotle and Demochares—it centres on Timaeus. It has been argued by Pédech[93] that Polybius' irritation against Timaeus was exacerbated by his discovery during a visit to Alexandria sometime during the decade 144–134[94] that, despite his own journeys in the west, the scholars of that city still held Timaeus to be the main authority on those parts; and he suggests that an elaborate comparison which Polybius makes in book xii between the art of the historian and the science of medicine[95] was the result of personal acquaintance with the medical schools of Herophilus and Callimachus derived from the same visit. This is ingenious but, I suspect, a little fanciful. Polybius' references to the medical schools give every impression of being drawn from some handbook of medicine[96] rather than from a trip to Alexandria, and he hardly needed to visit that city in order to find out that Timaeus was held in high repute, as he certainly was both in Greece and at Rome.[97] Nevertheless, Pédech is probably right in dating the book as a whole after 146 for the reasons mentioned above (p. 25).

[91] See above, pp. 24–5.

[92] xii. 11. 6–7.

[93] Cf. Pédech, *Polybe xii*, pp. xxxi–xxxiii.

[94] xxxiv. 14. 6 for Polybius' visit to Alexandria during the reign of Ptolemy VIII Euergetes II (Physcon), and so after 145; cf. Ziegler, col. 1461; Gelzer, 'Die Arbeitsweise des Polybios', *Kl. Schr.* iii. 168 n. 61; above, p. 12 n. 58.

[95] xii. 25 d. 2–25 e. 7.   [96] See my *Commentary*, ii. 388–9.

[97] See on this Walbank, 'Polemic in Polybius', *JRS*, 52 (1962), 10.

Book xii is essentially a book devoted to polemic; it therefore contains many examples of that censoriousness with which Polybius was particularly free, in others parts of his work too, when discussing his predecessors. I have already mentioned his attack on Theopompus;[98] he claims to be shocked and dismayed by the famous passage in which Philip II's *hetairoi* were denounced as a company of debauchees assembled from all over Greece. Dionysius[99] was later to commend Theopompus for his laudable exhibition of free speech, but Polybius could not stomach the attack on Philip II, whose career was still the object of controversy in Greece, but whom a loyal Arcadian naturally regarded as a benefactor who had brought freedom to a Peloponnese oppressed by Sparta. In this case[100] moral strictures serve to disguise the political prejudices of the historian of Megalopolis, who judges Philip II against criteria natural to an Arcadian. The example serves to show that Polybius' real motives in polemic are not always those which appear on the surface; and in the case of Timaeus we can trace several levels at which Polybius opposes him, and which when analysed throw as much light on the critic as on the object of his attack.[101]

It has recently been suggested[102] that Polybius' hostility to Timaeus springs from two divergent concepts of the nature of history: Polybius was concerned to train the statesman whereas Timaeus wrote within the framework of the Isocratean school, for

[98] See above, p. 40 n. 37.

[99] See Dion. Hal. *de imit.* 13, 31. 3, p. 428; *ad Pomp.* 6. 7–10; cf. Avenarius, 161–2.

[100] Polybius may also have resented the change in focus when Theopompus abandoned Ἑλληνικαὶ ἱστορίαι (running from 411 to 394) in order to write Φιλιππικά (the 58 books of which began in 360/59); cf. vii. 11. 3–4, where he affirms that ' it would have been more dignified and more proper to include Philip's achievement in the history of Greece than to include the history of Greece in that of Philip', and claims that the period after the battle of Leuctra, which was thus abandoned, constituted the most brilliant period of Greek history. It was of course the period when Epaminondas founded Megalopolis and established the Arcadian League; cf. Walbank, 'Polemic in Polybius', *JRS*, 52 (1962), 2.

[101] On Timaeus see Brown, *Timaeus*; M. A. Levi, 'La critica di Polibio a Timeo', *Studi alessandrini*, 195–202; Momigliano, 'Atene nel III secolo A.C. e la scoperta di Roma nelle storie di Timeo di Tauromenio', *Terzo contributo*, i. 23–53 (with bibliography); F. W. Walbank, 'Polemic in Polybius', *JRS*, 52 (1962), 3–12; 'The Greek historians of Sicily', ΚΩΚΑΛΟΣ, 14–15 (1968–9), 483–5 (also with recent bibliography).

[102] M. A. Levi, art. cit. (n. 101).

whom history was itself rhetorical and furnished the *exempla* of the orator. Now it is true that Polybius has some harsh criticisms of the speeches in Timaeus, especially those of Hermocrates and Timoleon, which he ridicules as puerile and time-wasting and even below the standard one would expect from a pupil in the rhetorical schools.[103] For a more favourable view we may turn to Cicero[104] who describes Timaeus as the most erudite of historians, *rerum copia et sententiarum varietate abundantissimus et ipsa compositione verborum non impolitus,* who brought great eloquence but no forensic experience to the task of writing. However neither Polybius nor Cicero seems to have provided evidence that Timaeus should be regarded as a rhetorician, and it seems to me that a significant connection between him and Isocrates has not been established; for the fact that his teacher Philiscus of Miletus is said to have been a pupil of Isocrates[105] does not really take us very far.

There are in fact many reasons more convincing than this why Polybius should have shown such hostility towards Timaeus. In the first place it seems reasonable to assume that he genuinely objected to the faults of procedure which he mentions as characteristic of Timaeus. He was given to cavilling and fault-finding,[106] making niggling criticisms of Theopompus and accusing Ephorus of faulty arithmetic, when it was quite obvious that the error was due to a copyist—the kind of thing which had in fact led to his nickname of Epitimaeus, the 'fault-finder'. Moreover he was ignorant and credulous,[107] accepting the story that the Alpheius dives under the sea to come up again in Syracuse,[108] or childishly explaining the Roman custom of sacrificing the October Horse as commemorating the role of the Wooden Horse in the capture of Troy—a piece of irrelevant pedantry, adds Polybius, turning against him the charge of ὀψιμαθία which he had himself levelled against Aristotle.[109] One could multiply examples: in Polybius they go on for chapters. Yet they are not so serious as his objection to Timaeus' concept of how a historian should set about his task, for this was an implied criticism of his own views on history.

The charge here is summed up in the statement[110] that Timaeus

103 xii. 25 k–26 a.
104 Cic. *de orat.* ii. 58.   105 *FGH* 566 T 1 = Suda, s.v. Τίμαιος.
106 xii. 4 a. 6, τὸ φιλεπίτιμον καὶ φιλέγκλημον.
107 xii. 4 b–4 c.   108 xii. 4 d. 5–8.
109 xii. 4 c. 1; for ὀψιμαθία cf. 8. 4.   110 xii. 25 d. 1.

imagined that by living for close on fifty years[111] in the libraries of Athens he had everything he needed for the writing of history at his disposal, and (Polybius alleges)[112] actually admitted to his complete ignorance of warfare and scanty knowledge of the outside world. It is on this that the contrast with his critic was especially marked, for Polybius, as we have seen,[113] took an especial pride in his practical experience of politics and warfare and in having travelled widely on land and ocean, in 'journeys through Africa, Spain and Gaul, and voyages on the seas that lie on the farther side of those countries'.[114] It is in this context that we have to consider a well-known passage[115] criticising Timaeus' bookish ways, in which Polybius not only contrasts the toil and expense involved in personal enquiry but quotes statements from Ephorus, Theopompus and above all Homer to support his contention that it is this that constitutes the most valuable and essential exercise for the would-be historian. Homer, he says,[116] defining his hero, the man of action, begins

'Tell me, o Muse, of the man of many wiles, who
    wandered far and wide'

and goes on

'and he saw the towns of many men and learned their
    minds and suffered many woes in his heart upon the sea'

and

'experienced wars of men and grievous waves'.

[111] In xii. 25 h. 1, Polybius says 'fifty years' without qualification. The dates of Timaeus' exile in Athens are uncertain, but the suggestion that he was already there when Agathocles banished him (Diod. xxi. 17. 1) is unlikely; see Momigliano, 'Atene nel III secolo A.C. e la scoperta di Roma nelle storie di Timeo di Tauromenio', Terzo contributo, i. 25, against Brown, Timaeus, 2–3, who also thinks he returned soon after Agathocles' death in 289 and that the fifty years fell within the period 339–278. Timaeus' lack of political and military experience (xii. 25 g. 1–3, 25 h. 1, 28. 6) and his inexperience as a speaker (Cic. de orat. ii. 58) would fit an early withdrawal to Athens; but there is no proof that he returned to Sicily at the end of fifty (or 'nearly fifty') years; indeed the word καταβιώσας (xii. 28. 6) might suggest that he died in Athens. See my Commentary, ii. 388; K. Meister, ΚΩΚΑΛΟΣ, 16 (1970), 53–9.

[112] It is difficult to believe that Timaeus actually made this admission in the terms Polybius cites—'living away from home at Athens for fifty years continuously and having, as I confess (ὁμολογουμένως), no experience of active war service or any personal acquaintance with places'—and it looks as if Polybius may have twisted a reference to Timaeus' long exile from Sicily (cf. Jacoby, commenting on FGH 566 F 34).

[113] See above, p. 11.   [114] iii. 59. 7.   [115] xii. 27–8.
[116] xii. 27. 10–11; see above, p. 25 and n. 128.

'It appears to me', says Polybius, 'that the dignity of history also demands such a man.'[117] As we shall see later,[118] Polybius included in book xxxiv an account of his journeys in the west and in the process embarked on another piece of polemic against Pytheas of Marseilles, himself a western Greek (like Timaeus) who claimed to have explored the northern seas and to have circumnavigated Britain. One might perhaps have expected a man so unlike Timaeus, and so active in travel and exploration, as Pytheas, to win Polybius' commendation. Not at all; quite obviously the rival claim is bitterly resented and Pytheas' credentials and honesty are alike assailed in a withering passage of critical venom.[119] The dignity of history demanded a man like Odysseus—but only one; and Polybius' foible will have been known to the Greeks of Megalopolis who set up an inscription recording how Polybius 'wandered over every sea and land' (ἐπὶ γῆν καὶ θάλασσαν πλανηθείη).[120] Indeed, if he had already begun drawing this grand, if slightly humourless, comparison after his crossing of the Alps and journey to Africa in 151/0, Cato may have been hinting at it in his jibe that, in asking for the restoration of their former honours in Greece for the returning Achaean exiles, Polybius was behaving like Odysseus going back into the Cyclops' cave to retrieve his forgotten hat.[121] At any rate, here undoubtedly is another important reason for Polybius' hostility towards Timaeus; behind the attack on the arm-chair scholar is his resentment that such a man should enjoy a reputation as the historian of the western lands.

Furthermore, Timaeus' history was one that put Sicily and Magna Graecia at the very centre of the picture. Despite his long exile in Athens, he had never come to terms with mainland Greece as she was. As Momigliano has shown,[122] he dissociated the contemporary Athenian statesmen such as Demochares, whom he attacked in the vilest terms,[123] from the city's anti-Macedonian past; and he declined to include continental Greece in his history. I have already mentioned[124] Polybius' criticism of the importance Timaeus attributed to Timoleon, who sought fame in a tea-cup—

[117] xii. 28. 1.   [118] See below, pp. 122–4.
[119] xxxiv. 5 ff.   [120] Paus. viii. 30. 8.
[121] xxxv. 6. 4 = Plut. Cato mai. 9. 3.
[122] 'Atene nel III secolo A.C. e la scoperta di Roma nelle storie di Timeo di Tauromenio', Terzo contributo, i. 23–53.
[123] xii. 13–14.   [124] See above, p. 3.

Sicily. Elsewhere he makes his point even more clearly.[125] In his account of Gelon's offer to assist the mainland Greeks against Persia, Timaeus, Polybius tells us, 'is so long-winded and so obviously anxious to demonstrate that Sicily was more important than all the rest of Greece, and that the events occurring in Sicily were more magnificent and more splendid than anywhere else in the world, and that of all the men of outstanding wisdom the very wisest were those in Sicily and that the most divinely favoured political leaders were those from Syracuse, that no young man in a school of rhetoric, who is set the task of composing a eulogy of Thersites or a diatribe against Penelope...could surpass him in paradox'. As for Timoleon, Polybius regards it as absurd that Timaeus should attack Callisthenes for trying to have Alexander deified,[126] 'a man whose soul, as all admit, had something super-human in it', only to make *him* 'greater than the most illustrious gods', a man who in contrast to Alexander undertook only one small journey, that from Corinth to Syracuse—rather, one can imagine Polybius hinting, as Timaeus had made his one small journey from Syracuse to Athens.

But this was not all. If we ignore Hieronymus,[127] who may have touched on the Roman background of the war with Pyrrhus, and Lycus of Rhegium,[128] whom Agatharchides mentions along with Timaeus, but who was probably an ethnographer, not a historian, there seems little doubt that Timaeus was generally regarded as the first historian of Rome. Aulus Gellius mentions his *Historiae de rebus populi Romani*,[129] as evidence for the Greek origin of the name 'Italy'; the context suggests that he has taken the reference from Varro, who is also mentioned in the same passage, and who else-where[130] quotes Timaeus for this statement. The reference must be to his books on Pyrrhus; and Momigliano has observed[131] that it

---

[125] xii. 26 b.   [126] xii. 23. 5.

[127] Cf. Dion. Hal. i. 6. 1 = *FGH* 154 F 13.

[128] *FGH* 570 T 3 = Agatharchides, *De mar. rubr.* 64.

[129] *FGH* 566 T 9c = Aul. Gell. xi. 1. 1.

[130] *FGH* 566 F 42 = Varro, *de r. r.* ii. 5. 3; cf. Momigliano, 'Atene nel III secolo A.C. e la scoperta di Roma nelle storie di Timeo di Tauromenio', *Terzo contributo*, 45 n. 68.

[131] Ibid. 44–51; Momigliano also discusses Lycophron's *Alexandra*, which makes the Romans in their conflict with Pyrrhus heirs to the Trojans, and has consequently been given a second-century dating by many scholars from Niebuhr onwards (cf. most recently, S. Josifović, *RE*, Suppl.-B. xi, 'Lykophron', cols. 925–30). The case for a third-century date would be strengthened if the

was to Timaeus that the Romans of the age of Varro and Cicero still turned for their history of Sicily and the Pyrrhic War. Could Polybius have foreseen this, it would have caused him intense annoyance; for this was probably the basic reason for his hostility towards a historian whose merits he feels otherwise bound to concede. 'He seems to me', he writes,[132] 'to have cultivated both a talent for detailed research and a competence based on enquiry, and indeed in general to have approached the task of writing history in a painstaking spirit, though in certain matters I know of no author of repute (τῶν ἐπ' ὀνόματος συγγραφέων) who seems to have been more inexperienced and more careless.' Timaeus is to be taken seriously: and that is fundamentally why Polybius gives him no quarter.

I have spent some time on this somewhat sordid episode because it demonstrates the disingenuousness which sometimes lies behind Polybius' claim to defend high principles. It does not stand alone.[133] In the chapter of book xvi devoted to a brief criticism of the Rhodian historians Zeno and Antisthenes,[134] who covered some of the events in Greece and Asia Minor with which Polybius was himself concerned and were probably among his sources, he not only lists Zeno's topographical errors in detail but also informs his readers that he had not hesitated to write to Zeno in person pointing these out—but too late, since the book was already published (as Polybius must have known when he read it).[135] He makes a virtue out of this, observing that 'as far as possible we

Chian inscription which mentions Romulus and Remus and the cult of Rome (cf. N. Kontoleon, Πρακτικὰ 'Αρχ. 'Ετ. 1953 (1956), 270 f.; *Akte des IV. Internazionalen Kongresses für...Epigraphik (1962)* (Vienna, 1964), 192) were firmly dated to the third century, as the letter-forms suggest; but the support for a second-century date later than the Treaty of Apamea seems to be gaining ground (cf. J. and L. Robert, *Bull. ép.* 1965, 304; *SEG*, xvi. 486; J. Reynolds, 'Roman inscriptions, 1956–70', *JRS*, 61 (1971), 139 n. 25). But even if the author of the *Alexandra* were assigned a third-century date, this would not necessarily give him precedence over Timaeus as the first person to appreciate the importance of Rome in the world. The Callimachean anecdote of Gaius (fg. 106–7 Pfeiffer) probably derives from Timaeus (cf. Momigliano, art. cit. 49).   [132] xii. 27 a. 3.

[133] Cf. Walbank, 'Polemic in Polybius', *JRS* 52 (1962), 11–12.

[134] xvi. 14–20.

[135] There is no evidence that Polybius had seen a private copy before publication. On the relevance of this passage to the general problem of what 'publication' meant at this time, and what sort of changes were subsequently possible, see above, p. 23 n. 115.

should look after and correct other people's works as well as our own for the common advantage'; and some scholars have indeed accepted this interpretation,[136] and it has recently been quoted as proof of Polybius' 'rare sense of humility and ability to forget himself and consider others'.[137] But I fancy more readers are likely to accept von Scala's view that Polybius' behaviour on this occasion 'will hardly have had the effect of creating...increased popularity for his own writings in contemporary professional circles'.[138]

7.

However, it is very easy to get these matters out of proportion, and to assume that Polybius' polemic merely reflects rancour and jealousy. More important than this personal motivation of his attack on Timaeus and Phylarchus and Zeno is his genuine belief that the kind of writing in which they indulge—whether rhetorical or sensational or a mixture of both[139]—is inimical to the real standards of history, judged by the criterion of political utility. About this he has a great deal to say. In particular he distinguishes the kind of history which he himself writes, and which he regards as clearly the most profitable, from other sorts, with less ambitious aims and a different public in mind. In the course of his introduction to Olympiad 142, which stood at the beginning of book ix,[140] he contrasts his own kind of history with what he calls 'the genealogical sort' which attracts the casual reader (τὸν φιλήκοον),[141] and with 'accounts of colonies, foundations of cities and ties of kinship' which make their appeal to readers with antiquarian interests (τὸν πολυπράγμονα καὶ περιττόν). A little further on[142] he associates genealogies with myths, and it is clear that by 'the genealogical sort' of history he meant the kind that dealt with the early legends in all their fabulous aspects, and elaborate genealogical links: the first volume of Jacoby's *Fragmente* assembles specimens from many of them, Hecataeus, Acusilaus, Hellanicus and others,

---

[136] Cf. Susemihl, ii. 117 n. 121.

[137] So Roveri, *Studi*, 81–2.   [138] Von Scala, 294.

[139] Polybius did not mention this more fundamental objection to Zeno's work—that he put style before accuracy—in his letter to the author, presumably because he could say nothing useful about this.

[140] ix. 1–2; cf. J. P. V. D. Balsdon, 'Some questions about historical writing in the second century B.C.', *CQ*, 3 (1953), 159, and my *Commentary*, ii. 116–18.

[141] See my *Commentary*, ii. 116, on ix. 1. 4.

[142] ix. 2. 1.

whose histories involved the working over of epic material and reduction of it to chronological order.[143] Colonies, the foundation of cities, and kinship ties are especially to be found in local histories like the *Atthis*, but also in general works like those of Ephorus and Timaeus.[144] In contrast to both is the sort of history Polybius writes, dealing with the affairs of peoples, cities and rulers (ἐθνῶν καὶ πόλεων καὶ δυναστῶν)[145] and consequently of interest and profit to the statesman.[146]

For this Polybius has a special word, πραγματικὴ ἱστορία or ὁ πραγματικὸς τρόπος,[147] a phrase which has often been misunderstood.[148] From the passage which I have just been discussing it seems clear that πραγματικὴ ἱστορία can be defined as political —and military—history; and in contrast to the other kinds mentioned there it is contemporary history.[149] What it includes seems to depend very much on Polybius' own predilections, since the overriding consideration, that it shall benefit the statesman and the general, is a fairly wide one. But it is interesting to find Polybius referring in this context to the great progress made by the arts and sciences in his own time, and suggesting that consequently the study of history will provide the means of solving any problems that may arise virtually by a formula (ὡς ἂν εἰ μεθοδικῶς).[150] This

[143] Cf. Jacoby, *Atthis*, 134.

[144] Cf. xxxiv. 1. 3–4 = Strabo, x. 465 for Ephorus; xii. 26 d. 2 for Timaeus; cf. Pédech, *Méthode*, 27.

[145] The phrase is common in Hellenistic official phraseology, with slight variants; cf. Diod. xix. 57. 3; *OGIS* 229 line 11; 441 line 132; *Syll.* 590 lines 12–14; 760; Rostovtzeff, *Hellenistic world*, 502–3, 1347, 1439–40 on the meaning of ἔθνη. Since ἔθνη included federal states (cf. Larsen, *Representative government*, 22–3), πόλις and ἔθνος were often used together to cover comprehensively all types of state (cf. Aeschin. iii. 110; *IG* iv². 1. 68 line 78; *Syll.* 613 lines 4–5).

[146] ix. 1. 4, τὸν πολιτικόν; Paton in the Loeb edition renders this as 'the student of politics', incorrectly. See further Petzold, *Studien*, 7.

[147] ix. 1. 4–5, 2. 4.

[148] For discussion of the meaning of the phrase see Gelzer, 'Die pragmatische Geschichtsschreibung des Polybios', *Kl. Schr.* iii. 155–60; Walbank, *Commentary*, i. 8 n. 6; Pédech, *Méthode*, 25 f.; *Polybe i*, p. xxi; Petzold, *Studien*, 3–24. πραγματικὴ ἱστορία does not in itself imply a practical and didactic purpose. Petzold, loc. cit., has argued that by his use of it in such contexts as i. 2. 8, 35. 9, xxxvi. 17. 1 and xxxix. 1. 4, Polybius stamped the phrase with a didactic connotation; but clearly to say that πραγματικὴ ἱστορία is of direct practical and didactic use is not the same thing as saying that πραγματικὴ ἱστορία *means* 'history with a direct practical and didactic use'.

[149] See above, p. 42.

[150] ix. 2. 5. Pédech, *Méthode*, 27, says that thanks to scientific and technical progress it is now possible to write history methodically (μεθοδικῶς); but Polybius

implies that an account of such improvements in the arts and sciences will be properly included in his πραγματικὴ ἱστορία—though in practice the only examples we find are of a military character, for example Polybius' own improvement to the art of fire-signalling.[151] He also regards a brief account of the cycle of constitutions, as outlined by some of the philosophers, as relevant to πραγματικὴ ἱστορία[152] and includes it in book vi. In general, however, his subject matter is the traditional material—politics and war—the world in which he had grown up; for this is most likely to appeal to and to benefit his readers.

It was an essential feature of political and military history that it should explain why things came about. This Polybius regards as very important, and I shall have more to say about it later. But in view of some misunderstanding it is worth pointing out that the phrase πραγματικὴ ἱστορία does not itself mean 'history which investigates causes'. Polybius comes nearer to expressing this idea in another phrase, ἀποδεικτικὴ ἱστορία,[153] which means literally 'demonstrative history', that is 'history which expounds things in detail'. He uses this phrase or its equivalent—μετ' ἀποδείξεως—to describe his main history as distinct from the cursory introduction in books i and ii[154] or to contrast it with his encomiastic biography of Philopoemen,[155] and he uses the word ἀποδεικτική referring to his account of the Black Sea[156] and the reasons which are leading to its silting up, because it is based not on unsupported statements, but on the principles of natural

does not say this. The question of *method* arises not in relation to the writing of history, but in relation to the solution of problems facing the statesman or general, who is envisaged as the reader of Polybius' work; and in fact Polybius has a cross-reference to this passage in x. 47. 12–13 after his account of the technique of fire-signalling (see the next note). Cf. the valid remarks of Petzold, *Studien*, 5.

[151] On this system, devised by himself, see below, p. 88.

[152] vi. 5. 2.

[153] Cf. ii. 37. 3; Pédech, *Méthode*, 46 n. 108. The phrase seems to mean 'demonstrative history', i.e. history which includes evidence and argument (rather than 'history which investigates causes', as I said in *Commentary*, i. 8 n. 6); see J. A. North, *JHS*, 87 (1967), 154. It also, necessarily, involves a contrast with history that is 'summary', κεφαλαιώδης, and Petzold, *Studien*, 17, argues that the sense of 'demonstrative' grew out of the idea of 'detailed presentation'. It is not in practice possible to write 'demonstrative history' without considering causes (see below, p. 58 n. 158).

[154] ii. 37. 3; iii. 1. 3.   [155] x. 21. 8.

[156] iv. 40. 1.

science. Detailed exposition of this kind naturally involves the consideration of cause and effect, as can be seen from a passage in book xviii,[157] where Polybius elucidates his statement that he has narrated Philip's moral deterioration by remarking that he has explained 'when, why and how' the stages in his change took place.[158]

8.

Polybius regards the study of the past as essentially a way to attain practical ends by learning lessons; some of these are of the kind useful to the politician, while others have a moral content—they assist men to bear the various blows of fortune by describing those that have befallen others in the past.[159] Broadly, this means that in human affairs a good deal is calculable even if a residuum is not; the whole programme of learning through the study of history implies a rational world in which—by and large—comparable causes produce comparable results and comparable efforts give comparable rewards. Describing the battle of the Aegates Islands Polybius remarks: 'As the condition of each force was just the reverse of what it had been at the battle of Drepana, the result was also naturally (εἰκότως) the reverse for each'; and so it proved. But when Aemilius Paullus encouraged his forces before Cannae by referring to Trebia and Trasimene, and concluding: 'since then all the conditions are now the reverse of those in the battles I spoke of, we may anticipate that the result of the present battle will likewise be the opposite', Polybius is surely indicating ironically that there is a limit to what can be assured by calculation and reasoning from the past.[160] But this merely means that Fortune must be allowed for, not that there are no lessons for reason to learn from history.

On this point it is fruitful to compare Polybius with Herodotus and Thucydides. Herodotus[161] is convinced that all that men do

[157] xviii. 33. 6.

[158] πότε καὶ διὰ τί καὶ πῶς ἐγένετο.

[159] i. 1. 2 (quoted below, p. 60 n. 169). Pédech, *Polybe i*, pp. xxxiv–xxxv, derives this aspect of Polybius' purpose from his own experience; 'les événements de l'histoire lui apparaissent continuellement ballottés par les caprices de la fortune, comme lui-même l'a été au cours de son incomparable destinée'.

[160] i. 61. 2 (Aegates Islands)—quoted below, p. 96 n. 186; iii. 109. 3 (Cannae). Cf. Walbank, *Speeches*, 13, for discussion of these two similar passages.

[161] Cf. Strasburger, 'Die Entstehung der politischen Geschichte durch Thukydides', *Thukydides*, 435.

and achieve is subject to the guidance of supernatural forces; the role that these play does not conform to any consistent pattern, but operates sometimes on the assumption of a predestined fate for all men, sometimes as an expression of divine malice or alternatively of an avenging justice which assigns to men their fitting lot. In Herodotus' world dreams and oracles play an important part and men's lives demonstrate the way in which the divine purpose is fulfilled. Thucydides describes a world[162] entirely governed by human rules and calculations, in which there is no place for divine powers. Whether he believed in the gods himself we cannot tell: but, if he did, he kept them entirely out of his history. In so doing, he reflected an attitude also to be found in sophistic circles, but certainly not among ordinary men; and the two hundred years or so that separated the death of Thucydides from the birth of Polybius had brought about no substantial change in this.

Polybius has been described as irreligious; yet he has not completely thrown off a belief in the gods. In a striking discussion of his religious attitudes the Spanish scholar Álvarez de Miranda[163] remarks that irreligiosity is not a coherent system, but is rather like the remains of a shipwreck. This may be true. But if one compares the religious attitudes of Polybius with those of Herodotus, one finds the same incoherence and inconsistency in both. This perhaps suggests that the incoherence is characteristic of popular Greek religious thought in general, and not merely an aspect of its collapse in the Hellenistic age.

A good many of Polybius' religious attitudes are only superficially relevant to him as a historian. He accepts what has been called the political view of religion, namely, that whether the gods exist or not, it is expedient that the people should believe that they do. This notion of religion as a clever trick devised for political purposes is first found in the late fifth century in the *Sisyphus* of Critias,[164] though the idea of a belief in divine law and divine sanctions as constituting a socially useful concept may go back to the Pythagoreans. Polybius believes that where absurd

---

[162] Ibid. 436–7.

[163] 'La irreligiosidad de Polibio', *Emerita*, 24 (1956), 27–65. Pédech, *Méthode*, 397 n. 296, defends Polybius' religious beliefs as coherent, but not, I think, convincingly. See also H. F. Allen, 'Polybius and the gods', *TAPA*, 39 (1908), xiii.

[164] Cf. Diels–Kranz, *Frag. Vorsok.* ii. 88 B 25; see further my remarks in *Commentary*, i. 741–2 on vi. 56. 6–12.

tales of miracles contribute towards the maintenance of religious piety among the common people, they are permissible, provided that they do not go too far—though the difficulty, he admits, is knowing how far is too far.[165] Specifically, he approves the use made of religious pageantry at Rome, and describes superstition, δεισιδαιμονία, as the force that holds together the Roman state.[166] In the main this attitude has little effect on him as a historian; but there is one exception, namely his interpretation of Scipio Africanus,[167] whom he sees as a man who, to his credit, cynically exploited the religious credulity of his troops in order the better to capture New Carthage. For his own part, he seems to have accepted Euhemerus' view of the traditional gods as having once been human beings, dead long ago but honoured for their benefactions to mankind.[168]

At the same time he refers to the divine powers on many occasions in terms which make it difficult to be certain whether he believed in them or not; and this is particularly true of Fortune or *Tyche*. The Hellenistic world had made Fortune a great goddess, and not inappropriately at a time which had seen the fall of Persia and Alexander's march to India, and the subsequent collapse of his kingdom and the varied fortunes of his successors.

The problem of Fortune is quite fundamental for Polybius' history; for if the logical sequence of cause and effect are more than marginally disturbed by chance—and obviously chance must play some part in an imperfect world—if in short human destinies are directed on a large scale by the whim of some incalculable and capricious power then the whole concept of πραγματικὴ ἱστορία as the nursery of the statesman and general is endangered. On the other hand, it was not too easy to play down the role of *Tyche* when a secondary purpose of writing history was to impart moral lessons by giving examples of how to meet the vicissitudes which she sent.[169] Up to a point, this could be managed, for the *Tyche* which brought vicissitudes need not be more than, as we should say, chance or bad luck: it could, logically, remain an impersonal

---

[165] xvi. 12. 9–11.   [166] vi. 56. 6–12.

[167] See my *Commentary*, ii. 191–6 on x. 2. 1–20. 8; 'The Scipionic legend', *Proc. Camb. Phil. Soc.* 13 (1967), 59–69.

[168] Cf. x. 10. 11; xxxiv. 2. 5; Pédech, 'Les idées religieuses de Polybe', *Revue de l'histoire des religions*, 167 (1965), 44.

[169] Cf. i. 1. 2 describing history as ἐναργεστάτην...καὶ μόνην διδάσκαλον τοῦ δύνασθαι τὰς τῆς τύχης μεταβολὰς γενναίως ὑποφέρειν.

force, the incalculable element in human affairs. In fact in Polybius this is often so; for if one analyses his use of the word,[170] it very quickly becomes apparent that it possesses a variety of meanings and that these operate at what might be termed different levels of intensity. Often the usage is quite formal: *Tyche* did something, but one could just as well have said that something happened. For example, the Mamertine plunderers seized the wives and families of the men of Messana ὡς ποθ' ἡ τύχη διένειμε...ἑκάστοις, meaning 'as they happened upon them'.[171] Elsewhere *Tyche* seems to take on more reality; and fortunately there is a passage (in book xxxvi)[172] in which Polybius sets out to define the situations in which events can properly be assigned to fate and fortune (τὴν τύχην καὶ τὴν εἱμαρμένην). When men find it difficult or impossible to grasp the causes of some events, he explains, one is justified in referring these ἐπὶ τὸν θεὸν...καὶ τὴν τύχην, 'to the divine power ...and to fortune'; examples are the destruction of crops from drought, outbreaks of plague, and what today would be termed 'acts of god'. But when one is dealing with something like the low birth-rate in Greece,[173] the causes of which are natural and ascertainable, such an explanation is quite improper. He then goes on to discuss human behaviour, as exemplified in the support the Macedonians afforded to Andriscus, which defies rational explanation, and he concludes (in a passage unfortunately riddled with lacunae) that this can only be characterised as 'heaven-sent infatuation and an expression of divine wrath'.[174]

Polybius here reserves to the domain of *Tyche* the area which lies beyond human control together with those events of which the causes are hard to detect or for which there are apparently no rational causes at all—in short all that lies outside the sphere of rational analysis. Such events can be described in terms of τύχη, θεός τις, μῆνις ἐκ θεῶν, τὸ δαιμόνιον or ταὐτόματον, and these phrases though not entirely synonymous—τὸ δαιμόνιον, for instance,

---

[170] The relevant passages are conveniently assembled by Hercod, 100–1; cf. Warde Fowler, 'Polybius' concept of τύχη', *CR*, 17 (1903), 446 ff.; P. Shorey, 'Τύχη in Polybius', *CP* 16 (1921), 281.

[171] i. 7. 4; for further similar cases see for example v. 42. 8; x. 33. 4–5—but they are frequent throughout the *Histories*.

[172] xxxvi. 17: Polybius seems to find such a discussion slightly out of place in his πραγματικὴ ἱστορία: cf. 17. 1, νῦν βούλομαι περὶ τούτου τοῦ μέρους διαστείλασθαι καθ' ὅσον ὁ τῆς πραγματικῆς ἱστορίας ἐπιδέχεται τρόπος.

[173] xxxvi. 17. 4–11.   [174] xxxvi. 17. 15.

seems especially concerned with divine vengeance[175]—are certainly used with a considerable overlap of meaning.

Within this general field *Tyche* might be expected to operate quite widely. In practice, however, it is possible to define rather more closely the occasions on which Polybius invokes her help. Frequently events which are quite explicable in themselves, but are external to the particular sequence of cause and effect under discussion, are attributed to *Tyche*.[176] For instance, Hannibal's attack on Rome came to nothing[177] because by pure coincidence an abnormally large number of troops happened to be present at Rome and could be led out against the enemy. Their presence could of course be quite rationally accounted for; but in relation to Hannibal's attack this was 'an unexpected stroke of Fortune'. But even more *Tyche* is felt to be involved when events of a striking or capricious kind occur to upset the balance of history and where fortunes are suddenly and sensationally reversed.[178] Indeed it can be taken as axiomatic that Fortune will allow no one to prosper indefinitely; it was through recognising this truth that Demetrius of Phalerum was able to make his dramatic prophecy of the downfall of Macedon.[179] In view of the instability of Fortune Polybius concludes that men should be moderate in success; and this somewhat trite moral is repeatedly emphasised.[180] The reason for displaying such moderation is not that it will have any effect on Fortune, but simply that it is more decent.[181] In fact Fortune,

[175] Cf. Pédech, *Polybe i*, 133 n. 1. On the other hand, in iv. 81. 5 Polybius uses τύχη to describe the power which visits the ephors at Sparta with the penalty appropriate to their crime, and it looks as if he was prepared to use either expression without distinction in such a context.

[176] See the examples quoted in my *Commentary*, i. 17–18.

[177] ix. 6. 5.

[178] See my *Commentary*, i. 18–19.

[179] xxix. 21; see above, p. 2. It was dramatic to Polybius, who thought he had seen the prophecy fulfilled, but in fact no great perceptiveness was required to subscribe to the general proposition that all institutions (including empires) ultimately come to an end, and then to apply this to Macedonia.

[180] For examples see my *Commentary*, i. 19.

[181] There is an apparent exception in xxvii. 8. 4, where Perseus' friends urge him to offer peace-terms to the Romans, who might well accept them in view of their recent set-back; and if they did not, νεμεσήσειν τὸ δαιμόνιον, while Perseus himself by his μετριότης would win over τοὺς θεοὺς καὶ τοὺς ἀνθρώπους. However, Polybius almost immediately (xxvii. 8. 8 ff.) explains that Perseus' friends had misunderstood the way the Romans behaved, and Perseus' fate shows equally that they had misunderstood the way τὸ δαιμόνιον behaved. Polybius himself believed neither that a politic exhibition of moderation could

as the power making for instability in human affairs, is impervious to human behaviour, and this might be held to justify the conclusion that Polybius regarded it as an impersonal force—the way things happen.

However this is not the whole story: for in many passages Fortune is depicted as punishing wrongdoing, and so presumably conscious. A notable example is that of Philip and Antiochus, whose dynasties were destroyed in condign punishment for their wicked conspiracy against the boy king Ptolemy Epiphanes;[182] and in this case Polybius elaborates the ruin of Philip himself with references to furies and metaphors taken from the stage, in a manner calculated to recall the sensational kind of writing which he elsewhere condemns in Phylarchus.[183] In such passages as these Fortune seems to be personified and purposive in her actions, so much so that several scholars have compared this *Tyche* with the Stoic concept of Providence, πρόνοια;[184] and Warde Fowler[185] not very convincingly suggested that she was to be identified with φύσις, nature,[186] which plays so large a part in the discussion of the Roman constitution in book vi. Now the most striking example of Fortune being represented as a purposive power is of course to be found in the central theme of the whole history, where the rise of Rome to world-dominion in nearly fifty-three years is singled out and consistently represented as the finest show-piece—a metaphor from the theatre—and the achievement of Fortune most excellent and profitable to contemplate.[187] And yet, elsewhere the rise of Rome is depicted as essentially something rational. 'By schooling themselves in vast and perilous enterprises,' writes Polybius,[188] 'it

influence the gods nor that arrogance in itself necessarily attracted divine vengeance (that is rather the penalty of prosperity). See further my *Commentary*, i. 20.

[182] Cf. xv. 20. 5–8; xxix. 27. 11–12 (where *Tyche* so arranges events that the fall of Perseus meant the salvation of Egypt). Philip was led to murder his son Demetrius, and if (as Schmitt, *Antiochos*, 18, argues) the story in Livy (xxxv. 15. 3–5), that Antiochus executed his homonymous son, goes back to Polybius, the fate of the two villainous kings is made remarkably parallel.

[183] See my *Commentary*, i. 20–1; *Speeches*, 55–68; above, p. 39 n. 34.

[184] So Hirzel, *Cicero*, ii. 862–9 (appendix 7), arguing that Polybius' *Tyche* is frequently the equivalent of the Stoic πρόνοια; but in that case why could he not use the technical term rather than the ambiguous *Tyche*? See further Hercod, 76–103; Mioni, 199 n. 32; Erkell, 140–1.

[185] 'Polybius' concept of τύχη', *CR*, 17 (1903), 446–7.

[186] So too Nilsson, *Religion*, ii². 189, 194.

[187] i. 4. 4, τὸ κάλλιστον ἅμα καὶ ὠφελιμώτατον ἐπιτήδευμα τῆς τύχης.

[188] i. 63. 9; see my *Commentary*, i. 129–30 ad loc.

was entirely natural (εἰκότως) that the Romans not only gained the courage to aim at universal dominion but actually executed their purpose'—thus showing that their progress was not due to chance or something that just happened on its own, as some of the Greeks believed.

The contradiction is patent, but all attempts to resolve it by postulating some sort of development in Polybius' philosophical view run up against the objection that they depend upon an entirely arbitrary division of a whole range of passages, many of which can be shown to belong closely together. To quote a single example, the failure of Regulus in Africa during the First Punic War is explained as due to two identifiable causes, neither in any way supernatural, viz. his psychological error in demanding unconditional surrender and the arrival of Xanthippus in the Punic camp; yet it is also adduced as an illustration of the whim of Fortune.[189] Equally unconvincing is the attempt to explain the contradiction as the result of some kind of schizophrenia in Polybius—a sort of Jekyll–Hyde 'with two souls in his breast', as Siegfried sees him,[190] switching without difficulty or conscious discomfort from a scientific world ruled by cause and effect to a religious world dominated by *Tyche*—and back again. This implausible theory ignores the fact that Polybius presents not two but several versions of *Tyche*; and whether *Tyche* is envisaged as capricious or retributive, or indeed whether *Tyche* figures in a particular situation at all, may well depend on the direction in which our sympathies are engaged. As we saw,[191] Macedonian support for Andriscus was an example of heaven-sent infatuation, and it was the wrath of heaven that descended on the old age of Philip V, to punish him for his past crimes. It is not easy to dissociate Polybius' interpretation of these events from the Achaean commitment to the Roman side in the wars against Philip V and Antiochus. Moreover this commitment was not simply a matter of political affiliation (on that I shall have more to say later), but it was even more a commitment which matched his central belief that the rise of Rome to world dominion was somehow part of the world-order and the beneficent design of *Tyche*.

Seen in this context *Tyche* certainly seems to take on divine lineaments. Yet one cannot ignore purely verbal and rhetorical

[189] i. 30–5.   [190] Siegfried, *Studien*, 47 ff.
[191] See above, p. 61.

elements in Polybius' remarks generally about the action of *Tyche*. It has been pointed out by Ziegler that such references are frequently qualified by words like ὥσπερ and ὡσανεί. Of two examples of sacrilege punished by swift and condign punishment Antiochus died struck down by madness, 'as some say', ὡς ἔνιοί φασι, and after despoiling temples Prusias' troops are afflicted by hunger and dysentery, 'so that it *seemed* as if heaven's vengeance visited him instantly'.[192] The doubts that these passages raise concerning Polybius' belief in an objectively existing *Tyche* are strengthened by the passage already mentioned,[193] in which he treats the word as a convenient label to attach to acts of God and the irrational and fortuitous interventions of men. Nevertheless, in the case of his main theme it is very hard to resist the impression that as he looked back on the remarkable and indeed unique process of Rome's swift rise to power, and recollected the words of Demetrius of Phalerum, he was led to confuse what had happened with what was destined to happen, and so to invest the rise of Rome to world power with a teleological character. Hence the personification of *Tyche* in his original programme and his use of such words as σκοπός, οἰκονομία, and συντέλεια, which, as Warde Fowler long ago remarked,[194] points clearly to the activity of a power working towards a conscious goal.

[192] xxxi. 9. 4; xxxii. 15. 4.
[193] xxxvi. 17; above, p. 61 n. 172.
[194] 'Polybius' conception of τύχη', *CR*, 17 (1903), 446.

III

'Pragmatike historia'

1.

In the previous chapter I suggested that in several respects Polybius' programme for new standards in the writing of history represented a return to the principles of Thucydides. πραγματικὴ ἱστορία, as we saw, meant the political and military history of Polybius' own time based on his own practical experience; and so far it followed the Thucydidean pattern. Where it broke away was in its rejection of the historical monograph. Thucydides had conceived his work as an account of the war between Athens and Sparta; but its incompleteness had obscured the unity of the conception, and when Xenophon resolved to continue it on the chronological basis of summers and winters, there seemed no reason why he should stop when he reached the end of the war. Nor did he. In fact he turned the monograph into a *historia perpetua*, a continuous narrative history capable of indefinite prolongation[1]—as he indicated when after Leuctra he ended his work with the words: 'Let my narrative end here: what follows will perhaps be the concern of someone else.'[2] This 'misunderstanding of Thucydides', as Strasburger has described it,[3] was also inherited by Ephorus, who adapted the narrative parts of his work to the needs of universal history, and turned the speeches into occasions for rhetorical dexterity in the manner of Isocrates, his teacher. At the same time, by perpetuating Thucydides' emphasis on military operations both Xenophon and Ephorus gave to this aspect of history a prominence which it was to retain throughout antiquity and beyond, not least in Polybius.

---

[1] Cf. Strasburger, 'Die Entdeckung der politischen Geschichte durch Thukydides', *Thukydides*, 467; *Wesensbestimmung*, 19. For the concept of *historia perpetua* cf. Cicero, *fam.* v. 12. 2, 12. 6.

[2] Xen. *Hell.* vii. 5. 27.   [3] Ibid. (n. 1).

The expansion of the monograph into continuous, and ultimately universal, history destroyed its unity. It is Polybius' claim, and indeed his achievement, that he succeeded in writing universal history in the footsteps of Ephorus, but at the same time produced a work with a subject and a pattern, which made it 'as it were an organic whole' (οἱονεὶ σωματοειδῆ).[4] Von Fritz has remarked[5] that Herodotus' history, with its two themes—to preserve the memory of the great and wonderful actions of the Greeks and barbarians and to explain why they fought each other—could fairly easily have been adjusted to give a systematic presentation of these but in fact was not. But this is not perhaps surprising when one bears in mind that the concept of an organic whole, a unified composition, which we find in Polybius, reached him from the school of Plato and Aristotle, for whom it was a canon of literary composition[6]—though in fact Aristotle excludes history from its application. In the century between Aristotle and Polybius the notion that a work of art should constitute a unity had become part of the common currency of Hellenistic history-writing; essentially it implied a limited theme and so in fact a monograph. We can see its principles best illustrated in Cicero's famous letter to Lucceius,[7] in which he urged him to compose a history of his (Cicero's) own achievements: 'from the beginning of the (Catilinarian) conspiracy down to my return from exile', he writes, 'could, it seems to me, be made into a unified work of medium proportions (*modicum quoddam corpus*)'. But Polybius had already transferred this idea and vastly extended its scope when he applied it consciously to the writing of a universal history.

This he did by projecting the idea of the unity of the historical composition on to the actual events he was describing; and he was able to perform this sleight-of-hand only thanks to the role which he assigned to *Tyche*, Fortune, in the rise of Rome to world dominion. It was an established tradition for a historian to begin his work by crying his own wares—how much more important was the theme of *his* history than that of any of his predecessors'. Thucydides' claim for the Peloponnesian War is a good example, but it by no means stands alone.[8] Polybius went beyond this: for

---

[4] i. 3. 4; cf. xiv. 12. 5.   [5] *Geschichtsschreibung*, i, Text, 448–9.
[6] Cf. Plato, *Phaedr.* 264 c; Aristotle, *Poet.* 23. 1, 1459 a 17 f.; see my *Commentary*, i. 43 on i. 3. 4.   [7] *Fam.* v. 12. 4.
[8] Dion. Hal. i. 1; Appian, *Hist.* praef.

he claimed not merely to be recording greater events than anyone before (though he does that),[9] but also to be describing a process unique in kind, namely the unification of the *oecumene*. Fortune herself, *Tyche*, is responsible for this operation, which has made the whole world one under the control of Rome—her finest and most beneficent achievement. All this of course incidentally redounds to the credit of the historian. *Tyche* and Polybius are shown as being in a sense complementary to each other: each is a creative artist in the relevant field, the one producing the unified *oecumene*, the other its counterpart in the unified work of history— σωματοειδῆ. In this way Polybius gives a new meaning to universal history, in so far as he identifies it with the history of his own time and no other; in addition he restores the pattern which Thucydides had intended his monograph to possess, but which Ephorus and his successors in continuing his work had lost. I have stressed this aspect of Polybius' theme for two reasons: first because it shows how *Tyche* stands in an absolutely fundamental relationship to his whole conception—without her, the pattern collapses; and secondly, because it demonstrates how much Polybius owes to the canons of Hellenistic historiography and its literary antecedents.

2.

Once it becomes clear that Polybius' claim to be writing the history of the unification of the *oecumene* under Rome derives some elements from a literary device, it is natural to enquire to what extent he forces the evidence in order to create this impression of universality. In book v, after describing the conference of Naupactus in 217— a conference, it should be noted, between Philip V of Macedonia and the Achaeans and the other members of the Hellenic Symmachy on the one hand and the Aetolians on the other, the result of which was to bring to an end the so-called Social War between the Greek confederacies—in short an event of mainly local significance—Polybius has this passage:[10] 'it was at this time and at this conference that the affairs of Greece, Italy and Africa were first brought into contact'. This is on the face of it an extraordinary claim to make for this meeting—even though it was marked by the famous speech of Agelaus warning the Greeks about the cloud

---

[9] i. 2, comparing Rome with former empires; on such συγκρίσεις see Lorenz, 15, 81 n. 74.   [10] v. 105. 4–10.

in the west.[11] Polybius justifies it by saying that from now onwards all eyes in Greece were turned on Italy; and that very soon the same was true of the islands and the Greeks of Asia Minor, who began sending embassies to Carthage and Rome, while the Romans in turn being afraid of Philip began sending embassies to Greece. This claim seems somewhat dubious. In fact many years were to pass before any islanders or Asian Greeks sent envoys to Rome; the neutral embassies from Egypt, Rhodes, Chios, Mytilene and Byzantium during the First Macedonian War did not approach the Romans; no embassy to Carthage is known from the islanders or from the Asian Greeks opposed to Attalus; and no Roman embassy crossed the Aegean before 200. In defence of Polybius it has been urged by Pédech[12] that even if actual contacts with Asia are delayed, what really matters is what men thought; the importance of Naupactus lies in the fact that Philip now began to think of action against Rome and so precipitated the συμπλοκή,[13]

[11] v. 104; on this speech see Gelzer, 'Die Anfänge des römischen Weltreichs', *Kl. Schr.* ii. 4; Walbank, *Speeches*, 15–16; Pédech, *Méthode*, 506; Deininger, 25–9. O. Mørkholm, 'The speech of Agelaus at Naupactus, 217 B.C.', *Class. et med.* 28 (1969), 240–53, argues that Agelaus' speech is a fictitious composition introduced by Polybius to support his belief that the συμπλοκή of east and west took place at this time. It is true that Carthage presented no real threat to mainland Greece; but there was a long history of Punic hostility to the Greeks, both locally in Sicily and Magna Graecia and, tradition had it, in combination with Persia at the time of the Great Persian Wars. The Greeks, who saw Roman policy as far more purposeful than it really was, may equally well have seen a potential danger to Greece, not only if the Romans won (a prospect which seemed remote in 217), but also if Italy fell to Hannibal. Against the view that the speech is fictitious are these considerations: (*a*) Polybius introduces it with circumstantial details: it was delivered at the first session of the conference (v. 103. 9); (*b*) Polybius repeatedly inveighs against the writing of fictitious speeches by historians and insists that they should give the substance of what was actually said (ii. 56. 10; iii. 20. 1; xii. 25 a–25 b, 25 i–25 k; xxix. 12. 9–10; xxxvi. 1. 2–7; cf. Walbank, *Speeches*, 7–18); (*c*) if Polybius wanted to invest a speech with great importance, it is difficult to see why he should have put it in the mouth of one of the hated Aetolians. Mørkholm notes that Agelaus said precisely the kind of things Philip wished to hear, 'Demetrius having previously prepared the ground by his advice (v. 105. 1)'. One can envisage real situations in which this may have happened; for example, in view of Demetrius' attested role in these events, one cannot rule out the possibility that Demetrius also used influence (perhaps through the go-between Cleonicus of Naupactus, who had been taken prisoner and released without ransom (v. 95. 12, 102. 5)?) to inspire from the Aetolian side the kind of proposal which Philip would find acceptable. I merely put this forward hypothetically—there is no evidence for it—to show that it is not necessary to assume that the coincidence of content marks the speech as fictitious.

[12] *Méthode*, 506–7.   [13] i. 4. 11.

the involvement of events in all the different theatres of history. Thoughts, so the argument runs,[14] are as much πράξεις[15] as actual deeds.

This may sound like special pleading; but Pédech has a sound point. To a mainland Greek Philip's decision to look westward marked a critical moment in the sequence leading to the Roman domination first over Greece and then over Asia. On the other hand, when he speaks of sending embassies, Polybius is talking about more than mere thoughts, and when every allowance has been made, it remains true that there is something slightly parochial about his choice of the conference at Naupactus—rather than, for example, the First Illyrian War[16]—to mark the moment when events throughout the whole *oecumene* began to intertwine; and it was to be many years before what happened in Asia impinged on the consciousness of Rome or affected Roman policy.[17] In fact, it is only by taking a very long view and by using the word *oecumene* in a very restricted sense[18]—after all the world was known as far as Bactria and India—that Polybius can claim either that the whole of its affairs became intertwined from Olympiad 140 onwards or that the Romans became masters of it in just over fifty years.

We must of course beware of exaggerating the difficulty. Polybius' subject is a real one. Between some date in the third century (which might have been variously put at 264 or 241 or 220

---

[14] Cf. Siegfried, *Studien*, 46.   [15] v. 105. 4.

[16] ii. 12. 7 makes this an ἐπιπλοκή, not a συμπλοκή; there is a real difference.

[17] In a remarkable analysis of the growth in the use of *victor*, *victoria* and *invictus* in Roman dedications from around 300 B.C., S. Weinstock, 'Victor and invictus', *Harvard Theological Review*, 50 (1957), 211–47 (cf. *RE*, 'Victor', cols. 2485 ff.; 'Victoria', cols. 2501 ff.), has brought this development into relation with the Hellenistic world and forms of cult and worship there which can be traced back to Alexander the Great's concern with Nike and his claim to be acknowledged with the title of ἀνίκητος θεός; but he wisely draws back from a possible conclusion that the Romans were already planning to follow in Alexander's footsteps. In fact, the use of these concepts of victory, whatever their origin, is in an Italian context; as Weinstock rightly observes, it was the time of the long Samnite wars, and the Romans were fighting for survival. Weinstock has added one more piece of evidence to the growing list of Greek influences on late fourth- and early third-century Rome; but it does not upset the picture of a Senate hardly concerned with the affairs of Asia until the last decades of the third century (when the active collaboration with Attalus of Pergamum in the First Macedonian War is a factor not to be minimised).

[18] iii. 36–8, especially 37, for a geographical disquisition on the divisions of the *oecumene* (which does not, however, say what it includes).

or 217 or 215 or 212 or 205 or even 200) and some date in the second (which might have been put in 189 or 167 or 146) the Romans became masters of the Mediterranean world in the sense that henceforth they were the decisive force in it; and a good case can be made for choosing 220 and 167 as the beginning and the end of that process. But the pattern which Polybius superimposes upon it and the role which he attributes to *Tyche* are both contrived and belong to the artistry of his composition. As we saw in the previous chapter, it is an aspect which may to some degree clash with the straightforward claims which he makes for his πραγματικὴ ἱστορία—contemporary political and military history; but it is to this more important side of his work that I shall now turn.

3.

The writing of contemporary history was nothing new, and consequently the problem of assembling material for it was not new either. What is new in Polybius is his systematic exposition of the methods to be used. A statement of these is to be found in a passage in book xii[19] in which he draws a rather forced comparison between the methodology of history and that of medicine. History—πραγματικὴ ἱστορία—he says, consists of three parts, 'the first being the study and collation of written sources,[20] the second the survey of cities, places, rivers, harbours and generally the peculiar features of land and sea and the distances between them, and the third political experience'. Of these, he explains, the first is of limited value to anyone writing contemporary history. Looking through old memoirs is useful as a means of discovering what views men of former times had on general conditions, places, nations, states and events, and the fortunes and circumstances that

[19] xii. 25 e. 1–7.

[20] I take ὑπομνήματα in this context to be a general word for written sources, for Polybius uses it of his own work (i. 1. 1 and elsewhere) and that of Timaeus (xii. 25 a. 4); I see no reason to restrict it here (cf. xii. 25 e. 1, 25 i. 2, 27. 3, 28 a. 4, 28 a. 7) to 'Aufzeichnungen, Schriftquellen ohne literarischen Anspruch' with Gelzer, 'Über die Arbeitsweise des Polybios', *Kl. Schr.* iii. 164–5 n. 29. The writing of memoirs and the obtaining of them from others may indeed be an important part of Polybius' literary technique, and such memoirs may have been among the ὑπομνήματα which Timaeus assembled καθήμενος ἐν ἄστει (xii. 28 a. 4); but the comparison which Polybius draws between the 'theoretical' doctor and the armchair historian (xii. 25 e. 4–5) shows that histories to be found in libraries are also included (especially if 25 e. 5 is correctly restored as τὰ πρότε⟨ρον ὑπομνήματα⟩ (with Heyse) or τὰ ⟨τῶν⟩ προγε⟨γονότων ὑπομνήματα⟩ (with Pédech)).

existed—all of which are of general help to the historian, 'since past events direct our attention to the future, if studied with proper care and detail'. But alone such studies are quite inadequate, not because these sources do not cover the period which the contemporary historian is concerned with—this is of course self-evident—but because contemporary history demands a kind of investigation which cannot be learnt in the library, any more than a painter can learn the technique of painting simply from the study of old masters.[21]

Polybius then goes on to define this difference in technique. It is, he says, really a matter of whether one uses one's eyes or one's ears; and of these organs, as Heracleitus had observed,[22] the eyes are the more accurate witnesses. To understand Polybius' point one must remember that reading was regularly thought of as something audible which was registered through the ears and not the eyes; so in effect to prefer the eyes to the ears means to put autopsy before library research, and the point is underlined in the passage culminating in the praise of Odysseus, the historian's model, mentioned in the previous chapter.[23] In this passage, which contains yet another polemical attack on Timaeus, the library-scholar, Polybius draws a further distinction which proves to be fundamental to his notion of the historian's task, and incidentally shows that the threefold distinction which he has just enunciated is by no means the full analysis which it purports to be. Indeed, it looks rather as if the three parts—study of memoirs, visiting of places, and political experience—owe their existence partly to Polybius' desire at that point to make a formal compari-

[21] Polybius' point is that a historian, like a painter, needs practical activity to master his craft—in his case active investigation and experience of politics. Wunderer, 'Gleichnisse aus dem Gebiet der Malerei', *Phil.* 66 (1907), 471–5, argued that Polybius was here referring to animal-painters (for so he translates ζωγράφος). The contrast between scholarship and practical experience, he argues, is meaningful only if Polybius is speaking of animal-painters, since painters of people, being concerned with the individual personality, can in any case paint only from real life (and not from old masters) whereas one animal is much like another. This curious thesis is based on a misunderstanding of Polybius' argument, for in this passage he is thinking of library research less as an investigation of sources than as a (less than adequate) method of acquiring a necessary skill—in the same way as one becomes a painter by painting, not by studying old masters.

[22] Cf. Diels–Kranz, *Frag. Vorsokr.* i. 22 B 101 a (cf. Polyb. xii. 27. 1 with my *Commentary*, ii. 408).

[23] xii. 27. 2 ff.; see above, pp. 51–2.

son with medicine; and there is of course always a special attraction in the figure three when one is making such comparisons.

Now, however,[24] it appears that knowledge derived from hearing, διὰ τῆς ἀκοῆς, is not restricted to the reading and collating of books, as the former passage suggested, but also includes something far more important. This is the interrogation of eyewitnesses, and about this Polybius shows a certain inconsistency. One of his reasons for choosing the period 220–167 for his *Histories* was that he had been present at some of the events contained in it and had the testimony of eyewitnesses for others;[25] and elsewhere he describes[26] the art of interrogating witnesses as the most important aspect of history, in so far as it is impossible for any one man to be everywhere at once or indeed to visit every place in the world at all, so that usually all that a historian can do is to enquire from as many people as possible and sift their evidence. However, when in what is now the last chapter of book xii he reverts to his criticism of Timaeus, he says[27] that having had no experience of personal participation in historical events and the deriving of material from this source—ἐξ αὐτουργίας καὶ...ἐξ αὐτοπαθείας, doing and experiencing—Timaeus thinks that what is really the least important and the easiest part of history—the collation of documents and enquiring from those personally acquainted with the facts (πυνθάνεσθαι παρὰ εἰδότων ἕκαστα τῶν πραγμάτων)— is in fact the most difficult (there is a slight lacuna here but the meaning is unambiguous).[28] The inconsistency will be apparent: the questioning of eyewitnesses cannot be both the most important part of history, albeit one involving great labour and experience— and at the same time the least important and the easiest. This contradiction seems to arise because in the one passage Polybius is concerned to distinguish between personal participation (the use of the eyes) and library work (the use of the ears), and in the other, rather more realistically, he is distinguishing between the study of documents and interrogation of eyewitnesses. When he discusses the latter technique, it is the practical historian speaking and his remarks are of considerable relevance to his methods. 'The interrogator', he says,[29] 'contributes as much to the interview as

---

[24] xii. 27. 3.
[26] xii. 4 c. 3.
[28] xii. 28 a. 7, where Spengel adds μέγιστον καὶ χαλεπώτατον.
[29] xii. 28 a. 9–10.

[25] iv. 2. 2.
[27] xii. 28 a. 6–7.

the informant since the latter is at the mercy of free association of ideas[30] without the discipline which the trained interviewer brings to the occasion.' Clearly, over the years, Polybius had in person developed a considerable skill in conducting enquiries of this kind from eyewitnesses, and when he describes this as the most important part of history, he is expressing his real belief. The contradiction mentioned above is there because he wants to make a forced and rhetorical comparison between history and medicine in order to score a point against Timaeus; it is not uncharacteristic of the slightly disingenuous criticism which appears at several points in book xii.[31]

4.

In practice, the interrogation of informants of various kinds must have been of vital importance in Polybius' technique;[32] and there is some indication that occasionally he also enlisted his friends' help in making enquiries on his behalf—if Scipio's fruitless interrogation of the Massaliotes and the inhabitants of Narbo and Corbilo on the Loire about Britain was undertaken at Polybius' request.[33] For this purpose, as I have already mentioned,[34] his internment in Rome was a positive advantage. Mahaffy[35] once compared the colony of Greeks παρεπιδημοῦντες at Rome to the nineteenth-century English colonies in Naples or Florence, 'a public in themselves, with an opinion of their own, which was clearly expressed'; and in an important and perceptive study of Polybius' methods of work, Gelzer[36] has described in some detail his position within this community, where his former role as a statesman in

---

[30] The phrase ἡ τῶν παρεπομένων τοῖς πράγμασιν ὑπόμνησις means 'the recollection of the concomitant details': it is this that leads on the narrator from incident to incident (χειραγωγεῖ τὸν ἐξηγούμενον ἐφ' ἕκαστα τῶν συμβεβηκότων), if he is left without the guidance of a trained inquisitor. Pédech, *Polybe xii*, ad loc., translates: 'car le souvenir des conditions dans lesquelles se déroulent les événements politiques conduit l'informateur à préciser chaque détail'; but this would not explain, as it should, the role of the inquisitor who 'contributes as much to the narration as his informant'. The sense is also missed by both Paton and Shuckburgh.

[31] See further Walbank, 'Polemic in Polybius', *JRS*, 52 (1962), 5 ff.

[32] Cf. Gelzer, 'Über die Arbeitsweise des Polybios', *Kl. Schr.* iii. 161–90.

[33] xxxiv. 10. 6–7; see above, p. 11 n. 52, below, p. 127 n. 159.

[34] See above, pp. 8–10.

[35] J. P. Mahaffy, *Greek life and thought* (London, ed. 2, 1896), 610–11; cf. xxx. 4. 10; xxxii. 6. 6; von Scala, 273–4 n. 1.

[36] 'Über die Arbeitsweise des Polybios', *Kl. Schr.* iii. 173.

Achaea and his influence in leading circles at Rome must have made him an outstanding figure. It can hardly be doubted that contemporary notes and memoranda which he made in Rome—a noteworthy example is his account of the flight of the Syrian prince Demetrius—later helped him in the composition of the extension of his *Histories* down to 146.[37] But the fact of living in Rome was important not merely for the light it could throw on current events. Among his fellow internees and the constant stream of visitors and envoys from Greek cities and states were men who had themselves played an active part in the history of the previous thirty or forty years, sometimes on the other side to Polybius himself.

For example, in his account of the negotiations between Perseus and Eumenes, which form an obscure episode in the Third Macedonian War and broke down owing to the mutual mistrust and avarice of the two kings,[38] he quotes Perseus' friends among his sources. These may have included Pantauchus, one of Perseus' πρῶτοι φίλοι, who had played an important part in the negotiations with Genthius, and another Friend, Hippias, who also surrendered to the Romans along with Pantauchus after the battle of Pydna.[39] But they were not the only Macedonians to be brought to Rome, for Livy following Polybius tells us[40] that in 167, as a preliminary to the setting up of republican government in Macedonia, the whole of the Macedonian court, including anyone who had so much as taken part in an official Macedonian embassy, was deported to Italy. So Polybius will have had a wide choice of informants about what was going on at the Macedonian court during Philip's last years, a subject on which he is very knowledgeable.[41] But besides the Macedonians there were in Italy internees from most Greek states. The thousand Achaeans who were deported along with Polybius had fallen to three hundred at the time of their repatriation.[42] According to Pausanias[43] many fled

---

[37] Ibid. 168; see above, pp. 9 and 18.   [38] xxix. 8. 10.

[39] xxix. 3. 3; cf. xxvii. 8. 5; Livy, xliv. 45. 2.

[40] Livy, xlv. 32. 3–6.

[41] Cf. Walbank, ' Φίλιππος τραγῳδούμενος', *JHS*, 58 (1938), 64–5; Gelzer, 'Über die Arbeitsweise des Polybios', *Kl. Schr.* iii. 170–1.

[42] Paus. vii. 10. 11–12; cf. also Polyb. xxxii. 3. 15, which implies that by 160 the only eminent men left among the internees were Polybius and Stratius. However this hardly implies (so von Scala, 274) that the rest of the survivors were too insignificant to be of any use to Polybius in his enquiries. Had they been very insignificant, they would not have been deported at all.

[43] Loc. cit. (n. 42).

while on the way to Italy and others from the Etruscan towns where they were interned; but even so the small number remaining in 150 suggests that they were mostly elderly men in 167—which indeed one would expect—hence useful informants to the historian. It is true that they were interned away from Rome, especially in Etruria,[44] but Polybius seems to have enjoyed considerable freedom of movement,[45] as his relations with Demetrius of Syria and his visit to Epizephyrian Locri[46] demonstrate, and he can easily have had access to them. There were Aetolians too, like Nicander of Trichonium, who may have provided information about Philip V's invasion of Thermum in 218[47] as well as details of the Romano-Syrian War;[48] such men could give Polybius a version of events which was not available to him when he was still in Achaea.

Clearly in Rome Polybius was surrounded by scores of Greeks from the mainland and Asia Minor, internees or transient visitors, who could furnish him with verbal information or even memoranda on events of the recent past: though it is wiser not to indulge our imagination—as von Scala does in his *Studien des Polybius*—by attempting to attribute particular passages to information passed on to the historian by (for example) Praxo of Delphi,[49] his close friend Menyllus of Alabanda,[50] Stratius the doctor of Eumenes,[51] or finally some unnamed informant from Athamania, who is supposed to have given Polybius an account of the affairs of king Amynander, of Philip of Megalopolis, the pretender to the Macedonian throne, whom he sponsored,[52] and even of Egypt —where Amynander's son Galaestes became one of Ptolemy Philometor's φίλοι.[53]

As well as the Greeks there were of course Romans. As the political influence of Scipio grew, and he entered the Senate, he

[44] Ibid.

[45] Contested by Cuntz, 55–6; but see Mioni, 13; Walbank, *Commentary*, i. 4–5.

[46] xii. 5. 1–3; cf. De Sanctis, iii. 1. 209–10.

[47] v. 7. 7–14. 7; but we do not know Nicander's age, and the likelihood is that Polybius could get information about this campaign only at second hand.

[48] xxvii. 15. 14; xxviii. 4. 6; see Woodhouse, 258 n. 1.

[49] Livy, xlii. 15 ff.

[50] xxxi. 12. 8; cf. Livy, xliii. 6. 5; von Scala, 270, thinks he may have been one of those who testified to the great worth of Ptolemy VI (xxxix. 7. 1, κατὰ μέν τινας μεγάλων ἐπαίνων καὶ μνήμης ὧν ἄξιος).

[51] xxx. 2. 2–4.

[52] Livy, xxxv. 47. 5–8; xxxvi. 14. 7 (Polybian).

[53] Diod. xxxiii. 20.

will have been able to tell Polybius more and more of what was happening—though the actual proceedings in the Senate were often declared confidential.[54] But for earlier events too, Romans, and often elderly Romans, must have been invaluable. An outstanding example is C. Laelius, the friend of Scipio Africanus, whom Polybius quotes as his authority for the capture of New Carthage,[55] though in fact his account of this famous assault can be shown to be based on a complicated mixture of sources including the pro-Carthaginian history of the Greek historian Silenus, a memoir specially written by Scipio himself and sent to King Philip V of Macedonia, and possibly Fabius Pictor.[56]

5.

In fact, despite his sneers at Timaeus,[57] Polybius could hardly avoid making widespread use of written sources, even for the main part of his *Histories*: unfortunately they are usually unidentifiable, since he weaves his material into a close and homogeneous fabric.[58] For the period before 220 he mentions four historians at some length; these are, for Greek events, Aratus of Sicyon and Phylarchus, and for the First Punic War Philinus of Acragas and Fabius Pictor. Polybius nowhere states that he has used Philinus and Fabius as his sources,[59] and there have been attempts to show that he made little or no use of one or the other or both of these.[60]

---

[54] Cf. Gelzer, 'Über die Arbeitsweise des Polybios', *Kl. Schr.* iii. 170 nn. 68–9, for examples (e.g. Livy, xlii. 14. 1; Val. Max. ii. 2. 1). See also my *Commentary*, i. 332–3 on iii. 20. 3.

[55] x. 3. 2 ff.; the evidence was probably oral. R. Laqueur, 'Scipio Africanus und die Eroberung von Neukarthago', *Hermes*, 56 (1921), 207–25, argues unconvincingly for a written account.

[56] For details see Walbank, 'The Scipionic legend', *Proc. Camb. Phil. Soc.* 13 (1967), 54–69.

[57] xii. 4 c. 3, 27, for Timaeus' use of books rather than enquiry.

[58] See my *Commentary*, i. 26.

[59] Cf. i. 14–15 (Fabius and Philinus), iii. 26. 3–4 (criticism of Philinus); see above, p. 43 n. 57, p. 47 n. 79.

[60] Polybius' use of Fabius has been substantially queried by Bung, *Fabius*, and Pédech, 'Sur les sources de Polybe: Polybe et Philinos', *REA*, 54 (1952), 246–66, rejected both Fabius and Philinus as sources for Polybius' introductory books. However in *Polybe i*, 8–9, he appears to have changed his opinion, and now admits that Polybius used both these authors, though supplemented by others. For the reasons mentioned in the text doubts such as are still expressed by Momigliano ('Linee per una valutazione di Fabio Pittore', *Terzo contributo*, i. 66–7) seems to me to be unfounded. La Bua, *Filino*, has recently argued that Fabius' history was a reply to that of Philinus, and was published shortly after

However, in his discussion of the two writers Polybius describes them as having the reputation of being the best authorities on the war, and his only criticism of them is that of excessive partiality—of Philinus towards Carthage, and Fabius towards Rome; it therefore seems reasonable to assume that he used their narratives as a check on each other rather than that he neglected them in order to follow some other unknown and unnamed authority or authorities, which would on his own admission be of inferior quality.[61] Philinus probably wrote a monograph on the First Punic War. This seems to follow from the fact that Diodorus, who used him for his account of that war,[62] went over to Polybius as his source for the subsequent Mercenary War.[63] Q. Fabius Pictor was, of course, the first Roman historian, and a contemporary of the Hannibalic War, and Polybius seems to have used him for his account of the Gallic Wars in book ii[64] and for the early part (at any rate) of the Hannibalic War itself; Fabius' views about the causes of that war are discussed in detail. For the First Punic War these two sources would give Polybius all he needed; but he has combined their versions in a way which makes it virtually impossible to assign passages to one or the other. Indeed any such operation is hampered still further by the likelihood that Fabius himself used Philinus.[65]

The position is a little clearer regarding Aratus and Phylarchus, for here Polybius does not feel the same need to balance prejudices

241; but this would imply piecemeal publication of Fabius' work, and for this there is no evidence. Against La Bua's thesis (it has further ramifications involving Silenus and Diodorus) see Walbank, 'The historians of Greek Sicily', ΚΩΚΑΛΟΣ, 14–15 (1968–9), 493 ff.

[61] Cf. E. Badian, 'The early historians', *Latin historians*, 5. It would, I suppose, be possible—though a somewhat forced argument—to take Polybius to be saying that Philinus and Fabius have the reputation of being the best sources on the war, but in fact they are not (that distinction being reserved for X and Y—unnamed—whom he is therefore following). But it is surely because they are the best sources that Polybius feels obliged to point out their shortcomings.

[62] Cf. Diod. xxiii. 8. 1.

[63] So Jacoby, *FGH* ii. D, p. 598; the theory that Diodorus' account of the Carthaginian Mercenary War goes back to Silenus of Caleacte, who is supposed to have dealt with it in the introduction to his *Hannibalic History* (and so to have produced a continuation of Philinus), was recently proposed by La Bua, *Filino*, but is to be rejected; see Walbank, 'The historians of Greek Sicily', ΚΩΚΑΛΟΣ, 14–15 (1968–9), 493–7.

[64] ii. 14–35; we do not know the terminal point of Fabius' history (cf. Badian, 'The early historians', *Latin historians*, 5).

[65] See my *Commentary*, i. 65.

against each other, and specifically mentions Aratus as his source for the Cleomenean War.[66] However, Aratus did not tell everything, as Polybius admits,[67] and notwithstanding his criticisms of Phylarchus for a sensational, emotional and inaccurate history,[68] in default of other evidence Polybius seems to have made use of him.[69] Phylarchus' *History* covered the period from 272, when Pyrrhus invaded the Peloponnese, down to Cleomenes' death in Egypt in 220/19, and Polybius' account of this event in a digression in book v uses Phylarchus along with other sources.[70] Timaeus is another historian whom Polybius criticises extremely harshly, yet is prepared to follow for some events in his introductory books;[71] and when in his narrative proper he digresses to mention events of the fourth century and earlier, there is some evidence that he uses Callisthenes and Ephorus.[72]

The main history starts from 220, where Aratus' *Memoirs* ended,[73] and Polybius implies when discussing his starting-date, that it initiates a period for which eyewitness accounts will be available.[74] The first definite reference to this kind of evidence occurs in a passage where Polybius speaks of questioning people who had actually been present when Hannibal crossed the Alps in 218—

[66] ii. 56. 2, Ἀράτῳ προῃρημένοις κατακολουθεῖν περὶ τῶν Κλεομενικῶν.

[67] ii. 47. 11, ἔνια τούτων οὐδ' ἐν τοῖς ὑπομνήμασι κατέταξεν.

[68] ii. 56–63; see above, pp. 34 ff.

[69] See my *Commentary*, i. 247 (on ii. 47. 11), 290 (on ii. 70. 6), 565–7 (on v. 35–9) for specific examples.

[70] v. 35–9.

[71] For the preliminaries of the First Punic War including the rise of Hiero (i. 8. 3–9. 8; see my *Commentary*, i. 53–5 ad loc. and i. 47–8 on i. 6. 2) and also for a digression on the Pythagoreans in South Italy (ii. 39. 1–6).

[72] Callisthenes is used on early Messenian history (iv. 33. 2) and perhaps for references to the Spartan seizure of the Cadmea in 382 and the peace of Antalcidas (iv. 27. 4–7; perhaps via Ephorus, see my note in *Commentary*, i. 475–6 ad loc.); Ephorus is also perhaps the source for a digression on Elis (*Commentary*, i. 525–6 on iv. 73. 6–74. 8). Both historians are criticised by Polybius (xii. 17–22, Callisthenes; xii. 22. 7, 25 f.; cf. vi. 45–47. 6 (with my note in *Commentary*, i. 726–8) for a passage on the Cretan constitution, which criticises an account which is almost certainly that of Ephorus (despite Polybius' reference to Xenophon, Callisthenes and Plato); see below, pp. 152–3.

[73] i. 3. 2; iv. 2. 1. I find unconvincing the suggestion of Petzold, *Studien*, 99–100, that Polybius originally intended Aratus' *Memoirs* to suffice as an introduction to his own work, and that although he wrote his Achaean chapters before 146, it was only later that he incorporated them in the introduction to his *Histories*.

[74] iv. 2. 2, συμβαίνει τοῖς μὲν αὐτοὺς ἡμᾶς παραγεγονέναι, τὰ δὲ παρὰ τῶν ἑωρακότων ἀκηκοέναι; see above, pp. 42–3.

but whether Gauls, Greeks or Carthaginians he does not say.[75] However he still uses published sources, preferably Greek. I have mentioned Fabius, and on the other side there were Chaereas and Sosylus who retailed 'the gossip of the barber's shop'[76] and Silenus of Caleacte, who like Sosylus accompanied Hannibal to Italy 'quamdiu Fortuna passa est',[77] and may be Polybius' source for Hannibal's campaigns in Spain before he left for Italy,[78] as well as for Scipio's capture of New Carthage.[79] There were no doubt countless others, who are not mentioned,[80] for instance L. Cincius Alimentus,[81] who was praetor in Sicily in 210/09; he had the misfortune to be taken prisoner, but used his captivity to obtain historical information directly from Hannibal.[82] But just what use Polybius made of him—or of C. Acilius and A. Postumius Albinus (whom he attacks for his vanity, loquaciousness, love of pleasure and insufficient knowledge of Greek)[83]—or the *historia graeca* of Africanus' son, mentioned in Cicero's *Brutus*[84]—we simply do not know. The relevant parts of Cato's *Origines* probably appeared too late to be used;[85] and indeed how far Polybius made use either of

[75] iii. 48. 12; the reference is to oral informants, not to Silenus' *History*, as Mioni, 121, suggests. Polybius may well have met such informants in Italy, Greece or Numidia; he nowhere says that he questioned them while actually crossing the Alps himself, as Pédech, *Méthode*, 528, assumes. (For his crossing of the Alps see iii. 48. 12.)   [76] iii. 20. 5; see above, p. 34 n. 14.

[77] *FGH* 175 T 2 = Nepos, *Hann.* 13. 3. On Silenus see Walbank, 'The historians of Greek Sicily', ΚΩΚΑΛΟΣ, 14–15 (1968–9), 487–97, where it is suggested that Silenus' role in the tradition is a modest one, and that his *Sicelica*, of which only three attested fragments survive, may well have been a periegetic or paradoxographical work dealing with the wonders of Sicily rather than a history.

[78] See my *Commentary*, i. 316 on iii. 13. 5–14. 8 for evidence; Silenus seems also to have been used by Coelius, to whom Ziegler, col. 1562, suggests that Polybius may have introduced his works. On the hypothesis that Silenus wrote an account of the Carthaginian Mercenary War see above, p. 78 n. 63.

[79] Cf. Livy, xxvi. 49. 3; the reference in Walbank, 'The Scipionic legend', *Proc. Camb. Phil. Soc.* 13 (1967), 62 n. 8, needs correcting.

[80] iii. 47. 6; v. 33. 2; see Jacoby, *FGH* 83 'Anonymoi des Polybios'; 180 'Unbestimmbare Hannibalhistoriker'.   [81] *FGH* 810.

[82] Cf. Livy, xxi. 38. 3–5, quoting information which Cincius claimed to have got from Hannibal personally.   [83] xxxix. 1.

[84] Cicero, *Brut.* 77. Gelzer, *Kl. Schr.* iii. 203, thinks this *historia Graeca*—i.e. a history written in Greek—may be the source of much of the pro-Scipionic material in Polybius' *Histories*; but much of this may of course go back to Aemilianus.

[85] If Polybius had written down to book xv before 146, he could hardly utilise Cato's later books, which were in all probability published after their author's death; cf. R. Helm, *RE*, 'Porcius (9)', cols. 160–1. There was

him or of other Latin sources, such as the virtually unknown L. Cassius Hemina[86] or even the poet Ennius,[87] must have depended in part on how proficient he was at reading Latin. He certainly understood it to some extent;[88] but it seems unlikely that he made great use of Latin sources, and even if Gelzer is wrong in supposing[89] that he never even learnt to read it during his sixteen years at Rome, I think we can feel fairly certain that he did not consult the Carthaginian treaties, couched in archaic and almost incomprehensible Latin, *in situ* in the 'treasury of the aediles'.[90]

For events in Greece and Asia the search for names is even more unproductive. Polybius' contemporary, Zeno of Rhodes, seems to have written more than a history of his own city; Polybius criticised his account of the battles of Chios and Lade, his version of Nabis' attack on Messene (in which the geography was quite incomprehensible) and his description of the siege of Gaza and the battle of Panium, but he may have used him fairly widely for all that.[91] Otherwise, it is largely a matter of guesswork;[92] and where

apparently a gap in publication between books i–iii and book iv, and another before books v–vii (which carried the narrative down to a few months before Cato's death in 149 (cf. Badian, 'The early historians', *Latin historians*, 7–8)). There is no reason why Polybius should have had access to Cato's work in advance of publication.

[86] He seems to have treated the Second Punic War in book iv, which he wrote before the outbreak of the Third Punic War (since he entitled it *bellum Punicum posterior* (sic)), but perhaps after the publication of the first three books of Cato's *Origines*; see De Sanctis, iv. 2, part 1, 66 n. 147.

[87] Ennius dealt with the Second Punic War in *Annales* ix and x, but there is no evidence that Polybius used him (whether he had read him or not); for Ennius' part in the creation of the Scipionic legend see Walbank, 'The Scipionic legend', *Proc. Camb. Phil. Soc.* 13 (1967), 56–9.

[88] ii. 15. 9; iii. 87. 6; vi. 26. 6; xi. 23. 1.

[89] Gelzer, *Kl. Schr.* iii. 203.

[90] iii. 26. 1; the 'treasury of the aediles beside the temple of Capitoline Zeus' has been the object of much discussion. Mommsen, *Staatsrecht*, ii. 1. 500 n. 1, identifies it plausibly with the *aedes thensaurum* (*CIL* iii, p. 845 line 22; cf. Suet. *Vesp.* 5. 7), where the apparatus for religious processions was kept under aedilician control. See further my note ad loc. in *Commentary*, i. 353–4. It is highly unlikely that Polybius consulted the text of the treaties in this treasury; he certainly does not claim to have done so.

[91] xvi. 14. 5–15. 8 (Chios and Lade), 16. 1–17. 7 (Nabis' attack on Messene), 18. 1–19. 11 (Gaza and Panium). He probably used Zeno for events in Crete and Sinope (iv. 53–6) and for the earthquake which did such damage to Rhodes (v. 88–90), as well as for other events in which Rhodes was actively involved (cf. Gelzer, 'Über die Arbeitsweise des Polybios', *Kl. Schr.* iii. 188).

[92] Cf. iii. 32. 3, 32. 8; viii. 8. 5; xvi. 12. 4 (perhaps); xxii. 18. 2–5, for writers of monographs on Philip and Perseus and their wars against Rome (cf. *FGH*

one can attempt some sort of source analysis—for instance in the description of Cleomenes' death, where Plutarch provides a separate version—the result is so complicated as to suggest that Polybius' sources and how he used them are alike problems without an answer.[93] For of course he did not limit his written sources to published histories. Gelzer has shown how likely it is that he used memoranda provided by collaborative acquaintances on matters of which they had special knowledge,[94] and, as we saw, Polybius had access to a letter which Africanus sent to Philip V, describing his Spanish campaign and in particular his capture of New Carthage,[95] and another sent by Scipio Nasica to some Hellenistic king, unnamed, about the campaign against Perseus in the Third Macedonian War.[96] Material of this kind may have been commoner than our evidence indicates, and to supplement it there will have been published speeches,[97] though not perhaps very many.[98]

Finally, there is the question of archives and inscriptions. Polybius' use of these has probably been exaggerated. His jibe at Timaeus as the man who 'discovered inscriptions on the backs of buildings and lists of *proxeni* on the doorposts of temples'[99] suggests that he did not rate this kind of research very high—though he is quite ready to boast of his own discovery of an inscription left by Hannibal[100] in the Temple of Hera on the Lacinian Promontory and to use the statistics which it contained. In any case, Gelzer seems quite right to doubt[101] whether any Greek city would

83 F 2–4). They will have included the Strato mentioned by Diog. Laert. v. 61, the Poseidonius mentioned by Plutarch, *Aem. Paul.* 19, and the writers mentioned by Livy, xl. 55. 7 (following Polybius) who gave various versions of the death of Philocles, the murderer of the Macedonian prince Demetrius.

[93] v. 35–9; cf. Plut. *Cleom.* 33 ff. For discussion see my *Commentary*, i. 565–7 and references quoted there.

[94] Cf. Gelzer, 'Über die Arbeitsweise des Polybios', *Kl. Schr.* iii. 164 ff.

[95] x. 9. 3; Polybius probably had access to it through Aemilianus, for Cicero (*off.* iii. 4) seems not to know of any published versions: 'nulla enim eius ingenii monumenta mandata litteris, nullum opus otii, nullum solitudinis munus exstat'. See further my *Commentary*, ii. 204 ad loc.

[96] xxix. 14. 3; Nasica's report is most recently discussed by G. A. Lehmann, 'Die Endphase des Perseuskrieges im Augenzeugenbericht des P. Cornelius Scipio Nasica', *Altheim Festschrift*, i. 387–413.

[97] For instance, those of Astymedes of Rhodes (xxx. 4. 10–11) and Cato's speech on the Rhodians (Livy, xlv. 25. 3; Aul. Gell. vi. 3. 7), which he inserted in the fifth book of the *Origines*.

[98] Cf. Gelzer, 'Über die Arbeitsweise des Polybios', *Kl. Schr.* iii. 182–3.

[99] xii. 11. 2.   [100] iii. 33. 17–18, 56. 1–4.

[101] 'Über die Arbeitsweise des Polybios', *Kl. Schr.* iii. 168 n. 61.

normally have opened its archives to curious foreigners. Polybius supports his polemic against Zeno and Antisthenes by quoting the dispatch sent after the battle of Lade by the Rhodian admiral to the Council and Prytaneis of Rhodes 'which', he says, 'is still preserved in the Rhodian Prytaneum';[102] but he does not say he saw it there himself, and it is quite possible that Zeno quoted it, but tried to draw what Polybius regarded as unacceptable conclusions from it.[103] Aetolian or Macedonian archives[104] will have been equally inaccessible. Indeed his main use of official records is likely to have been restricted to Achaea[105] and Rome, where some records may have been kept of embassies sent or received by the Senate. But for these it is on the whole more probable that Polybius used reports provided by Greek friends; and the sort of material available in the pontifical archives in the *regia*—the records which were later to be published as the *annales maximi*[106]— can hardly have been of much interest or use to him.[107] Besides, he was after all an internee and a foreigner and it may be doubted

---

[102] xvi. 15. 8.

[103] Polybius is apt to argue from what is 'reasonable' or 'likely' (see for example his criticism of Timaeus' views on Locri, xii. 5–12, 16) and he may well have employed this criterion to reject Zeno's account, without having himself seen the documents to which Zeno refers. Pédech, 'Un nouveau commentaire de Polybe', *REG*, 71 (1958), 441, suggests that Polybius consulted the Rhodian records 'par un intermédiaire qui voyageait entre Rhodes et Rome', but he adduces no evidence for the existence of this hypothetical personage. See further my *Commentary*, i. 31–2.

[104] See my *Commentary*, i. 32 n. 4, for various hypotheses based on the assumption that Polybius used these records.

[105] On the Achaean records kept at Aegium cf. *Syll.* 665 line 15, τὰ γράμματα τὰ δημόσια; their existence is implied in xxii. 9. 10, where the general Aristaenus produces all the treaties made between Achaea and the Ptolemies in a carefully organised manoeuvre designed to discredit Philopoemen and his henchman Lycortas, who had reported his renewal of the treaty and was then unable to say which treaty he referred to. Polybius probably drew on this source for his detailed description of the conference of Locris between Flamininus and Philip in 198; and his account of the decree of the allies at the opening of the Social War (iv. 25. 6–7), which echoes official terminology, may be based on a document taken from the same records.

[106] On the publication of the *annales maximi*, perhaps by P. Mucius Scaevola (pontifex maximus from 131/0 to some date between 123 and 114) see J. E. A. Crake, 'The annals of the pontifex maximus', *CP*, 35 (1940), 375–86; Badian, 'The early historians', *Latin historians*, 15. But Cicero, *de orat.* ii. 56, is merely evidence that Scaevola ceased displaying the annual *tabula dealbata* (cf. M. I. Henderson, *JRS*, 52 (1962), 277–8).

[107] The *annales maximi* seem to have consisted of records of magistrates, elections, commands and sacerdotal minutiae.

whether he would have found it easy to penetrate behind the doors of Roman record-houses before the late 150's when his patron Scipio Aemilianus had reached a position of influence in the state. In the main, as he says and as we have seen, his chief source of information will have been the men whom he met and questioned in Rome (down to 150) and elsewhere afterwards using techniques which he had developed; and he will no doubt have supplemented these with memoranda prepared by himself or by others.

6.

These sources, as far as we can tell, were the raw material out of which Polybius constructed his πραγματικὴ ἱστορία, political in concept and in purpose. As I mentioned earlier, it was pre-eminently for Greeks that Polybius was writing and for them that the lessons of history were intended. The long digression on the Gallic wars of Rome in book ii is justified as encouraging his Greek readers not to be daunted should there be a repetition of the Galatian invasions which have frequently alarmed Greece in his own time;[108] and at any rate in that part of his *Histories* which he composed before 150, he not infrequently turns aside to make comments of a purely parochial nature—on the merits of the Acarnanians as allies[109] or how important it is that the Arcadians and Messenians should combine to show a firm front against Sparta.[110]

In these and similar instances Polybius does not draw a clear distinction between political and moral issues. For example it is the great merit of the Acarnanians that they have always regarded duty (τὸ καθῆκον) as a prime consideration; in contrast to the Epirotes, they are renowned both in public and in private for their steadfastness and their love of liberty. However in the period with which Polybius was dealing, duty was not always very easy to define, and especially where Achaea was concerned, he sometimes seems to flounder in his attempt to reconcile expediency with morality. The most striking example of this occurs in book xviii,[111] where he devotes a special digression to the question of treachery, which, he says, along with the other human failings, has long

---

[108] ii. 35. 9.   [109] iv. 30. 5.
[110] iv. 31. 3–33. 12; see above, p. 20.
[111] xviii. 13–15. On this digression see my *Commentary*, ii. 564–70; 'Polybius and Macedonia', *Ancient Macedonia*, 300–2.

given him cause to ponder. The position of this passage among the fragments[112] makes it difficult to accept the common hypothesis[113] that it was introduced here apropos of the defection of the Achaeans under the leadership of Aristaenus from Philip to the Romans, since this event must have been described earlier, in the previous book; and the most likely explanation of its appearance here is that suggested by Aymard,[114] who argued very plausibly that it arose out of the secession of Argos from the Achaean confederation to join Philip—an act which met swift retribution when Philip callously handed the Argives over to the scant mercy of Nabis, the tyrant of Sparta.

Now although it was not Aristaenus' action which provoked the digression, the relevance of that action to the question of treachery was clearly in Polybius' mind, and he spends half the first chapter of his digression justifying it; he does so on grounds of expediency. Had Aristaenus not carried through his policy, the whole nation would have been destroyed; whereas in fact they not only secured their safety at the time as a result of his action, but the power of Achaea was considerably increased. This argument would pass muster if Polybius had not then gone on to discuss the policies of Demosthenes and several of his contemporaries in various Greek states who, in opposition to him, had thrown in their lot with Philip II of Macedonia. These men, Polybius declares, were certainly justified in joining Macedon, especially those from Arcadia and Messenia, for by bringing Philip into the Peloponnese they humbled Sparta and allowed all the Peloponnesians to breathe freely and entertain the thought of freedom (ἀναπνεῦσαι καὶ λαβεῖν ἐλευθερίας ἔννοιαν).[115] These words have a familiar ring; and indeed if one turns back three chapters one at once sees why. It is because they have been used in a passage describing the speeches that were made by Greek envoys who had been sent to Rome after the Council of Nicaea in Locris. These Greeks pointed out to the

---

[112] Its position between the Locrian conference and the battle of Cynoscephalae is firmly established from its place in the *excerpta antiqua*; see my *Commentary*, ii. 26.

[113] So Schweighaeuser, vii. 331; Nissen, *Untersuchungen*, 326 n.; E. Gabba, 'Studi su Filarco', *Athen.* 35 (1957), 30 ff.

[114] 'Le fragment de Polybe "sur les traîtres" (xviii. 13–15)', *Études*, 354–63; but Aymard draws invalid conclusions about the composition of the *Histories* from this passage (see above, p. 19 n. 89).

[115] xviii. 14. 6.

Senate that so long as Chalcis, Corinth and Demetrias, the fetters of Greece, remained in Macedonian hands, the Greeks could not have any thought of freedom (λαβεῖν ἐλευθερίας ἔννοιαν) and the Peloponnesians could not breathe freely (ἀναπνεῦσαι) with a royal garrison in Corinth.[116] Polybius' discussion of treachery in terms of expediency—and a very short-sighted idea of expediency at that, since Sparta no longer represented the major threat to the Peloponnese after Leuctra[117]—has led him into the patent contradiction of describing in the very same words the policy of expelling the Macedonians from the strongholds of Greece in the second century and the policy of the fourth-century collaborators who had contributed to putting them there. The point is underlined when Polybius comments[118] that Aristaenus was honoured for his policy ὡς εὐεργέτην καὶ σωτῆρα τῆς χώρας 'the benefactor and saviour of the land'—forgetting that only twenty-three years earlier these same cult titles had been widely accorded to Antigonus Doson upon his reimposing the Macedonian yoke on southern Greece after the battle of Sellasia.[119]

However, Polybius' troubles do not end here. For he goes on to propose a definition of traitors as men who in time of danger purchase safety or advantage by handing over their cities to an enemy or who, to further their own ambitions, admit a foreign garrison and use outside aid to submit their country to a superior power. The second definition would apply to the Argives; but, as Aymard has observed,[120] it might be held to apply just as well to Aratus of Sicyon, who handed over the Acrocorinth to Antigonus Doson so as to secure the defeat of Cleomenes of Sparta. Moreover, Aristaenus and his party by joining Rome contributed to securing her domination just as effectively as if they had handed over their citadels to the Romans; and the Argives had at least remained faithful to their oaths and the Achaean laws. The very unsatisfactory nature of this whole digression on treachery springs from Polybius' attempt to apply moral criteria to decisions which it is quite clear that he is really judging purely in terms of expediency. It has been said[121] that a politician must sometimes be right and

[116] xviii. 11. 4, 11. 6.
[117] Cf. Treves, 'Démosthène d'après M. Werner Jaeger', *LEC*, 9 (1940), 289–93.   [118] xviii. 13. 10.
[119] Cf. v. 9. 10; ix. 36. 5 (Sparta); *IG* v. 2. 299 (Mantinea).
[120] Loc. cit. p. 85 n. 114 above.
[121] The remark is that of J. K. Galbraith.

yet fail: this would have been incomprehensible to Polybius, for whom failure is tantamount to proof of error. Where this criterion finally takes him appears from his comments on the Greeks at the time of the Third Macedonian War. When Polybius came to describe this war he had already spent several years in the household of Scipio Aemilianus and, as I hope to show later,[122] had come to identify himself to a large extent with Roman attitudes. His treatment of Perseus no longer suffers from the ambiguities concerning Macedonia which we have seen in his discussion of Aristaenus' switch from Macedon to Rome. Perseus he regards as the instrument of his father's policy and though that policy could marshal a good deal of sympathy in Greece it could marshal none in Polybius.

When the Boeotians supported Macedonia, Roman envoys used their influence to secure the arrest and suicide of the pro-Macedonian partisans and the breaking up of the confederacy; Polybius, who has decided that political realism means choosing Rome, condemns the Boeotians for 'rashly and inconsiderately espousing the cause of Perseus'.[123] Towards the pro-Macedonian party in Rhodes he is even more brutally uncompromising; he attributes the political affiliations of their leaders to debt and unscrupulous avarice,[124] holds up their policy to abuse and contempt, and rails against them for not having shown the courage or self-respect to kill themselves. Judged *ex eventu* they had, like Demosthenes, committed the ultimate sin—they had failed. Other views were held, and I shall return to them in a later chapter.[125]

7.

Πραγματικὴ ἱστορία was intended to furnish both political and military lessons; and when he is dealing with military affairs Polybius is a decidedly less doctrinaire and more sympathetic character. Like Thucydides he finds himself much involved with warfare, not only because his rejection of the more colourful kinds of history favoured by Duris and Phylarchus tended to leave him with a rigid programme of war and politics,[126] but also because

---

[122] See below, pp. 176 ff. [123] xxvii. 2. 10.
[124] xxix. 10–11, 19. [125] See below, pp. 178–9.
[126] See Strasburger, 'Die Entdeckung der politischen Geschichte durch Thukydides', *Thukydides*, 469; and for the argument that war as a main topic of the historian was part of the Homeric legacy to Thucydides see his *Wesensbestimmung*, 27 ff.

after all his chosen theme was the rise of Rome to world dominion. Not all wars interest him equally, and in fact personal predilection plays a large part in his selection of material. As far as we can tell from what has survived, he was not very much concerned with Roman wars in the west (unless they involved Scipio and his family); but he describes in loving detail the war of 220–17 between the Hellenic Alliance and the Aetolian confederacy and also various Syro-Egyptian wars which were only indirectly relevant to Rome and her rise to hegemony.

His passion for the professional techniques of warfare emerges very clearly from his detailed description of campaigns and the frequently somewhat pedantic comments which accompany them. The successful general, he insists, is the one who can best exploit his adversary's weakness, and choose the manner and means of attack best suited to this end.[127] Fabius' success in extracting Minucius' forces from the difficulties into which his rashness had got them, made it clear to the Romans how far the foresight, good sense and calm calculation of a true general differ from the reckless bravado of a mere soldier.[128] Philip's surprise attack on Melitaea failed because when he set up his ladders against the wall, they proved to be too short;[129] this incident is a general warning to us not to enter upon such projects without due care, and in particular it illustrates the importance of measuring one's ladders correctly. There is a simple way of doing this, and Polybius will explain it in due course—as indeed he does four books later in a long and substantial digression on the art of the general. There is much to be learnt from the Romans—for instance, their method of dividing up booty so as to ensure a fair division without any risk that the soldiers will break rank.[130] It is also useful to take note of the precise forms of cavalry manoeuvre which Philopoemen taught the Achaeans as their hipparch;[131] for it is this kind of detail that makes a well-drilled force. Fire-signalling, too, is an essential part of warfare, and four chapters are devoted to a detailed account of the most up-to-date system—which happens to be Polybius' own invention.[132] How should one calculate the area of a city?[133] In

---

[127] iii. 81. 10.   [128] iii. 105. 9; cf. i. 84. 6; ix. 14. 1–4.

[129] v. 98; cf. ix. 18. 5–9 (the slightly different account in this passage is preferable to the summary version in book v).

[130] x. 16. 1–17. 5.   [131] x. 23. 1–8.

[132] x. 43–7; see also xxvii. 11 on the *cestrus*, a novel type of javelin fired from a sling.   [133] ix. 26 a.

what respects is the legion superior to the phalanx?[134] And is it fair to criticise the Romans for recklessness at sea?[135] Such questions receive the competent answer of the expert; and they are accompanied by a long series of edifying *exempla* incorporated in the narrative of sieges, campaigns and battles. This is all highly professional and it is not without reason that Pritchett, after testing his accounts of Sellasia, Caphyae, Mantinea and Cynoscephalae on the spot,[136] and vindicating him against sundry criticism, concludes that in him we have the best military historian not merely of Greece (as Fougères had claimed),[137] but of antiquity generally.[138]

In addition Polybius is especially interested in the social impact of forms of warfare. He is fascinated by mercenaries and the special problems which their employment raises both for the employer and for others.[139] Mercenaries are more appropriately employed by tyrants than democracies, since when they defeat the enemies of a democracy they are apt to put themselves out of work, whereas the stronger a tyranny grows, the more it needs its foreign soldiers. Polybius relates the Carthaginian Mercenary War at such length[140] in book i partly, it is true, for the light it sheds on Carthage,[141] but more especially because of the lessons it affords to employers of mercenaries.[142] The behaviour and the psychology of the mercenaries in revolt show clearly that in certain circumstances mercenary service could constitute a threat to civilised life. Take for example Rhegium and Messana, where mercenaries seized the cities by violence.[143] Frequently mercenaries were at a lower cultural level than Greeks in general, and so an event like the Carthaginian Mercenary War serves to illustrate the fundamental differences between civilised men and barbarians,[144] and the horrors to which civilisation can be exposed in what Demos-

---

[134] xviii. 28–32. [135] i. 37. 6–10.

[136] Pritchett, *Studies*, i. 59–70 (Sellasia); ii. 37–72 (Mantinea), 120–32 (Caphyae), 133–44 (Cynoscephalae).

[137] Fougères, *Mantinée*, 581. [138] *Studies*, ii. 37.

[139] xi. 13. 5–8; C. Thirlwall, *History of Greece* (London, 1835–47), viii. 273 n. 2, quotes similar comments by Guicciardini on the Italian mercenaries of the fifteenth century.

[140] i. 65–88.

[141] See Pédech *Polybe i*, 7.

[142] Especially i. 67; cf. Roveri, *Studi*, 122–4.

[143] i. 7. 1–12; cf. Musti, *Annali di Pisa*, 36 (1967), 205–7.

[144] i. 65. 7.

thenes and Aeschines had termed a 'truceless war',[145] that is, a war shorn of all the usages of international law.

International law is perhaps a misnomer. War is itself a resort to violence;[146] but during recent centuries and especially in the early Hellenistic age accepted conventions had gone a long way to cushion and modify its worst excesses. To Polybius such conventions are part of the social aspect of warfare,[147] and he refers to them as 'the laws of war'. One may, and should, do anything that will harm the enemy. To burn crops, destroy buildings, and carry off men and herds as plunder is all legitimate;[148] but it is wrong to violate temples[149] and commit wanton injury that does nothing to further the aims of the war—for instance to destroy trees and agricultural installations,[150] at any rate when they belong to fellow-Greeks(ὁμόφυλοι).[151] What is more, wars ought to be based on justice (or at least its semblance),[152] and properly de-

[145] i. 65. 6 for the term ἄσπονδος πόλεμος (cf. Demosthenes, xviii. 262; Aeschines, ii. 80—in both cases the word ἀκήρυκτος is also used).

[146] Cf. Diod. xxx. 18. 2, πᾶς γὰρ πόλεμος ἐκβεβηκὼς τὰ νόμιμα καὶ δίκαια τῶν ἀνθρώπων ὅμως ἔχει τινὰς ἰδίους καθαπερεὶ νόμους, οἶον ἀνοχὰς μὴ λύειν, κήρυκα μὴ ἀναιρεῖν, τὸν τὸ σῶμα αὐτοῦ πρὸς τὴν τοῦ κατισχύοντος πίστιν ⟨παραδίδοντα μὴ vel simile⟩ τιμωρεῖσθαι. This passage is almost certainly derived from Polybius; cf. von Scala, 307.

[147] Cf. v. 11. 3-4, οἱ τοῦ πολέμου νόμοι.

[148] Livy, xxxi. 30. 2-3 (based on Polybius): 'esse enim quaedam belli iura, quae ut facere ita pati sit fas: sata exuri, dirui tecta, praedas hominum pecorumque agi misera magis quam indigna patienti esse'.

[149] iv. 62. 3, τοῖς θεοῖς πόλεμον ἐξενηνοχώς. See Polybius' criticism of the Aetolians (iv. 67. 3-4; ix. 34. 8), of Philip V (v. 11. 1 f.; vii. 14. 3; xi. 7. 2; Livy, xxxi. 30. 4 (Polybian)), of the Phocians (ix. 33. 4), of Prusias (xxxii. 15. 7) on this score.

[150] xxiii. 15. 1, τὰ δένδρα καὶ τὰ κατασκευάσματα. The trees will be primarily olives, a meaning which δένδρον still commonly bears in modern Greek (as Professor Homer Thompson informs me). κατασκευάσματα often means buildings, but in v. 11. 3 Polybius condones the destruction of the enemy's forts, harbours, cities, men, ships, crops and τἆλλα τὰ τούτοις παραπλήσια, the loss of which will weaken him. Buildings could hardly be excluded from this category. Mauersberger translates κατασκευάσματα 'Ergebnis der Bodenbestellung, pl. Kulturen', i.e. cultivated plants; but it is hard to distinguish between destroying plants and destroying crops (which is permissible). On the whole it seems likely that Polybius is thinking of agricultural installations such as terracing, drainage channels and irrigation works, and also olive mills, wine vats and agricultural machinery of a larger kind, the destruction of which would prove disastrous over a long period.

[151] xxiii. 15. 1, εἰς τοὺς ὁμοφύλους.

[152] xxxvi. 2. 3; see below, pp. 170-1 nn. 92-3, for discussion of the Roman attitude before the Third Punic War. The background of the Roman concern—here cynically regarded—is the doctrine of the *iustum bellum*.

clared.[153] The main interest in all this is not its novelty, for indeed it provides no novelties. Von Scala once argued that it showed the influence of Plato;[154] but Polybius' 'laws of war' are a good deal harsher than the code envisaged in the *Republic*, and reflect, if anything, the conditions and experience of his own time. Here, though he claims to teach, he is very much the mirror of his age.

8.

I have said that in his narrow formulation of political and military history Polybius was in part reacting against Hellenistic methods. But many valuable lessons could come only from observing the behaviour of individuals, and in his portrayal of people Polybius was himself very much a Hellenistic historian. In the previous chapter I drew attention to the increased importance now attributed to personality. But this was of course a development that had begun much earlier.[155] Already Thucydides gives brief biographical sketches, and among his contemporaries Ion of Chios incorporated personal reminiscences of famous men in his memoirs,[156] while Stesimbrotus recorded biographical details of Themistocles, the other Thucydides and Pericles.[157] In the fourth century biography received a further impulse from Xenophon and Isocrates,[158] while Plato's characterisation of Socrates is too well-known to require comment. But it was mainly in the Peripatetic school that most progress was made.[159] Theophrastus' *Characters* were bound to influence writers of history; and his contemporary Aristoxenus of Tarentum[160] and his pupil Duris of Samos[161] both added their contribution. Strasburger has written of the 'rich

[153] xiii. 3. 4, with my note in *Commentary*, ii. 416 ad loc.

[154] Cf. von Scala, 299–324, especially 313 ff.

[155] See on this von Fritz, 'Die Bedeutung des Aristoteles für die Geschichtsschreibung', *Histoire et historiens*, 101; A. Momigliano, *The development of Greek biography* (Harvard, 1971), 23 ff.

[156] Cf. Jacoby, *FGH* 392 F 6, 11, 12, 13, 15 for gossipy comments on Cimon, Pericles and Sophocles; see Stuart, *Epochs*, 35, 175.

[157] *FGH* 107 F 1–11 for fragments of his study of these three statesmen.

[158] In Isocrates' *Evagoras*, and the *Memorabilia* and *Agesilaus* of Xenophon.

[159] Von Fritz, 'Die Bedeutung des Aristoteles für die Geschichtsschreibung', *Histoire et historiens*, 101, emphasises the interest which the Peripatetics displayed in different styles of life—the active life, a life of scholarship, a life of pleasure, as Aristotle had discussed them in *Eth. Nic.* x. 6. 6 f., 1176 a 30 f.; the path to Theophrastus' *Characters* is clear.

[160] Cf. Wehrli, *Aristoxenos*.   [161] See above, pp. 34 ff.

blossoming of biography in the Hellenistic age which still finds
its most remarkable expression in Plutarch'.[162] This development
inevitably involved Polybius, who through it inherited a tradition
of historical writing which contrasted strongly with what had so
far been achieved at Rome. I am thinking of Cato, who probably
originated Latin historiography and who, Nepos tells us,[163] did
not even mention the names of military commanders—though he
did name Syrus, the elephant which fought most bravely for
Hannibal in the Second Punic War; in this he was perhaps
following a practice of anonymity general among the early
annalists.[164]

The intrusion of personality into historical writing presents
certain problems. There is the question of the development of a
man's character over a period of time, and there is also the
question how the historian ought to deal with it. It has been
pointed out[165] that historians broadly speaking fall into two classes.
There are those who, like Livy—or Thucydides—let their characterisation of the men and women whose actions they are describing
arise indirectly out of the narrative; and there are those who like
Xenophon in the *Anabasis*, express their views directly in their
own persons. It is not surprising that Polybius, who can rarely miss
any opportunity to address his readers personally[166] for their own
good, adopts the second method. Indeed, not content to discuss the
characters of the persons he is writing about, he also discusses the
problem of character development in general. His practice, he
says,[167] in a passage about Philip V, is not to attempt to give
a general characterisation when a person first crops up in his
narrative, but to make comments on character and, it goes without saying, to pass moral judgements on each separate incident.
This approach is of course better suited to his didactic purpose
than a more generalised description of a man's personality would
be.[168] In book ix, however, he goes a little further, and after

---

[162] 'Die Entdeckung der politischen Geschichte durch Thukydides',
Thukydides, 469.
[163] Nepos, *Cato*, 3; cf. Pliny, *Nat. hist.* viii. 11 (= Peter, *HRF*, 'M. Porcius
Cato', T 2 and F 88).
[164] See F. Bömer, 'Naevius und Fabius Pictor', *Symb. Osl.* 29 (1952), 39 n. 4.
[165] Cf. Bruns, *Persönlichkeit*, v f., 1–11 (Polybius' method).
[166] See above, p. 47 nn. 86–90.
[167] x. 26. 9 , with my *Commentary*, ii. 231.
[168] Cf. Petzold, *Studien*, 19.

discussing in detail some of Hannibal's traits which are most commonly matters of dispute, he is led to some general remarks on the development of character.[169]

Some people, he says, believe that a man's real character is revealed by circumstances, whether these take the form of the acquisition of power—here he may have in mind the old proverb ἀρχή ἄνδρα δείξει[170]—or the blows of misfortune. This is of course the view which we find expressed in Tacitus' famous characterisation of Tiberius:[171] 'Then fear vanished and with it shame. Thereafter he expressed only his own personality—by unrestrained crime and infamy'—'postremo in scelera simul ac dedecora prorupit, postquam remoto pudore et metu suo tantum ingenio utebatur'. Polybius rejected it, on the grounds, first, that circumstances are often complex and lead men to act and speak in a manner contrary to their real inclinations, and, secondly, that the influence of their friends can have the same effect. When, for example, he is discussing the character of Philip V[172] and his famous 'change for the worse', his μεταβολή, he says that no former king possessed more of the qualities that make a good or a bad ruler than Philip, and that in his opinion his good qualities were natural to him (φύσει...ὑπάρξαι) but his defects were acquired as he advanced in age—as sometimes happens, he adds, no doubt from experience, in the case of old horses. Here, quite clearly, the development of Philip's character is not regarded as a gradual revealing of his nature. On the contrary, this—his φύσις—is treated as something given, indeed as just one of the several factors which together determine his character. In Philip's case his μεταβολή was caused, not by his φύσις, which was good, but by the force of circumstances and especially by bad advice such as he received from Demetrius of Pharos[173] or Heracleides of Tarentum.[174]

In practice the influence of such advisers, good or bad, was one to which kings were especially exposed; and it has been observed that the theme is frequent in Hellenistic historians, who borrowed it from the philosophers. Polybius stresses the role of courtiers and

---

[169] ix. 22. 7–26. 11.
[170] Bias quoted in Aristotle, *Eth. Nic.* v. 1. 16, 1130 a 1.
[171] Tac. *Ann.* vi. 51. 6.
[172] iv. 77. 1–4; vii. 11. 10, 13. 7, 14. 1–6; x. 26. 7–10.
[173] Cf. vii. 14. 3.
[174] xiii. 4. 1–5. 6; Livy, xxxii. 5. 7; Diod. xxviii. 2.

flatterers in the Antigonid, Ptolemaic and Seleucid courts,[175] and it would be wrong to dismiss this as a τόπος. The men he mentions are real enough and their influence was bound to be strong in the context of court life. At the same time the importance he attributes to them seems to owe something to tradition. It has been claimed[176] that Polybius' way of regarding a man's personal character development derives from Aristotle[177] who, in the *Nicomachean Ethics*, traces a man's character or ἦθος not from his nature but from a series of decisions freely taken, which in accordance with their tendency lead him along the path towards virtue or its opposite. In that case his nature is part of the background against which the decisions are taken. The resemblance to Polybius' view is striking and the suggestion up to a point plausible; but, as usual, the origins of Polybius' thought are not to be determined so easily. For in fact there seems also to be a Stoic element in his formulation.

According to Chrysippus[178] 'there are two causes of perversion, one arising out of communications with many men, the other out of the very nature of circumstances'; and Diogenes Laertius[179] records the same Stoic view that 'a rational being is perverted, sometimes by the persuasiveness of external affairs and sometimes through the communications of those with whom he associates'. Attempts to trace Stoic beliefs in Polybius have in the past led to a great deal of exaggeration,[180] but it is hard to imagine that these two factors—force of outside circumstances and the counsel of friends—turn up entirely by coincidence in Polybius' theory of character development.[181]

In fact, Polybius here shows his usual eclecticism and his ability to combine the views of various schools successfully in a pragmatical compromise. Before leaving this subject I should however add a word on a passage which at first sight seems to

---

[175] On the theme of the evil counsellor see Pédech, *Méthode*, 234 with n. 141.

[176] Cf. von Fritz, 'Die Bedeutung des Aristoteles für die Geschichtsschreibung', *Histoire et historiens*, 103–6.

[177] *Eth. Nic.* ii. 1 ff., 1103 a 14 ff.

[178] apud Galen, *de Hipp. et Plat. plac.* v, p. 462 (who attributes the view to Chrysippus).

[179] Diog. Laert. vii. 89.

[180] Especially by von Scala, 201–55, 325–33, and by Hirzel, *Cicero*, ii. 841–907.

[181] Cf. Hirzel, *Cicero*, ii. 858–60; Susemihl, ii. 104 n. 91.

contradict his theory. In book ix,[182] after describing inconsistencies in the behaviour of Agathocles of Syracuse and Cleomenes of Sparta, both of whom he regards of course as tyrants, he remarks that 'we can hardly suppose dispositions (διαθέσεις) so diametrically opposite to have existed in the same natures—περὶ τὰς αὐτὰς φύσεις'; consequently he interprets the differences in behaviour as the reaction to different circumstances. In book iv however, in a passage[183] about Aratus of Sicyon, he contrasts his great skill in stratagems and *coups de main* with his slowness, lack of courage and ineffectiveness on field operations; and he concludes that there is something multiform in a man's φύσις which causes him to display the most contradictory behaviour even in similar pursuits, ἐνεργήματα ὁμοειδῆ.[184] At first sight the two views seem to contradict each other. But the examples which Polybius quotes at the end of the chapter on Aratus show that this is not so.[185] There he parallels Aratus' behaviour by pointing out that Thessalian cavalry are irresistible in squadrons and brigades, but slow and awkward when dispersed and tackling the enemy single-handed, whereas the opposite is true of Aetolian cavalry. Similarly Cretans are excellent in ambuscades but cowardly in pitched battles, while the opposite is true of Achaeans and Macedonians. These examples show that Polybius is concerned to break down the concept of 'similar enterprises', ἐνεργήματα ὁμοειδῆ, by showing that there can be differences between them. Hence, since a man's φύσις is multiform, πολυειδής, he will in consequence frequently react differently to situations which are superficially similar, ὁμοειδῆ, but in fact are different—just as pitched battles are in reality quite a different matter from secret stratagems. His remarks on Aratus would contradict his main theory of character

---

[182] ix. 23. 1–4.   [183] iv. 8. 1–12.

[184] Pédech, *Méthode*, 237, would resolve the difficulty by drawing a distinction between περιστάσεις, events which accidentally contradict the tendencies of a man's character, and ἐνεργήματα, which engage the very heart of a man's being ('le tréfonds de l'être'). I am not sure that I understand this distinction; but certainly in iv. 8. 7 Polybius is saying that both in mind and in body a man's nature (φύσεις) is inherently multiform, so that even when he is engaged in ὁμοειδῆ ἐνεργήματα he may display himself in a contradictory light at different times. This must mean that differences of behaviour are due to differences of disposition within a man's own nature (and not to different περιστάσεις). As I have suggested above, the solution of the apparent contradiction must lie rather in the closer definition of what *seem* to be ὁμοειδῆ ἐνεργήματα (but are not really so).   [185] iv. 8. 10–11.

development only if he were obliged to admit that Aratus behaved differently in the *same* circumstances, that is if in the course of stratagems he had behaved sometimes boldly and sometimes with cowardice. And this Polybius, who is a great believer in the tendency of like causes to create like results (and the reverse),[186] does not do.

In conclusion it is perhaps worth noting that Polybius' theory of how character develops is eminently reasonable and not out of step with modern theories which, whatever their particular emphasis, generally attribute importance to both innate and environmental factors. It was also a theory well adapted to his own purpose of drawing political and military lessons from history, and in that way it contributes in no small degree to the ultimate success of his πραγματικὴ ἱστορία.

---

[186] Cf. i. 61. 2, τῆς δ' ἑκατέρων παρασκευῆς τὴν ἐναντίαν ἐχούσης διάθεσιν τῇ περὶ τὰ Δρέπανα γενομένῃ ναυμαχίᾳ, καὶ τὸ τέλος ἑκατέροις τῆς μάχης εἰκότως ἐναντίον ἀπέβη; iii. 109. 1 (a false prognostication). See above, p. 58 with n. 160.

IV

Some structural problems: Time and Place

1.

Any historian, whether he consciously sets out to produce a work of literary merit or not, has to solve a number of problems affecting the structure and organisation of his material. When like Polybius he claims to be writing a history that is σωματοειδής, an organic whole, this becomes even more of an obligation to his readers. Much of this chapter will therefore be devoted to the architectural structure of Polybius' *Histories*.

We must assume that when he planned to end the work in 168/7 with Pydna and its aftermath, he had a scheme of books to fit that plan. Since in the work as it finally appeared the years from 220 to 167 (together with the two introductory books) took him down to book xxix, it looks as if the original version, including the index-volume, was designed to occupy thirty books. On the other hand, this would imply that the first scheme included at any rate some version of book xii and did *not* include any equivalent of book xxxiv, which is devoted to questions of geography. Both these assumptions may well seem reasonable, but neither is certain. There is indeed a reference forward to book xxxiv in a passage in book iii[1] dealing with the place of geographical information in history, but this passage was certainly written after 146 since it mentions Polybius' journeys on the outer ocean.[2] Likewise the chapter in the same book in which Polybius promises to speak about the barbarians who live along the Atlantic[3] is also a late insertion. In fact there are no references to book xxxiv in any part of the *Histories* that can be assigned with certainty to the original plan. As regards book

---

[1] iii. 57–9; the relevant passage is 57. 5.
[2] iii. 59. 7–8.   [3] iii. 37. 11.

xii, I have argued above that it was undoubtedly composed after 146 in its present form,[4] but that this does not exclude an earlier version. However, as I have indicated,[5] there is no reason to think that this first version of the *Histories* going down to 167 only was ever published in its entirety; and we simply do not know whether the original publication up to book xv included any equivalent of the present book xii or not.

Polybius' decision to extend his *Histories* to include the years 167–145 will also have involved a decision to increase the proposed total number of books from thirty to forty; at any rate, forty was the final number in the revised edition. It has been argued[6] that these forty books are arranged roughly in groups of six. In support of this one can point to vi and xii, both digressions, one on the Roman state and army, the other on Timaeus and other previous historians, and at the other end xxxiv and xl, devoted the one to geography and the other to the index. Further, it can be argued that xviii brings the narrative to a decisive point—the Roman victory at Cynoscephalae and the proclamation of Greek freedom. On the other hand, book xxiv takes the story down to 180, which provides no sort of historical climax, since the death of Philip V, which was later to serve Livy as the culminating event of his fourth decade, rounding off book xl, fell in 179 and must have been related by Polybius in book xxv. Similarly the year 164, which ended book xxx, was completely undistinguished by any event of importance. The so-called hexadic arrangement also gives us an awkward four books (instead of six), xxxi to xxxiv, or at the best a 'half-hexad' of books xxxi to xxxiii, leaving xxxiv to xxxix to constitute the final hexad, with xl hanging forlornly at the end, as a kind of supernumerary.[7] The evidence derived from the individual books is somewhat inconclusive. Book vi had to come after Cannae for this is the place which logically demands it. But of course books iv and v need not have recounted Seleucid and Ptolemaic affairs at such length: so perhaps there is a formal element involved in placing the study of the constitution in book vi. Book xii on the other hand appears to interrupt Ol. 143 in the middle because it arises out of Timaeus' statements on Africa—an area which now comes to the fore as the scene of Scipio's final campaign; and as a subsidiary reason for dealing with Timaeus

---

[4] See above, pp. 24–5, 48.   [5] See pp. 16–22.
[6] See Lorenz, *Untersuchungen*, 66 ff.   [7] See the table on p. 129.

now there were his inaccurate statements about Locri, a town with which Scipio was to be very much involved in book xv (the relevant passages have not survived). So, at first sight there seem to be good reasons arising out of the content of book xii for its position at this point in the work.

However, the problem takes on a different complexion according to whether book xii was in the first draft or not. If it was, the reasons for putting it there will be those just mentioned. But if it was not, and merely appeared as an afterthought in the second edition, it seems clear that Polybius' real reason for including it will have been his growing hostility to Timaeus, due to causes which I indicated in the second chapter—one being his claim to be regarded as the true historian of the west; the misstatements about Africa will then be merely an excuse for introducing the polemical book at this point, and the hexadic structure could be a factor in the decision. Book xxxiv starts conveniently at the point in 152 B.C. between Olympiads 156 and 157, when the period which is to serve as a kind of test of how Rome exercised her universal power gives way to a time of trouble and disturbance (ταραχὴ καὶ κίνησις);[8] and I will say more about this shortly when I come to discuss the place of geography in Polybius' work.[9] To sum up, it seems that even if Polybius shows a slight inclination to arrange some of his books in sixes, he has no strong feelings about this, and certainly does not attempt to force a hexadic arrangement on those parts where it does not easily fit.

2.

It was obviously far more important in a universal work covering seventy-five years (excluding the period described in the introductory books) and designed to serve a practical purpose for its readers, that the chronological structure of the history should be rational and effective. There are two aspects to this. First, over a long period such as, for example, that covered by the account in book ii of the Gallic Wars of Rome stretching from 387 to 225, there must be a clear way of indicating the time intervals between successive incidents, and equally a way of relating either the starting point or the finishing point of the sequence to some externally established event. This might be the beginning of an era (such as the Seleucid Era) or it might be some firmly anchored

<hr />

[8] Cf. iii. 4. 12; above pp. 29–30.   [9] See below, pp. 122 ff.

event like the battle of Aegospotami or the battle of Leuctra,[10] both of which were well known in the Greek tradition and could in turn be easily related to the reader's own date. At the time Polybius was writing there was, however, no era that would command general and obvious recognition throughout the Greek world, and the second alternative was therefore clearly preferable. The other problem is to divide up events in the detailed narrative and relate them to the seasons, so that the reader knows not only in what year they happened but whether they took place in summer or in winter —or according to the degree of accuracy required, what month or what day or even at what time of day a particular event occurred.

Herodotus made a great but largely inconspicuous contribution to chronology in the sense of determining intervals; he used the reigns of the Persian and Lydian kings and, as Jacoby and Strasburger have shown,[11] he thereby laid the foundation for most of our chronology of the seventh and sixth centuries. Thucydides employed years of the war for his monograph, dividing them into summers and winters (though he left some ambiguity about whether these were to be reckoned as 6 and 6 months or 8 and 4).[12] He indicated starting points by the use of the eponymous priests or magistrates at Argos, Sparta and Athens to date the Spartan entry into Plataea, and those of Sparta and Athens for the Peace of Nicias[13]—though he comments on the awkwardness of this device.[14] Unfortunately, *eponymi* are only useful if the reader has access to a list which will enable him to count backward and forward, and to that extent their use is inferior to that of an era.

Ephorus' problem was different. In his universal history he had to cover vast periods stretching from the return of the Heracleidae to the siege of Perinthus in 341, and he divided his material up under various cities and countries, the chronology of which he treated separately κατὰ γένος.[15] Polybius was to use the same method for the first four years (220–216) of his main period, before the events of the *oecumene* had become intertwined; but after that he adopted a chronological system derived from Timaeus. For, he

[10] Cf. i. 6. 1–2.

[11] Jacoby, *Atthis*, 382 n. 10; Strasburger, 'Herodots Zeitrechnung', *Herodot*, 677–725 (a corrected and expanded reprint of the first version in *Historia*, 5 (1956), 129–61), with the supplementary bibliography on p. 677 n. 1.

[12] Strasburger, *Herodot*, 717, with nn. 95–6.

[13] Thucyd. ii. 2. 1; v. 25. 1.   [14] Thucyd. v. 20. 2–3.

[15] Diod. v. 1. 4 = *FGH* 70 T 11; see Jacoby's note ad loc.

tells us,[16] it was Timaeus who 'compared the dates of the ephors with those of the kings in Lacedaemon from the earliest times, and the lists of Athenian archons and priestesses of Hera at Argos with those of the victors at Olympia'. The list of Olympionicae preserved at Olympia and covering the period from 776 onwards had been published by Hippias of Elis in 400.[17] Timaeus made this list—whether taken from Hippias or not—the foundation of his chronology, and in this way he produced an 'Olympiad' era dating from 776; but whether he drew up two chronological tables or one comprehensive one embracing Spartan kings and ephors, Athenian archons, and Argive priestesses of Hera depends on the precise meaning of the rather ambiguous passage from Polybius which I have just quoted.

It was from Timaeus that Polybius took over the idea of dividing up his history into Olympiad years—though indeed we cannot be sure whether any other historians had used it in the meantime.[18] This system had the obvious advantages of an era for indicating intervals of time, though as we shall see in a moment Polybius did not use it primarily for that purpose. As a framework for a narrative which contained much military campaigning, had it been strictly interpreted it would have had the disadvantage of splitting up each summer's campaigns between two Olympiad years; and for us it has the further disadvantage that our surviving evidence is inadequate to fix the dating of the Olympic games closer than to a full moon in the high summer.[19] Now whether in recounting a campaign in Italy or Spain or even the Peloponnese Polybius would have had sufficient information to enable him to say whether a particular event fell before or after the Olympic games in an Olympic year or—what was more difficult—whether it fell before or after what could only be the quite arbitrary date in summer which separated, say, the second from the third year of a given Olympiad, is extremely doubtful.[20] But in practice the

[16] xii. 11. 1.
[17] Plut. *Numa*, 1. 6 = *FGH* 6 F 2; Plutarch regards it as unreliable.
[18] Cf. Ziegler, col. 1565.
[19] See R. Sealey, 'The Olympic festival of 324 B.C.', *CR*, 10 (1960), 185–6; Errington, 'The chronology of Polybius' *Histories*, Books i and ii', *JRS* 57 (1967), 99, against Pédech, *Méthode*, 457, who would date it between 25 July and 23 Aug. (Julian).
[20] Pédech (*Méthode*, 456–61) postulates that Polybius used a luni-solar *octaeteris*—an eight-year cycle covering two Olympiads—and divided up his

question was not very important since what Polybius really used was an adapted or manipulated Olympiad year,[21] which allowed him to continue a campaign to the end of the summer in which it began, as if it all belonged to the same 'Olympiad year'.[22] Thus Polybius' 'Olympiad year' normally closed at the end of the campaigning year and the retirement of troops into winter quarters; and this terminal point had the advantage for Greek readers at any rate that it often coincided roughly with the end of the Aetolian 'general' year, that is the year of office of the chief Aetolian magistrate, and for the greater part of the period covered by the *Histories* with the end of the Achaean 'general' year as well.[23]

In practice this system proved very good, since it was operated with considerable elasticity, as one or two examples will demonstrate. In books iii–v Polybius recounts the events of Ol. 140, that is 220–216. For Greece and Asia Minor he ends in the summer of 216 but he also includes the death of L. Postumius Albinus who apparently fell at the end of winter 216/15, when he was consul designate for 215;[24] hence it looks as if this event was included under Ol. 140 to complete the picture of woe after Cannae. Books vii and viii between them cover the next Olympiad, 141, which embraced the years 216/15 to 213/12; the fall of Syracuse occurred in late autumn 212,[25] and was recounted in book viii, which was

Olympiad years according to lunar months; but although such an *octaeteris* is mentioned in Geminus (*Elementa*, 8. 27–50), and Eratosthenes wrote a treatise on it (Geminus, ibid. 8. 437), it is extremely doubtful if any Greek state actually *used* it (cf. Bickerman, *Chronology*, 29–30), and there is no indication anywhere in Polybius that he took account of it. See further Errington, art. cit. (n. 19), 99.

[21] Cf. Ziegler, col. 1565.

[22] For various views on how he organised this see Pédech, *Méthode*, 449–50, discussing the works of Nissen, Unger, Steigemann and Seipt. The most likely solution is that of De Sanctis, iii. 1. 219–23, and is the one adopted above; it assumes a flexible procedure, adapted to the special problems of each year.

[23] When the change in Achaea took place is uncertain. Timoxenus, whose election as Achaean general after the Social War of 220–217 is mentioned in v. 106. 1, may have entered office in autumn, 217; but this would have involved the curtailment of Aratus' generalship of 217/16, and it is possible that the change was not made until Aratus' death in 213 (cf. Walbank, *Philip V*, 300 n. 3; *Commentary*, ii. 5, 87–8; Aymard, *Assemblées*, 238–47). What is certain is that Philopoemen entered his first generalship in autumn, 208 (cf. my *Commentary*, ii. 279, on xi. 8–18); so the change must have been introduced sometime between 217 and 208.

[24] iii. 118. 6; for discussion of Postumius' status at the time of his death see my *Commentary*, i. 448–9 ad loc.

[25] Some scholars date this to 211; for the argument in favour of 212 see my *Commentary*, ii. 6–8.

thus extended to include events beyond the end of the fourth Olympiad year and even beyond the end of the normal campaigning season, in order to round off the Sicilian campaign. Book xiv appears to begin with the winter of 204/3 at least for the African theatre of war, for the section dealing with this starts with Scipio in winter quarters;[26] and this suggests that book xiii contained events down to the end of the campaigning season of 204. These examples could be extended—though especially in the later books the fragments are often too scanty to allow us to say with certainty at what point a particular book began or ended.[27] In general, however, it is clear that in assigning events to any particular Olympiad year Polybius would call a halt at the most logical point—winter quarters, the end of a campaign, a decisive battle—and in consequence would start the next Olympiad year from there.

3.

For Olympiad 140, covering the years 220 to 216, the detailed treatment is rather different from that in the rest of the *Histories*. There Polybius usually follows what he calls his normal procedure, τὴν εἰθισμένην τάξιν[28]—by which the events of the various regions are dealt with in a fixed order, only rarely broken, viz. Italy, Sicily, Spain, Africa, Greece and Macedonia, Asia and Egypt.[29] But this begins to be applied only from Olympiad 141, since it is from then onwards that the events of the *oecumene* are intermingled.[30] During Olympiad 140 events are merely moving towards this situation, and Polybius still feels it proper to treat them κατὰ γένος.[31] He therefore devotes book iii to the events of Spain

[26] xiv. 1–2.

[27] Cf. Pédech, *Méthode*, 451 ff.; vol. iii of my *Commentary* will contain a detailed analysis of the arguments for the assignment of the known fragments of books xx to xxxix.   [28] xxxii. 11. 2; cf. xv. 25. 19.

[29] See Lorenz, *Untersuchungen*, 66. In reality, of course, events in all fields were occurring simultaneously, and Duris had complained that the 'imitation' achieved by the historian therefore inevitably fell short of reality in πάθος (see above, p. 35 n. 18). Polybius' scheme in all its flexibility is intended to surmount this difficulty (as far as possible) and the modifications which he introduces into it show him to have been alive to the need to sustain the reader's interest.

[30] Cf. iv. 28. 2–6; v. 105. 4–10; on the validity of this claim see pp. 68 ff.

[31] See especially v. 31. 4–5, where Polybius claims that in order to achieve clarity it is essential that during this Olympiad he should *not* interweave the histories of the various countries; for discussion see my *Commentary*, i. 562 on v. 31. 6.

and Italy from the outbreak of the Second Punic War down to Cannae, and then in books iv to v recounts the parallel events of the Social War in Greece, the Fourth Syrian war for Coele-Syria, and various other wars like that of Rhodes and Bithynia against Byzantium, the fighting in Crete, and the attack by Mithridates of Pontus on Sinope, down to the same date—that of the battle of Cannae in summer 216.[32] To some extent the various eastern theatres are juxtaposed for variety. In book iv the events in Greece are carried down to the end of winter 220/19 and are then followed by an account of the war against Byzantium, the Cretan war and the attack on Sinope.[33] The narrative then returns to Greece to cover the events of 219 down to the end of the following winter in the remaining chapter of book iv;[34] and in book v Polybius first relates Greek events from spring 218 to spring 217,[35] then prefaces his account of the Syrian War with a digression of 27 chapters describing various revolts in Egypt and Molon's revolt against Antiochus, some of which fall outside the Olympiad altogether.[36] The Syrian War itself, which occupied the years 219–217, is also broken at a point between 218 and 217 by an account of the activities of Antiochus' general Achaeus and of Attalus of Pergamum, which are only marginally relevant to it.[37] Finally after describing the Raphia campaign which brought the Syrian War to a close,[38] and after a short digression on Rhodes,[39] Polybius reverts to Greece to bring the narrative of the Social War down to the Peace of Naupactus.[40] The remaining chapters of book v deal quite shortly with the Greek, Egyptian and Syrian events of 217/16,[41] and then after giving a slightly fuller account of Philip's advance by sea to Illyria[42]—which was important because it brought a confrontation with Rome nearer—Polybius concludes[43] with the mention of a successful attack on some Gauls by Prusias of Bithynia.

Thus books iv and v to some extent use the method of the later books in juxtaposing the events in the various theatres east of the

---

[32] iii. 2. 1–5.
[33] iv. 3–37 (Greece); 38–52 (Rhodes, Bithynia and Byzantium); 53–5 (Crete); 56 (Mithridates and Sinope).   [34] iv. 57–87.
[35] v. 1–30.   [36] v. 31–57.
[37] v. 72–8; the first stages of the Syrian War are described in v. 58–71.
[38] v. 79–87.   [39] v. 88–90.
[40] v. 91–105.   [41] v. 106–7.
[42] v. 108–10.   [43] v. 111.

Adriatic, but east and west are still treated separately and the divisions into Olympiad years are not strictly kept. Instead Polybius employs a system of synchronisms, which, as I have already mentioned,[44] he explains[45] as intended to render his narrative clear and easy to follow by relating events at convenient points both to the Olympiad years and to contemporary events in Greece—thus plainly indicating that it is primarily for a Greek public that he is writing.

4.

For the two introductory books the problem is different again, for here Polybius was sketching on a wider canvas and felt it necessary to describe events which occupied periods of varying length in different parts of the world. His account of the early history of Achaea, for example, took him back briefly to the time of the Heracleidae,[46] and in a little more detail to the fifth century confederation of the Crotonians, Sybarites and Caulonians in Magna Graecia;[47] but his first real date for early Achaean events comes with the revival of the Confederacy in Ol. 124 (284/3–281/0).[48] On the other hand his account of the conflicts between Rome and the Gauls, introduced in relation to the invasion of 225, is set in a chronological framework going back to the famous sack of Rome by Brennus, which he dates to 387/6.[49] Relations between Carthage and Rome are taken back to 264,[50] at the beginning of Ol. 129, and preceded by a short discussion of the Mamertine seizure of Messana and of the comparable occupation of Rhegium, neither event being very clearly dated.[51] Finally, these books contain an account of the First Punic War, the Carthaginian Mercenary War, the careers of Hamilcar and Hasdrubal in Spain, and the First Roman War against Illyria.[52]

It has been argued that for all this earlier material Polybius

[44] See above, pp. 5–6.

[45] v. 31. 3.

[46] ii. 41.

[47] ii. 39.

[48] ii. 41. 1–2; cf. 41. 11, 71. 6.

[49] ii. 18–35.

[50] i. 5. 1.

[51] See for discussion my *Commentary*, i. 52–3 on i. 7. 6–13. This digression also involves an account of the early career of Hiero of Syracuse; on the chronology of this see my *Commentary*, i. 54, on i. 8. 3, and Petzold, *Studien*, 149 ff.

[52] i. 10–64 (First Punic War), 65–88 (Carthaginian Mercenary War, preceded by the Roman action against the Falisci); ii. 1 (Hamilcar in Spain), 2–12 (First Illyrian War), 13 (Hasdrubal in Spain).

used a chronology based systematically on Olympiad years.[53] This is not the occasion to examine that thesis in detail.[54] There are, however, several points which weigh strongly against it. First, there are very few references to Olympiad dates in books i and ii; in fact, as Errington has pointed out, there are only six altogether, and all of these refer to the beginning or the end of a fairly long series of events.[55] Secondly, the hypothesis does not take adequate account of the variety of sources used by Polybius in his introductory books; yet it is clear that there were several of these and highly probable that they used different chronological systems. Fabius Pictor, who was most likely Polybius' source for the Gallic Wars[56] and certainly one of his sources for the First Punic War,[57] was evidently acquainted with Olympiad dating, since according to Dionysius of Halicarnassus[58] he put the foundation of Rome in the first year of the eighth Olympiad (748/7); but for his detailed narrative he must have recorded the consuls of each year.[59] Polybius' other source for the First Punic War was Philinus, and he apparently used 'years of the war' as a dating system for his monograph;[60] two examples of this have survived into Polybius' account.[61] For

[53] Leuze, *Jahrzählung*, 105 ff.; Pédech, *Méthode*, 432–95 (cf. 'La Méthode chronologique de Polybe d'après le récit des invasions gauloises', *CRAI*, 1955, 367–74); Werner, *Republik*, 42 ff.

[54] For a detailed criticism see Errington, 'The chronology of Polybius' *Histories*, books i and ii', *JRS*, 57 (1967), 96–108; his conclusions are rejected by Pédech, *Polybe ii*, 28 n. 1, but without discussion.

[55] They are i. 3. 1 (Ol. 140 marks the beginning of the main history), 5. 1 (Ol. 129 marks the beginning of book i); ii. 41. 1, 41. 11, 71. 6 (Ol. 124 marks the beginning of the revival of Achaea), 71. 6 (Ol. 139 ends the introductory section). Of these six, three, viz. ii. 41. 11, and 71. 6 (both dates), are qualified with περί; cf. Errington, art. cit. (n. 54), 96.

[56] Cf. De Sanctis, iii. 1. 305 n. 103; Leuze, *Jahrzählung*, 142–5; Beloch, *RG*, 139–40; Gelzer, 'Römische Politik bei Fabius Pictor', *Kl. Schr.* iii. 72 ff. Bung, *Fabius*, 151 ff., thinks other sources were also used for this section.

[57] i. 14. 1; see my *Commentary*, i. 64–5, on Polybius' use of Fabius and Philinus. On doubts expressed by some scholars see above, pp. 77–8, nn. 60–1.

[58] Dion. Hal. i. 74 = Peter, *HRF*, 'Q. Fabius Pictor', F 6 = *FGH* 809 F 3.

[59] Cf. Badian, 'The early historians', *Latin historians*, 3; against the view of R. Laqueur, *RE*, 'Philinos (8)', cols. 2180–93, that Fabius did not mention consuls, see Walbank, 'Polybius, Philinus and the First Punic War', *CQ*, 39 (1945), 2–3, and against the argument of Pédech, *Méthode*, 466, that 'l'éponomie n'est pas chez Polybe un procédé de datation' see—at least for its application in the introductory books—Errington, 'The chronology of Polybius' *Histories*, books i and ii', *JRS*, 57 (1967), 100–2.

[60] See Walbank, 'Polybius, Philinus and the First Punic War', *CQ*, 39 (1945), 1–5.

[61] i. 41. 4, 56. 2.

Achaean affairs both Aratus' *Memoirs* and any other sources Polybius may have used are likely to have been based on Achaean 'general' years.[62] Now it is *prima facie* unlikely that Polybius set out to convert the dates given in these various systems into Olympiad years, and that for several reasons. First, it would have been point-less; secondly, it would have been very difficult and sometimes even impossible; thirdly, as we have seen, such a conversion has left no traces in his narrative; and fourthly, the summary of his work which he appends at the end of book xxxix[63] distinguishes clearly between the *Histories* proper and the introductory books, and mentions the use of the Olympiad system only for the former.

The various chronological sequences given by Polybius in books i and ii create many problems. But the most likely assumption is that in each case he has simply followed the system which he found in the source he was using—general-years for Achaea, con-sul-years for the Gallic Wars, consul-years and years of the war for the First Punic War.[64] It is highly unlikely that he attempted to construct or make use of tables like that of Timaeus, but in-cluding Rome and worked out in greater detail, so as to enable him to determine whether an event which his source assigned to a particular consul-year was in fact to be put in the part of that year that fell before or after the beginning of the new Olympiad year—a matter of some importance if he wished to indicate in terms of Olympiad years the correct interval between events several years apart—or alternatively to enable him to make a rough and ready equation of consul and Olympiad years (and Achaean general-years) along the lines Livy later adopted when he came to use Polybius as his source for events in Sicily and Greece in his third decade (and it is well known what trouble it landed him in).[65] In these two introductory books Polybius

---

[62] See my *Commentary*, i. 234; Errington, 'The chronology of Polybius' *Histories*, books i and ii', *JRS*, 57 (1967), 97, contra Pédech, *Méthode*, 488–9, arguing for Olympiad dating.   [63] xxxix. 8. 4–6.

[64] One should moreover bear in mind that in these introductory books Polybius was concerned less with giving a carefully constructed sequence of events than with demonstrating their relationship and eliciting their causes; cf. Petzold, *Studien*, 184, '...eine gewisse Unbestimmtheit in der Chronologie zu Gunsten des für die Kausalität wesentlicheren Nacheinander und Neben-einander der Geschehnisse' (in reference to the First Punic War).

[65] See De Sanctis, iii. 2. 446, for Livy's equation of Ol. 142. 1 (212/11) with the consular year A.U.C. 542 (212) for Spanish events, with the result that they are recorded a year in advance of their real dates, so that the battle

was concerned primarily with explaining the causal sequence leading to the position in 220, and for this purpose such an elaborate correlation of different conventions could bring no conceivable advantage: his chronological structure needed only to be self-consistent within each sequence of events, it did not need to correlate them except very generally. After all the *oecumene* had not yet become one.

5.

When he reached his *Histories* proper Polybius adjusted the Olympiad system to the books, so as to suit the amount of detail available or important at different times. The norm, as he twice states it,[66] was to assign two books to each Olympiad—which would normally imply covering two years' events in each book. This gave a reasonable allowance of space, and Polybius refers to it as his uniform method of composition, τὸ μονοειδὲς τῆς συντάξεως.[67] However, he varied it, when required, in any one of three different ways—by redistributing the material contained in the Olympiad between the two books assigned to it, by assigning more than two books to a particularly crowded Olympiad, or by covering a whole Olympiad in a single book where events were thin.

Olympiad 140, covering 220–216, as I have already indicated, was dealt with on a basis of different theatres of war, κατὰ γένος, and had three books assigned to it, iii, iv and v; book vi was of course allotted to the account of the constitution of Rome and the Roman army. Out of the remaining eighteen Olympiad periods which covered the main *Histories* from 216/15 to 145/4 (Olympiads 141 to 158) only seven followed the 'normal' pattern of two books to the Olympiad. These included the first three, Ol. 141, Ol. 142 and Ol. 143, which between them covered the years 216/15 to 205/4. In these six books the arrangement was regular, two years to a book, and the only unusual feature was the insertion of book xii, with its criticism of Timaeus and other earlier historians, half

---

Baecula, for example, which took place in 208 (Polyb. x. 34. 1–40. 12) is dated by Livy (xxvii. 17–20) under 209. On the other hand Livy relates the Greek events of 209 and 208 under the years 208 and 207 (Livy, xxvii. 29. 9–33. 5; xxviii. 5–8; cf. De Sanctis, iii. 2. 443, with the valid criticisms of T. Walek-Czernecki, 'La chronologie de la première guerre de Macédoine', *Rev. Phil.* 54 (1928), 13 ff.), as the references to the Heraea, Nemea and Olympia show.

[66] ix. 1. 1; xiv. 1 a. 5.   [67] ix. 1. 2.

way through Ol. 143, between books xi and xiii, for reasons which
I have already discussed.

Ol. 144 covering the years 204/3 to 201/0 contained the culmina-
tion of the Hannibalic War including the great victories of Scipio
in North Africa. Accordingly the years 204/3 and 203/2 were
allowed a book each, and Polybius justifies this deviation from
normal practice in the preface to book xiv, where he claims that
Ol. 144 is particularly important and engrossing, both because in
it the wars of Italy and Africa are brought to an end—and, he
adds, everybody is eager to hear the end of a story[68]—and also
because the political aims of Philip and Antiochus leaked out during
these years.[69] However the years 202/1 and 201/0 were covered in
the usual manner in a single book, xvi, and Olympiad 145, containing the Second Macedonian War (200–196) also had two
books allotted to it, each covering the events of two years. The
normal pattern was again being followed. After 196, the treatment
becomes more flexible. Between 196 and 192 Polybius evidently
found less to recount, and so he dealt with the whole of Olympiad
146 in book xix, which is now lost. Olympiad 147 was dealt with
in two books, as usual, but the first of these, book xx, covered the
events of a single year, 192/1, and the second, book xxi, the remaining three years 191–188. This curious division was of course
caused by the multiplication of events in the War with Antiochus,
which began in 192. The next Olympiad, 148, covering the years
188/7–185/4 was assigned to a single book, xxii. Books xxiii and
xxiv almost certainly contained the events of Ol. 149, with the
normal two years to a book; and the following eight years 180/79–
173/2, that is Olympiads 150 and 151, were covered in two books,
each containing the events of four years. Polybius had now reached
the Third Macedonian War, and to Ol. 152, containing the years
from 172/1 to 169/8, he allotted three books (xxvii, xxviii and
xxix). Unfortunately the state of the fragments of these is such
that we cannot say with assurance whether the events of the second
year of the Olympiad, 171/0, were included along with 172/1 in
book xxvii or with 170/69 in book xxviii; Büttner-Wobst's arrangement of the fragments adopts the former alternative, and this is
probably right, since one would expect material to become fuller
as the war got under way; but the arguments are not decisive.
The events of 169/8 take up a whole book, xxix. The next sixteen

[68] xiv. 1 a. 3.   [69] xiv. 1 a. 4.

years, which separated the Third Macedonian War from the period of ταραχὴ καὶ κίνησις which seems to have begun in 152,[70] were devoted to testing out the results of Roman world dominion. Events were evidently few (there were no full scale Roman wars in the east) and consequently only the four books, xxx–xxxiii, were allotted to the four Olympiads 153–6.

Book xxxiv was devoted to geography and book xl provided an index. Of the intervening five books the first two, xxxv and xxxvi, covered Olympiad 157, that is the years 152/1 to 149/8, with two years to each book in the normal way. But the years 148/7 to 145/4 which included the fall of Carthage and the downfall of the Achaean Confederacy, together with much for which Polybius had been an eyewitness, were assigned to the three books xxxvii, xxxviii and xxxix; of these xxxvii, which is now lost, contained one year, 148/7, and xxxviii the next year 147/6, which left 146/5 for book xxxix. It is doubtful whether Polybius went down as far as the fourth year of the Olympiad, since there are no fragments from it: on the whole the likelihood is that he finished with the third year, 146/5. In this way, subject to the overriding rule, which is never broken,[71] that a new Olympiad always coincided with a new book, Polybius was able to make his scheme sufficiently flexible to deal with the varying amounts of relevant material. The result is significant for the character of the *Histories*, for the concentration comes at the end of the Hannibalic War, at the beginning of the war with Antiochus, in the war with Perseus and in the culminating period of the Third Punic War, and emphasises the primarily military aspect of Polybius' work. When Rome is at peace in the east, the narrative is more summary. Indeed one can fairly say that the pattern of the seventy years, which included the Second Punic War and the first half of the second century, as being the period of the Roman conquest of the Mediterranean was not only established by Polybius through his general theme, but was reinforced by the internal economy of the *Histories*.

6.

Within each year, as I have said, variety was achieved by the regular switch from one theatre to another, a rhetorical device which virtually converted the digression—intended to provide re-

[70] See above, p. 29 n. 149.
[71] See the table, p. 129.

laxation through change[72]—into a system. This method was not without its disadvantages, as Polybius himself remarks: for example, in his account of affairs in Egypt in 203/2 he mentions the sending of Ptolemy, the son of Sosibius, as an ambassador to Philip V of Macedon[73] to arrange a marriage alliance and to ask for help against Antiochus, if it were needed, and then observes that he has already described the reception of this embassy and apparently recorded what the ambassador said[74] under the Greek events of the same year, which by his own convention had to precede the affairs of Egypt. This worries him a little, for in a fragment which was restored to its proper position in this passage by the skill of Paul Maas,[75] he remarks: 'As I give an account of events that happen contemporaneously throughout the world each year, obviously the result will on occasion have to be recounted before the beginning, whenever in fact the general pattern of my work and the progress of my narrative requires the locality which is the scene of the conclusion of some action to occupy an earlier place than that which witnessed its initial stages.' Later he makes the same point again in book xxviii,[76] where he describes the sending of Rhodian envoys to the Senate in 170/69, having previously recounted their speeches at Rome under the affairs of Italy; and he hints that if we had the whole work before us we should have further examples of this since he says that he mentions it πλεονάκις. There were other difficulties too. Sometimes the conventional order in which the different localities were due to be mentioned clashed violently with the commonsense development of the narrative and might lead to an undesirable interruption. Thus, in book xxxii, dealing with the events of the year 157, Polybius tells his

---

[72] See above, p. 46 with n. 75.

[73] xv. 25. 13.   [74] xv. 25. 19.

[75] xv. 24 a; see P. Maas, 'Sosibios als Pseudepitropos des Ptolemaios Philopator bei Polybios', Annuaire, 9 (1949), 443–6, who argued that this passage should stand immediately after xv. 25. 19—a thesis happily confirmed by his subsequent realisation that the proposed combination of xv. 25. 19 with xv. 24 a corresponds with close verbal echoes to the passage xxviii. 16. 9–11, which refers back to it. Maas's view is queried by K. Abel, 'Der Tod des Ptolemaios IV. Philopator bei Polybios', Hermes, 95 (1967), 81–4, who would leave xv. 24 a in its present position and take the words ὡς ἐδηλώσαμεν (xv. 25. 19) as referring back to it. It is more likely that this phrase refers to the reception of the Ptolemaic envoy at Pella, details of which were probably included in the Macedonian events of this year. There may well have been some mention of this in the lacuna immediately preceding the words ὡς ἐδηλώσαμεν.

[76] xxviii. 16. 10–11.

readers that in describing Ariarathes' departure from Italy and return to Cappadocia to recover his kingdom he has been unable to separate the two areas of action and as a result has had to pass directly from the *res Italiae* to the *res Asiae*. Now therefore he proposes to return to the affairs of Greece and moreover—exceptionally and notwithstanding his Olympiad framework—to recount the story of Oropus (which had suffered some odd treatment at the hands of Athens) as a whole, 'partly reverting to the past and partly anticipating the future', he adds, 'so that the separate details being in themselves insignificant, I may not by relating them under different dates produce a narrative which is both trivial and obscure' (εὐτελῆ καὶ ἀσαφῆ).[77]

This is not the only place where Polybius deviated from his Olympiad scheme for reasons of clarity. Book xiv[78] seems to have included a single unified account of the whole of Ptolemy IV's reign after his reconquest of Coele-Syria, which according to a marginal note in the manuscript originally occupied forty-eight sheets. The reason was that for a large part of his reign Ptolemy spent his time in dissipation and then became involved in a savage internal war with native Egyptians which 'contained nothing of note, no pitched battle, no sea-fight, no siege'—in short, none of the features which traditionally served to make a narrative interesting.[79] In this case Polybius seems to have attached his account of Ptolemy Philopator's reign to that king's death (which probably occurred in summer 204);[80] and in order not then to overload his

---

[77] xxxii. 11. 1–6 (on the reading here see below, p. 113 n. 82).

[78] xiv. 12. 1–5.

[79] Cf. xxix. 12, where writers of monographs are accused of working them up for lack of serious material.

[80] K. Abel, 'Der Tod des Ptolemaios IV. Philopator bei Polybios', *Hermes*, 95 (1967), 72–90, has proposed a new solution to this ancient crux. He argues that the extracts xv. 26. 1–36. 11 (from F, the *excerpta antiqua*) and xv. 25. 3–37 (from Q, the Constantinian excerpts *de insidiis*) belong to book xiv, not book xv; and although he does not press the point, his thesis implies that xv. 1–2 (from P, the Constantinian excerpts *de virtutibus et vitiis*) was also displaced. Abel supports this bold hypothesis by pointing out that in xv. 33. 2 Polybius mentions a certain Philo, apparently for the first time (since he calls him τῶν...'Αγαθοκλέους ὑπηρετῶν καὶ κολάκων τις ὄνομα Φίλων), yet according to Athenaeus vi. 251 c (= Polyb. xiv. 11. 1) this man was mentioned in book xiv. I think that in fact a case can be made out for thinking that this Philo is the same man who is mentioned in xv. 30. 5 where Agathocles, taking τοὺς συγγενεῖς πάντας πλὴν Φίλωνος, goes to the king; Abel, art. cit. 87 n. 2, denies this, but if it is someone else, there is no apparent reason why Polybius mentioned his not going with the others. However I would not press this, for

Egyptian section in book xiv still further by going on to describe events subsequent to Ptolemy IV's death, he apparently postponed recounting the ceremony of Ptolemy V's accession until book xv, although it took place in Olympiad 144. 1 (204/3) and book xv was nominally devoted to the events of Olympiad 144. 2 (203/2). This unusual procedure, which has wrought havoc among students of Ptolemaic chronology, was designed to leave the account of Ptolemy Philopator's reign as a unified composition—and in fact Polybius uses the same word to describe it, σωματοειδής,[81] that he used of the unification of the history of the *oecumene* at the hands of Fortune.

These divergences from the normal Olympiad pattern seem to illustrate some degree of concern for stylistic criteria and for Hellenistic principles of literary composition. The affair of Oropus is dealt with all together because what happened to it was ἴδιον καὶ παράλογον, singular and strange; to split up the details would be to produce a narrative that was εὐτελῆ καὶ ἀσαφῆ.[82] By treating

in fact the more important point is that, whether through his negligence or a faulty manuscript tradition, no firm reliance can be placed on Athenaeus' references to the books of Polybius from which he is quoting. These are often right, but not always. Thus Athen. x. 439 b assigns to book xxxi a passage which must belong to book xxx (it is xxx. 26); and Athen. x. 445 d quotes and assigns to book xxvi a passage of Polybius which can be shown by its overlap with another extract to belong to Ol. 150. 2, and is quite properly printed as xxv. 3. 6–8. Abel's hypothesis would imply a dislocation in the archetype common to both the *excerpta antiqua* and the Constantinian excerpts, and such a dislocation would have had to occur at an early stage in the tradition without ever being subsequently corrected. Though clearly this is not absolutely impossible, Abel suggests no reason why it should have happened. Indeed, it seems highly implausible, and certainly the full weight of such a hypothesis can hardly be allowed to rest on a numeral in Athenaeus. Another difficulty in Abel's theory is that it does not explain why, if (as he unconvincingly assumes) Ptolemy IV died on 28 November 205 and Epiphanes' accession took place shortly afterwards, Polybius should have delayed his comprehensive narrative of Egyptian events from Raphia onwards to book xiv, which covered the events of Ol. 144. 1 (204/3 B.C.). For a more probable reconstruction of the historical sequence of events and of Polybius' procedure see my *Commentary*, ii. 434–7 on xiv. 11–12.

[81] xiv. 12. 5.

[82] xxxii. 11. 6. Pédech, *Méthode*, 504 n. 56, would read ἀτελῆ, 'incomplete', and compares xxxviii. 6. 6. But in that passage it is a narrative based on the Olympiad system which is described as leaving nothing ἀτελὲς μηδ' ἐλλιπές, whereas here Polybius is combining events of different years in a single narrative, lest divided under their separate Olympiad years they might produce a narrative that is 'trivial and lacking in clarity' (for εὐτελής means 'poor, trivial', not 'perfect, *achevé*', as Pédech translates it). If, however, the Olympiad

it as a whole Polybius could produce a narrative that possessed clarity, τὸ σαφές, and it is interesting to note that Lucian, in his treatise *How to write history*,[83] links the quality of clarity with the avoidance of breaks or a multiplicity of disjointed narratives.

The arguments which Polybius uses in these passages, which form an exception to his usual practice, can also be paralleled from Appian, who writes in the introduction to his *History*,[84] 'As I came to read these historians (i.e. of Rome) and tried to acquire some understanding of the achievements of the Romans in various lands in a connected manner, their writings frequently took me from Carthage to Spain, and from Spain to Sicily or Macedonia, or to some embassies sent to other peoples or alliances made with them; and they brought me back again to Carthage or Sicily as if I were wandering in exile (ἀλώμενον), then took me away again without finishing the matter.' That was why Appian decided to treat each area separately. His method was that of Ephorus; and the arguments Polybius adduces to justify describing Ariarathes' return or the affairs of Oropus or the reign of Philopator as a single whole can also be raised against the Olympiad arrangement, with its separate fronts, in general. His answer[85] is to be found in the very passage with which I began this digression—namely that the systematic switching from theatre to theatre provides the variety that Nature demands, and at the same time makes it easy for the student to go back to the point at which a particular theme was interrupted and so get a proper understanding of the whole field. And, of course, it is essential to the period when the history of the *oecumene* has become one.

7.

The argument that the Olympiad chronology is designed to provide in a systematic form the variety demanded by Nature is a slightly highfalutin way of saying that it is designed to conform to Hellenistic literary principles; and this device does not preclude the introduction of a large number of digressions in addition. As I indicated earlier,[86] these cover a vast range of topics, the only common feature of which is that Polybius believed that they

system avoids 'incompleteness' in one place, why should it produce it in another? There seems no reason for altering the MS reading at this point.

[83] Lucian, *Hist. conscr.* 55; cf. Avenarius, 119–27.
[84] Appian, *Hist.* praef. 12.
[85] xxxviii. 5–6; see above, p. 111 n. 72.   [86] See above, pp. 46–8.

would be useful to his readers. Among them an important category is that concerned with geography, and here Polybius shows a very typical blending of what is new with what is traditional.

From its earliest beginnings Greek history had contained a strong geographical and ethnographical strain.[87] Ever since the time of Hecataeus there had been no clearly defined frontiers separating geography from history, and both had been characterised by a common concern with human affairs.[88] The ἱστορίη or 'enquiry' which Hecataeus practised[89] was directed not only towards historical material in our sense, but also to what we should call geography or ethnography; and it has been argued that Herodotus' work was originally conceived as primarily geographical, whether in criticism of Hecataeus[90] or, less probably,[91] as an independent geographical study, and only gradually developed into the *History* as we know it. Much of Herodotus' geographical and ethnographical material is to be found in the form of digressions from his main theme. Indeed, Howald has likened his art to that of the popular story-teller, in which one excursus follows another, or indeed quite often one is included within another like the boxes in a Chinese puzzle.[92] This role of the geographical digression as a regular element in history was to persist. There is little of it in Thucydides' tightly organized structure; but his successors, Ephorus,[93] Callisthenes and other historians of Alexander who followed him to distant lands,[94] Timaeus,[95] Duris,[96] and later

[87] Cf. Jacoby, 'Über die Entwicklung der griechischen Historiographie', *Klio*, 9 (1909), 80 ff. = *Abhandlungen*, 16 ff.; Müllenhoff, i². 351; Pédech, *Méthode*, 515–16; O. Murray, *CR*, 18 (1968), 220–1.

[88] See Ninck, *Entdeckung Europas*, 33 ff.; Walbank, 'The geography of Polybius', *Class. et med.* 9 (1948), 156.

[89] *FGH* 1; cf. Strasburger, 'Die Entdeckung der politischen Geschichte durch Thukydides', *Thukydides*, 418. The word ἱστορίη is not actually found until Herodotus (i. praef. ἱστορίης ἀπόδεξις).

[90] So von Fritz, *Geschichtsschreibung*, i 'Text', 105–7, 442 ff.; P. Brunt, *CR*, 19 (1969), 199 calls this view 'persuasive'. But see above, p. 2.

[91] Jacoby, *RE*, Suppl.-B. ii, 'Herodotos', cols. 261, 279 ff.

[92] Howald, 42–3.

[93] Ephorus devoted books iv and v of his *History* to a geographical survey; cf. *FGH* 70 F 30–53, 128–72.

[94] Cf. *FGH* 124 F 7, 19, 20, 28, 29, 30, 38, 53, 54; Jacoby, *RE*, 'Kallisthenes (2)', cols. 1699 ff. For the other Alexander-historians see *FGH* 119 (Baiton), 120 (Diognetus), 121 (Philonides), 122 (Amyntas), 123 (Archelaus), 133 (Nearchus), 134 (Onesicritus). See Pédech, *Méthode*, 515; Pearson, *Lost histories*, passim.

[95] *FGH* 566; cf. Brown, *Timaeus*, passim.   [96] *FGH* 76.

Agatharchides[97] and various Roman historians from Sallust to Ammianus regularly introduced geographical excursuses into their work, often only superficially related to their narrative and serving purposes which varied with the kind of history they wrote. In many the purpose was primarily to entertain and impress the reader, in the manner later recommended by Theon of Alexandria, who in his *Progymnasmata*[98] explained how ἐκφράσεις of some country could be used to create ἐνάργεια, 'vividness'—'purple patches' we might say. Others however used the geographical digression to lay the scene for the events to be described, or simply as a subject of intellectual interest in its own right.

It is against this traditional association of history and geography that Polybius' geographical passages must first of all be considered. For him geography is a serious matter. In the passage from book xii discussed in the previous chapter,[99] 'the survey of cities, places, rivers, harbours, and all the special features of land and sea and the distance of one place from another' is described as one of the most essential parts of the historian's task; but he makes it quite clear that there is to be no concession to idle curiosity as there was in Duris or Phylarchus. Speaking of Spain and Africa in book iii he writes:[100] 'No one should be surprised when in the course of my history I reach such places if I avoid any description of them; and if there are any who expect a detailed account of each place, they do not perhaps realise that they resemble gourmands at a dinner-party who taste everything on the table without really enjoying any dish at the time, or indeed assimilating enough to derive any long-term food value from what they eat.' This does not mean that the places are not to be described at all, but that Polybius proposes to devote a separate book to geographical matters, so that these can be dealt with all together. This plan was effected in book xxxiv, and there is a strong likelihood that the idea of a separate geographical book was conceived only after his journeys and voyages between 151 and 146 had stimulated Polybius to a new interest in the subject.[101] The passage I have just

[97] *FGH* 86 F 1, 18–21; and for his *De mari Erythraeo* cf. *GGM*, i. 111–95; cf. Pédech, *Méthode*, 515.

[98] Theon, *Progymn.* 119, 27; cf. E. Burck, *Die Erzählungskunst des T. Livius* (Berlin, 1934; ed. 2, 1964), 199.

[99] xii. 25 e. 1, discussed above, pp. 71 ff.

[100] iii. 57. 6.

[101] See above, p. 24.

quoted from book iii will be one of a number of insertions in that book dating from the revised edition.

That Polybius' journeys did in fact augment his interest in geography after 146, there can be little doubt. I have already mentioned the part these journeys played in sharpening his hostility towards Timaeus[102] and encouraging him in the vanity of imagining himself to be a second Odysseus.[103] But his interest in geography always remained subordinated to his main purpose, which was the writing of universal history. In book xii, which as we saw was probably to a large extent, if not wholly, the result of the development of his interests after 146,[104] the very passage in which he makes his comparison with Odysseus is followed by an adaptation of Plato's famous saying about philosophers becoming kings, to this effect that 'it will be well with history either when men of action undertake to write it...or again when would-be historians regard a training in practical affairs as essential to their craft'.[105] There is no suggestion here that geography has taken the place of history in his scale of values, and I think one must reject a recent hypothesis that after 146 Polybius' intellectual development took a direction which involved him more and more in geographical research for its own sake.[106] The composition of the *Numantine War* sometime after 133 shows that Polybius' historical interests—as well as his friendship with Scipio Aemilianus—remained as strong as ever.

8.

From the very outset Polybius' narrative was faced with geographical problems. How is one to convey to the reader the nature of the places where the action is taking place? Sometimes a short sketch is enough. 'Aegira is situated in the Peloponnese on the Gulf of Corinth between Aegium and Sicyon, and is built on steep hills difficult of access, looking towards Parnassus and that part of the opposite coast, its distance from the sea being about seven stades.'[107] Nothing could be clearer or more succinct; and Polybius' descriptions of campaigning in the familiar districts of southern and central Greece are full of this kind of thing.[108] Diffi-

---

[102] See above, pp. 25, 50-4.   [103] See above, pp. 51-2.
[104] See above, pp. 24-5.   [105] xii. 28. 1-4.
[106] Cf. Pédech, *Méthode*, 515-97.   [107] iv. 57. 5.
[108] On this see Cuntz, 5 f.

culties arose however as he got further afield. When dealing with events that have occurred in remoter districts, the geography of which may even be obscure to the historian himself—for example Hannibal's crossing of the Alps before Polybius had actually made the journey[109]—it was tempting to convey a general impression of the area by falling back on geometric schematisation. Herodotus had done this when he described Scythia as a quadrilateral bounded on two sides by sea and two by land,[110] or divided up north Africa into a series of zones schematically arranged. Polybius uses the same method in book i to describe Sicily,[111] and in book ii[112] he has an elaborate account of the Italian peninsula and the Po valley in terms of triangles. Sicily and Italy were both reasonably well known, even to Greeks: but for more distant lands some other system is needed, since geometrical figures can indicate only the shape and not the locality. Names too are useless there. 'When we are dealing with unknown places', he writes,[113] 'the citing of names is just about as much use as uttering unintelligible, inarticulate sounds.' Polybius tackles this problem not very happily by proceeding from the general to the particular.[114] 'Everyone', he writes,'—even those of the most meagre intelligence—can recognise north, south, east and west from the heavens: so the first thing is to classify the various parts of the earth under each of these divisions': in other words, since we cannot use names, we must use compass-points. To illustrate this meaning, Polybius then goes on to define the three continents as situated, Asia between the Nile and the Don and under that part of the heavens which lies

---

[109] For Polybius' crossing of the Alps cf. iii. 48. 12, τῇ διὰ τῶν Ἄλπεων αὐτοὶ κεχρῆσθαι πορείᾳ γνώσεως ἕνεκα καὶ θέας.

[110] Herod. iv. 101.   [111] i. 42. 1–7.

[112] ii. 14–16. In ii. 14. 7 Polybius remarks that the Po valley shows a fertility greater than any other in Europe ὅσα πέπτωκεν ὑπὸ τὴν ἡμετέραν ἱστορίαν. This could mean 'which falls within the scope of my history' (cf. xv. 9. 5 and iv. 2. 2); but it can equally well be 'which have fallen within the scope of my enquiries' (though I would not accept Pédech's argument, Méthode, 567 n. 295, that it *must* mean that). I agree with Pédech, loc. cit., that these chapters imply autopsy; see especially ch. 15. But Polybius can have visited this part of Italy before 151 (as he visited Locri before then), and no conclusions are to be drawn about the date of composition. It should be noted that elsewhere (Méthode, 594) Pédech argues from the inconsistencies which exist between the figures here and those in book xxxiv that at the time he composed ii. 14–16 Polybius had not yet formed a firm picture of Italy; and this is more likely if this passage was written relatively early.   [113] iii. 36. 3.

[114] iii. 36. 6–38. 3.

between north-east and south, Africa between the Nile and the Pillars of Hercules and under the heavens stretching from south to west and south-west, and Europe extending from east to west from the Don to the Pillars. Strabo, who has some vigorous criticism of Polybius' account of a triangular Italy,[115] finds this passage even more intolerable.[116] 'The terms east and west, north-east and south-east', he complains, 'are not absolute but relative to our individual positions. If we shift our position to different points, the positions of sunrise and sunset...become different, though the length of the continent remains the same. Consequently, while it is reasonable to make the Don and the Nile limits of continents, it is something new to use the north-east or the east for such a purpose.' Strabo is of course quite right; and his criticism exposes a certain naïveté and amateurishness which underlie Polybius' theorising in this field. For this is not the only place where he makes the mistake of trying to use moving points to define fixed areas. There is another example in book xxxiv,[117] where he divides the earth into six zones, two under the arctic circle, two between there and the tropic circles and two between the tropics and the equator. The trouble with this definition is that to the Greeks the 'arctic circle' meant something different from what it means to us. The Greek arctic circle was a circle drawn in the heavens, at any latitude, with the celestial pole at its centre and the distance from the pole to the nearest point on the horizon as its radius, and so containing all the stars, which *at that latitude* never set. It follows of course that there was a different arctic circle for every different latitude, whereas our arctic circle is a circle of latitude drawn round the earth at the most southerly point at which the midnight sun can be seen on the night of the summer solstice. So once again Polybius is quite properly reproved by Strabo for assuming that what held good at one point—at Megalopolis?—was valid everywhere.

That the passage defining the continents in terms of compass-points is one of those inserted in book iii at a later date is clear from the reference forward to book xxxiv.[118] But by no means all Polybius' geographical comments and descriptions of places are necessarily late, not even where he mentions autopsy. As I have

[115] Strabo, v. 210.
[116] Strabo, ii. 108.   [117] xxxiv. 1. 14 = Strabo ii. 96.
[118] iii. 37. 10–11.

already remarked,[119] the description of New Carthage in book x was almost certainly written before he went there in 151; in fact, he only refers to autopsy when he gives the size of the circumference of the city in a sentence which is probably a later insertion.[120] There is a good parallel to this in his account of Hannibal's crossing of the Alps,[121] which was also based on a literary source, probably Silenus, but contains a similar reference to his own journey in Hannibal's footsteps. In both cases, the personal reminiscence seems to have been introduced subsequently to add authority to his account. Polybius' description of the battle of Telamon,[122] the topographical accuracy of which has recently been demonstrated by Sommella,[123] is early and derives from Fabius, not from his own investigation. There are also excellent topographical details of Tarentum[124] in his account of Hannibal's seizure of it in book viii, but this does not necessarily mean that they are based on personal acquaintance with the city.[125] Polybius may have visited Tarentum; who can tell? But a comparison with Livy's very similar version of the same events, which contains some details that are not in Polybius, yet do not look like Livian elaboration,[126] suggests that Polybius' account, written very noticeably from the Punic point of view, derives (like his account of Hannibal's Alpine crossing) from Silenus, whose version reached Livy via Coelius Antipater. These are by no means the only instances of excellent topographical details taken from a literary

[119] See above, p. 24; the description is at x. 9. 8–10. 13.

[120] Cf. ix. 11. 4 (quoted above, p. 24 n. 125).

[121] iii. 49. 5–56. 4; see Walbank, 'Some reflections on Hannibal's pass', *JRS*, 46 (1956), 37–45. The reference to autopsy is at iii. 48. 12.

[122] ii. 25–30.

[123] Cf. Sommella, 11–34. He argues that Καλούσιον in ii. 25. 2 is not Clusium, as generally assumed, but a lost city of the same name on the coast (perhaps to be identified with the large site near Magliano and Orbetello once wrongly identified with Vetulonia; cf. M. W. Frederiksen, *JRS*, 59 (1969), 318).

[124] viii. 24–34.   [125] As Pédech, *Méthode*, 526, asserts.

[126] E.g. Livy, xxv. 1. 1, Hannibal had remained near at hand 'spe per proditionem urbis Tarentinorum potiundae'; 8. 8, the Carthaginians undertake that the Tarentines shall not receive any Punic garrison against their will; 10. 8, Hannibal mentions his generosity towards Tarentines taken at Trasimene and Cannae (evidently added by Coelius, as there were no Tarentines taken at Trasimene or Cannae); 11. 18–19, a rather fuller account of the device used by Hannibal to get his ships across the isthmus. For further examples see Klotz, 165–7. Others believe Livy to be following Polybius here (cf. Kahrstedt, iii. 257; De Sanctis, iii. 2. 365–7); but even if that view were accepted, it need not affect the assumption that Polybius was following Silenus.

source: other examples are his discussion of the terrain of the battle of Issus,[127] and his description of Seleuceia.[128] It has been suggested that he visited these places in the course of a journey to Egypt which he made in the reign of Ptolemy Physcon,[129] but this seems improbable. Still less is it likely that he had visited Media and Ecbatana;[130] indeed it is dubious whether he was ever even at Byzantium,[131] for in his description of its situation he never says so.

It seems clear then that Polybius included short geographical passages, descriptions of towns and districts and somewhat schematic accounts of larger areas from the time when he began to compose; and one must be alert against the temptation to equate 'geographical' with 'late'. However, the travels of 151 to 146 undoubtedly extended Polybius' geographical knowledge, excited his proprietary feelings concerning his discoveries, and led him to insert several passages[132] in what he had already written, besides planning a book entirely devoted to geography among the additional ten books which were to carry his *Histories* down to 146.

[127] xii. 20. 2; Polybius discusses the battle of Issus between Alexander the Great and Darius in the course of polemic against Callisthenes, whom he accuses of incompetence in military matters.

[128] v. 59. 3–11.

[129] So Pédech, *Méthode*, 561, who thinks he visited Issus on the same occasion; for Polybius' visit to Alexandria see above, p. 12 with n. 58, p. 48.

[130] v. 44 (Media). The origin of Polybius' account of Media is not known. Schmitt, *Antiochos*, 50–61, thinks it goes back ultimately to Eratosthenes; Pédech, *Méthode*, 568, derives it from Callisthenes. Certainly it is not the same as that of his narrative, for it locates the Zagros range in a different place.

[131] iv. 38–52 (where Pédech, *Méthode*, 570–1, makes a good case for regarding chs. 39–42 as a later insertion). Whether Polybius had already visited Sardes when he wrote the account of Achaeus' fall (vii. 15–18) is not known; for his meeting with the Galatian chieftain's wife, Chiomara, there (xxi. 38. 7) is hardly to be dated to 189 (as Pédech, *Méthode*, 518–19, claims) but may have taken place either before (so Gelzer, *Kl. Schr.* iii. 202) or after (so Lehmann, *Untersuchungen*, 273 n.) 169.

[132] Cf. iii. 36–9 (see above, p. 119 n. 118 for a reference forward to book xxxiv); 57–9 (cf. 59. 4, a clear reference to the situation in Greece after 146); iv. 39–42 (probably; see above, n. 131); v. 21. 3–22. 4 (with echoes of iii. 36–9); and the bulk if not the whole of book xii. This is not of course a full list of all later insertions; and some would add to the geographical passages. See for example the considerably longer list in Pédech, *Méthode*, 572; and above, pp. 23–4.

9.

Book xxxiv[133] is foreshadowed specifically in two earlier passages, both in book iii and both almost certainly later insertions. In the first[134] Polybius promises to speak on a subsequent occasion about the barbarous tribes which inhabited the whole of Spain between the Mediterranean and the outer ocean, and in the second[135] he says that he will treat separately matters relating to the Pillars of Hercules, the outer sea, the British Isles and their tin mines, and the gold and silver mines of Spain; and he mentions as part of his credentials his own journeys in Africa, Spain and Gaul and his voyages on the outer ocean.[136] If this information is combined with various remarks of Strabo,[137] it becomes clear that book xxxiv also contained a τοπογραφία τῶν ἠπείρων, that is to say a description of the land masses, a χωρογραφία of Europe, that is a cartographic and descriptive account of that continent, with places and measurements and criticisms of Dicaearchus, Eratosthenes and Pytheas, and a περιοδεία of Africa, which again seems to mean a description of the places included in that region, described in order,[138] no doubt that of his journeys and voyages there. Since, moreover, Strabo does not quote Polybius for anything in Asia, and specifically says that he referred his readers to Eratosthenes for information on India,[139] Pédech rightly deduces from this that Polybius' geographical work comprised these three elements: a general physical description of the world, a more detailed account of the distances and dimensions of Europe and a description of its lands, and a *periegesis* of Africa;[140] his argument that the book which Geminus[141] mentions *On the habitability of the equatorial zone*

---

[133] On book xxxiv see the sensible discussion of Pédech, 'La Géographie de Polybe: structure et contenu du livre xxxiv des *Histoires*', *LEC*, 24 (1956), 3–24, on which the following pages draw heavily.

[134] iii. 37. 11.   [135] iii. 57. 5.

[136] iii. 59. 7–8.

[137] Strabo, viii. 332; ii. 104, 109. The first two are printed as Polyb. xxxiv. 1. i and 5. 1, the last is not included in standard texts of Polybius.

[138] Strabo, viii. 369; ix. 417, for other examples of his use of περιοδεία.

[139] Strabo, xiv. 663 = Polyb. xxxiv. 13 (where Paton in the Loeb edition translates ἐκείνῳ 'Artemidorus' instead of 'Eratosthenes', as it should be rendered).

[140] Cf. Pédech, 'La Géographie de Polybe', *LEC*, 24 (1956), 7; *Méthode*, 588–96.

[141] Geminus, *Elements*, 16. 32–8 = Polyb. xxxiv. 1. 7. See above, p. 15 n. 77; it seems to be a case for a verdict of *non liquet*.

was really part of book xxxiv is less compelling. Unfortunately scarcely any genuine fragments of book xxxiv survive: what goes under that name in the editions is little more than a list of *testimonia* together with paraphrases of some of Polybius' information or arguments retailed (sometimes with criticism) by Strabo, Athenaeus or the Elder Pliny. The choice of these and in particular the decision at what point a passage should break off have often been exercised somewhat arbitrarily. However, from these 'fragments', suitably extended where necessary, some impression of the book can be recovered and it is possible to say certain things about it.

The idea of a separate geographical book would be familiar to Polybius from Ephorus, who devoted books four and five of his universal history to geographical matters;[142] Strabo[143] links the two authors together in this context, and though Polybius undoubtedly used his geographical book to describe many of his own discoveries in the far west and along the African coast, the introduction of this personal element should not be taken, as it has been, to indicate that he was drawing away from history. On the contrary, book xxxiv stood at a point in his narrative at which the history itself was becoming more personal, since many of the events from 151 to 146 fell within Polybius' own experience and in many of them he had played a leading part. In that respect his geographical book acts as a very suitable point of demarcation, and serves to bridge the gap between the period from 168 to 152, the account of which was to provide the evidence for passing judgement on the administration of the empire in the aftermath of Pydna, and the subsequent period of trouble and disturbance, punctuated by incomprehensible and disordered risings, which interested Polybius not least because of his personal role in them. Book xxxiv probably opened with the τοπογραφία τῶν ἠπείρων, a physical sketch of the whole world: this had its place towards the end of a history of Rome's conquest of the *oecumene*. But Pédech is right to insist that the real *raison d'être* of book xxxiv was the exposition of Polybius' own discoveries and the correction of his predecessors on the basis of these. That he was able to reconcile this purpose with that of a book punctuating the two main divisions in his universal history is less difficult to understand if one bears in mind the extent to which the 'useful digression' is a regular feature throughout the

[142] See above. p. 115 n. 93.   [143] Strabo, viii. 332.

Histories. I have illustrated the character of such digressions in my second chapter and need not quote examples here. Most of them were more obviously directly related to the political and military purposes of the *Histories* than an account of geographical exploration or speculation could be. But that was because they grew largely out of Polybius' personal activities, which had in the past been directed towards such matters as cavalry training and fire-signalling. We are not entitled to assume that he believed the knowledge of geography to be less useful than these or that he had ceased to believe that knowledge should have a strictly utilitarian purpose. This view is asserted in book ix, and if he had ceased to believe it, it is difficult to see why he should have left it in his revised edition. 'I strongly disapprove,' he wrote there,[144] 'of any superfluous adjuncts to any branch of knowledge such as serve but for ostentation and fine talk...and I am disinclined to insist on any studies beyond those that are of actual use.' That this continued to be his view is confirmed by a passage in book iii,[145] which forms part of his new programme, and so belongs to a late stage in the development of the plan of his *Histories*, where he says precisely the same: 'no one takes up the study of arts and crafts merely for the sake of knowledge, but all men do what they do for the resulting pleasure, good or utility'.

Book xxxiv then serves as a kind of demarcation line in the transition from the testing time to the age of confusion. Schulten believed that it was designed to serve as an introduction to the Celtiberian War,[146] but this is too narrow a view of its function and can be disproved: for the passage marking the beginning of that war, which since Schweighaeuser has been assigned to the first chapter of book xxxv, in fact should stand in book xxxiii, since it originally preceded an account of the dispatch of Q. Fulvius Nobilior, the consul of 153, to Spain shortly after his entry into office on 1 January. Hence the beginning of the Celtiberian War fell in the third year of Olympiad 156, and must have been described by Polybius in book xxxiii.[147]

---

[144] ix. 20. 5–6.   [145] iii. 4. 10–11.

[146] Cf. A. Schulten, 'Polybios und Poseidonios über Iberien und die iberischen Kriege', *Hermes*, 46 (1911), 568.

[147] xxxv. 1. 1–6, a general comment on the πύρινος πόλεμος, the 'fiery war' between the Romans and Celtiberians, is from the Suda. Comparison with Diod. xxxi. 39–40, two chapters derived from the Constantinian excerpts *de sententiis*, of which the second closely corresponds to Polyb. xxxv. 1. 1–6, shows

10.

The so-called fragments tell us a great deal about the contents and tone of this book; they show clearly that Polybius' polemic against his predecessors was not limited to matters of factual description, but also involved the measuring of distances which were the basis for map-making, and in particular became involved in the Alexandrine dispute about Homeric geography. I can only indicate briefly one or two of the issues raised and where Polybius stood in regard to them.

One of the great arguments in Alexandrine scholarship concerned the authority to be attributed to Homer. The Stoics in particular believed that his poems contained the key to all ordered knowledge, and were disposed to regard him as the prototype of the Stoic wise man;[148] difficulties were swept aside, if necessary by textual emendation or by the assumption—later not unknown in biblical exegesis—that the sacred text must be interpreted allegorically. Scholars like Crates of Mallos, a contemporary of Polybius, thought that Homer already knew that the world was a globe;[149] and others, for example Asclepiades of Myrleia in the first century, tried to identify the places in Odysseus' wanderings as if Homer were recording a historical voyage.[150] This view of Homer was opposed by the great scholar Eratosthenes, who said that you would find the scene of Odysseus' travels when you discovered the cobbler who sewed up the bag of the winds.[151] Poetry, he believed, was designed not to instruct but to entertain;[152] and he asked, Strabo records, what contribution it makes to the excellence of a poet for him to be expert in geography, or generalship,

that the latter must, in the original text of Polybius (which Diodorus is here following), have come immediately after the Senate's cancellation of the treaty; and from Appian, *Hisp.* 44–5, it appears that this event preceded the dispatch to Spain of Q. Fulvius Nobilior, one of the consuls for 153, whose entry into office was brought forward to 1 January. Hence the Suda passage, which Ursinus identified as Polybian, must be from book xxxiii, where it should stand between chs. 15 and 16, to constitute part of the *res Hispaniae* of the third year of Ol. 156, i.e. 154/3. Book xxxv contains the events of Ol. 157. 1 and 2, i.e. 152/1 and 151/0.

[148] Cf. K. J. Neumann, 'Strabos Gesammturtheil über die homerische Geographie', *Hermes*, 21 (1886), 134–41.

[149] On Crates see Hansen, *Attalids*, 409–18; Mette, *Sphaeropoiia*, passim.

[150] Cf. Strabo, iii. 157 for his discovery of evidence for Odysseus' wanderings in the dedication in a Spanish temple in Turdetania.

[151] Strabo, i. 24 = Polyb. xxxiv. 2. 11.   [152] Strabo, i. 7.

or agriculture, or rhetoric or any of the special arts with which some people wanted to invest him.[153] Polybius' sympathies were strongly with the 'fundamentalists' on this issue. He believed in the utilitarian view of poetry; and in addition his somewhat romantic idea of himself as a second Odysseus predisposed him to join Crates and the Stoics, who were later to include Poseidonius and Strabo, in resisting the sceptical view of Homer's geographical accuracy inculcated by Eratosthenes. Odysseus was not to be dismissed as legendary; on the other hand, his journeys by being firmly located in well-known areas were to be kept within bounds. Crates had placed Odysseus' voyages on the ocean and in the land of the Lotus-eaters outside the Pillars of Hercules, and the word ἐξωκεανισμός,[154] frequently used by Strabo and apparently by Polybius to describe the transfer of Odysseus' adventures to the unknown world of the outer ocean, sounds like a bit of technical jargon used in a regular controversy on the subject. In a long section, probably linked to his account of Spain,[155] Polybius places Scylla and Charybdis at the Straits of Messana and identifies Scylla as a kind of epic forerunner of the Sicilians who hunted the swordfish thereabouts.

In this passage Polybius hopes to secure two objectives. First, he writes to establish the probability that Odysseus was a real man voyaging in real waters as Homer described him; and secondly, I would suggest, he wants to ensure that Odysseus is not regarded as having anticipated himself, Polybius, in exploring the outer ocean. This personal jealousy is also no doubt a factor in his hostility to Pytheas of Marseilles,[156] who had made his famous voyage from Gades north along the Breton coast to Ushant and Belerion, the western promontory of Britain, in four days. From here he had probably continued north to circumnavigate Britain in a clockwise direction, reaching a point where the summer night lasted only two hours, and natives told him of the midnight sun in Thule. His date is uncertain; for recently Rhys Carpenter argued that this should be brought down from about 323 B.C. to the end of the First Punic War in about 242–238.[157] But in any case

153 Strabo, i. 16.
154 Strabo, i. 26, 44, 46–7; Polyb. xxxiv. 4. 5.
155 So Pédech, 'La Géographie de Polybe', LEC, 24 (1956), 18.
156 See above, p. 52.
157 Rhys Carpenter, Pillars, 143–98; cf. R. Dion, 'Pythéas explorateur', Rev. Phil. 40 (1966), 191–216.

Polybius clearly regarded Pytheas as a rival, who must be discredited, and he does his best to do this by ridiculing the claims of 'a private individual and a poor man at that' to have traversed such distances—clearly in contrast to himself, who voyaged with all the resources put at his disposal by Scipio Aemilianus. Pytheas is a shadowy personality, but he is generally supposed, rightly I think, to have been a merchant as well as a great scientific explorer; and Polybius, himself a landed gentleman, did not like merchants. In his account of the geography of the Black Sea area he contrasts scientific reasoning with merchants' yarns;[158] when they wanted, merchants could tell 'false and sensational stories', but when you tried to get any real information out of them, as Scipio did from the Gallic merchants of Narbonne, Marseilles and Corbilo,[159] they lapsed into a convenient silence. Perhaps Pytheas was closely associated with these men in Polybius' estimation.

11.

The campaigns of Alexander had given a new stimulus to geographical studies; and following on the great extension of areas explored there had come new developments in geographical theory, which set the subject well on the way to emancipation from being merely an adjunct to history. The proposed world-map of Dicaearchus[160] had been revised and modified by Eratosthenes who, despite Hipparchus' criticisms, probably represents the high peak of Greek geographical achievement. In Hipparchus himself theory seems to have outstripped the resources which would have been necessary to translate his ingenious proposals for establishing longitude into reality. Polybius' attitude towards these developments is unsympathetic. I have already pointed out some of the shortcomings in his attempt to construct large-scale models of the various zones on the earth and to lay down principles for defining the situation of the continents. Whether in fact he attempted to make a detailed map of the *oecumene* there is not the evidence to determine with any certainty. The measurements which he gives for the distances between widely separated places concern Europe, not the whole *oecumene*. Examples are the distance from the Pillars

[158] iv. 39. 11.

[159] Strabo, iv. 190 = Polyb. xxxiv. 10. 6–7. It was probably on his way back from Spain in 150 that Scipio made these enquiries, perhaps instigated by Polybius (cf. Walbank, 'The geography of Polybius', *Class. et med.* 9 (1948), 161 n. 6; above, p. 74).   [160] Cf. Walbank, art. cit. (n. 159), 174.

of Hercules to the mouth of the Maeotis, 3437½ Roman miles—the figure comes via Pliny—from the Pillars to Seleuceia in Pieria,[161] 2340 miles, or from the Pillars to Cape Malea, 22,500 stades;[162] and these perhaps suggest that he conceived the continent as contained within a large triangle,[163] with its points at the Pillars, the Maeotis and Cape Malea: and certainly the discussion which Strabo records about his measurements of the western part of the Mediterranean and his criticism of Dicaearchus' distances shows that he conceived this area as a triangle with its angles at the Pillars, Messana and Narbonne. But we simply have not enough evidence to say in what detail this scheme was developed nor how far the various parts fitted together into a consistent whole: the figures which he gave in book ii for Italy do not tie in with those in book xxxiv.[164] The measurements themselves seem to have been taken from coastal journeys, recorded distances along roads and the like; for according to Strabo (though how he knew we cannot tell), the distance from the Danube to Cape Malea was based on an actual journey made by some general (it would be interesting to know who he was).[165] Altogether, then, this is not very impressive. Pédech rightly observes[166] that in the domain of theory Polybius' work was inferior to that of Hipparchus or Seleucus of Seleuceia.[167]

12.

The present chapter has been concerned with two questions: one of time—how Polybius solved the structural problems of

[161] xxxiv. 15. 2.   [162] xxxiv. 4. 6.

[163] Cf. Pédech, *Méthode*, 592.

[164] Compare ii. 14. 4–6 (and the figures in 14. 9–12) with xxxiv. 6. 1–10; discussion in Pédech, *Méthode*, 592–4.

[165] Strabo, viii. 335 = Polyb. xxxiv. 12. 12. Polybius, we are told, made the distance from the Danube to Cape Malea 10,000 stades, but Artemidorus 'corrected' this, bringing it down to 6,000 stades; so perhaps Artemidorus was responsible for the remark about the general who, incidentally, need not have marched or sailed the whole way for Polybius, following him (if he did), to get the distance too large.

[166] *Méthode*, 596; cf. Walbank, 'The geography of Polybius', *Class. et med.* 9 (1948), 175.

[167] Pédech, *Méthode*, 596 n. 471, believes that the ἀντιγραφὴ πρὸς τὴν Πολυβίου ἱστορίαν by a Scylax was directed against Polybius' geography. The Suda attributes it to Scylax of Caryanda (*FGH* 709 T 1), but it may indeed belong to the Scylax of Halicarnassus, *excellens in astrologia*, who is known as a friend of Panaetius (Cicero, *de div.* ii. 88); so Gisinger, *RE*, 'Skylax (2)', col. 624, following earlier scholars. But we can only guess at what aspect of Polybius' work Scylax attacked.

chronology presented by his *Histories*, and one of place—the role geography was designed to fill in his general conception, and more particularly in the special book which he devoted to this subject. Both topics have taken us some distance from the historical content of the *Histories*. In the next chapter I propose to return to this and to look in detail at one of the most important parts of his work, book vi.

Structure of Polybius' *Histories*

Olympiad	Year	= B.C.	Books	Comments
			I and II	Introduction
140	1–4	220/19–217/16	III, IV, V	Beginning of unification of *oecumene*
			VI	Roman constitution and military system
141	1–2	216/15–215/14	VII	
	3–4	214/13–213/12	VIII	
142	1–2	212/11–211/10	IX	
	3–4	210/9–209/8	X	
143	1–2	208/7–207/6	XI	
			XII	Polemic against Timaeus and others
	3–4	206/5–205/4	XIII	
144	1	204/3	XIV	
	2	203/2	XV	
	3–4	202/1–201/0	XVI	
145	1–2	200/199–199/8	XVII	Lost
	3–4	198/7–197/6	XVIII	
146	1–4	196/5–193/2	XIX	Lost
147	1	192/1	XX	
	2–4	191/0–189/8	XXI	
148	1–4	188/7–185/4	XXII	
149	1–2	184/3–183/2	XXIII	
	3–4	182/1–181/0	XXIV	
150	1–4	180/79–177/6	XXV	
151	1–4	176/5–173/2	XXVI	
152	1–3	172/1–170/69	XXVII	Uncertain whether Ol. 152. 2 = 171/0 is in XXVIII: probably in XXVII
			XXVIII	
	4	169/8	XXIX	
153		168/7–165/4	XXX	
154		164/3–161/0	XXXI	
155		160/59–157/6	XXXII	
156		156/5–153/2	XXXIII	
			XXXIV	Geographical book
157	1–2	152/1–151/0	XXXV	
	3–4	150/49–149/8	XXXVI	
158	1	148/7	XXXVII	Lost
	2	147/6	XXXVIII	
	3	146/5	XXXIX	Probably ended with 146/5 (= Ol. 158. 3)
			XL	Index (lost)

V

The Sixth Book

1.

Polybius' sixth book is the first of three—the others are of course xii and xxxiv—devoted entirely to a special range of topics outside the chronological framework of the *Histories*; but more than either of the other two it is an essential and integral part of his overall plan. For this was[1] to explain 'how and thanks to what kind of constitution' Rome had raised herself to world dominion. However, the Roman constitution forms only one element in a book which also contains for example a unique and invaluable description of the Roman army organisation[2] and method of castrametation in the mid-second century B.C. Its tightness of construction and to some extent its fragmentary state have left book vi bristling with problems. Its structure, its date of composition, its sources, and, not least, the validity of its conclusions about the Roman state have all been vigorously and almost incessantly debated.[3] Here I can only hope to sketch the outlines of some of

[1] See above, p. 13 n. 66; Polybius frequently states his programme: cf. i. 1. 5–6, 2. 7, 4. 1; iii. 1. 4, 1. 9, 2. 6, 3. 9, 4. 2, 118. 9; vi. 2. 3; viii. 2. 3; xxxix. 8. 7.

[2] vi. 19–42; for discussion see my *Commentary*, i. 697–723 (with addenda in ii. 647–8); G. Sumner, 'The legion and the centuriate organisation', *JRS*, 60 (1970), 67 ff. Brunt, 625, argues that Polybius' account of the army does not describe contemporary practice.

[3] For bibliography see my *Commentary*, i. 636; ii. 645; add Cole, *Democritus*, passim, a speculative and not always convincing attempt to reconstruct Democritus' 'anthropology', drawing on Polyb. vi among many other sources (cf. D. J. Furley, *JHS*, 90 (1970), 239–40); Graeber, *Mischverfassung* (which appears to be acquainted only with work in German); Aalders, *Theorie*; Petzold, *Studien*, 64–90 (cf. Walbank, *JRS*, 60 (1970), 252–3). The article by W. Theiler, 'Schichten im 6. Buch des Polybios', *Hermes*, 81 (1953), 296–302, is now reprinted in his *Untersuchungen zur antiken Literatur* (Berlin, 1970), 343–50; in an additional note on p. 345 he moves the *archaeologia* (see below, p. 132 n. 16) from the second of his three 'layers' to the first, but his arguments are otherwise unchanged.

these problems and perhaps indicate the direction in which one may look for a solution.

The pattern of the book can be reconstructed with some confidence from the order of the so-called *excerpta antiqua* contained in the *codex Urbinas*.[4] It opens with an extract from the introduction[5] which deals with the nature of political constitutions, and is designed to lead up to an account of the mixed constitution and the early history of Rome.[6] Polybius distinguishes three simple types of constitution, kingship, aristocracy and democracy,[7] but to these he adds the mixed constitution, such as Lycurgus introduced at Sparta,[8] and also the three corruptions of the simple forms, monarchy (or tyranny), oligarchy, and mob-rule (or ochlocracy).[9] He next goes on to outline a kind of political cycle, in which the three good forms and their three corruptions follow one another in a succession which he describes as natural (κατὰ φύσιν),[10] and which is made into a continuous and circular progression by the addition of primitive monarchy, which serves both to start off the cycle and also to bring it to an end—the order thus being monarchy,

---

[4] As was shown by Nissen ('Die Oekonomie der Geschichte des Polybios', *Rh. Mus.* 26 (1871), 253 ff.; cf. Büttner-Wobst, ii, pp. lxii–lxvi), these fragments follow the order of the original text closely in books i–v, the only dislocation occurring in book v, where fol. 54ʳ contains 79. 3–86. 7 and fol. 59ʳ 75. 2–6; it may therefore be assumed that the same degree of closeness to the original order exists throughout the rest of the *Histories*, where the fragments cannot be checked against a full text. On the *codex Urbinas* see Moore, 19–20.

[5] vi. 2; in our text it is preceded by vi. 1, which consists of what are no more than references to book vi taken from other parts of the *Histories*.

[6] In vi. 3. 1–11 a. 12, and 11–18. In 3. 3 Polybius explains that the Roman state is difficult to understand because it is so complicated (διὰ τὴν ποικιλίαν τῆς πολιτείας) and it is hard to foretell its future owing to ignorance about its past; it is these two defects in his readers' knowledge that he sets out to remedy with his account of the mixed constitution (this providing the ποικιλία that gives Rome stability) in vi. 11–18, and of the early history of Rome in the so-called *archaeologia* of vi. 11 a.   [7] vi. 3. 5.

[8] vi. 3. 6–8.   [9] vi. 3. 9–4. 6.

[10] vi. 4. 11. Since he can find only γένεσις, 'birth', and μεταβολή, 'change' (but no αὔξησις, 'growth', or ἀκμή, 'acme'), in the various stages of the constitutional cycle, Petzold, *Studien*, 72, argues that the phrase κατὰ φύσιν is here used, not to refer to the law of nature with its sequence of birth, acme and decline, but only to indicate what is natural in terms of human psychology, and so has a 'transferred sense' ('im Gegensatz zum Naturgesetz ist dieses "natürliche", auf menschlichen Motivationen beruhende Gesetz durchbrechbar'). This seems to me over-subtle and improbable. On the problem see Brink and Walbank, 'The construction of the sixth book of Polybius', *CQ*, 4 (1954), 110–12; and see below, pp. 135 ff., 143–4.

kingship, tyranny, aristocracy, oligarchy, democracy, ochlocracy, and finally monarchy once again, and so on *ad infinitum*.[11] Polybius next tells us that by observing where any particular state stands in the cycle one can foretell its future political development,[12] and that this method is especially applicable to Rome[13]—an assertion which is by no means self-evident, and will require consideration shortly; for after describing the cycle (or *anacyclosis* as he calls it),[14] Polybius returns to Lycurgus who, he says, devised his mixed constitution at Sparta in order to avoid the corruptions inherent in the single forms. What Lycurgus achieved by reason, the Romans had achieved by a natural political development, during which they had consistently used the experience gained in disaster to enable them to choose the better course in a series of struggles and crises. Thus Rome too, like Sparta, had ended up with a mixed constitution.[15]

How precisely this had come about must have been related in the next section,[16] which apart from a few fragments is now lost, but which seems to have contained a survey of early Roman history from the foundation of the city by Romulus to the time of the decemvirate of 450, presumably bringing out the detailed events and decisions which resulted in the setting up of the mixed constitution at that time. This section was followed by one which we still possess, and in which[17] Polybius analyses the system of political checks and balances operating within the framework of the mixed constitution, when at its prime; and he may have included a comprehensive account of the Roman constitution at this point though this is not certain.[18] There must however have been some transitional passage, for the next section—a large one[19]—is devoted to a detailed account of the recruitment and organisation of the Roman army and of its encampment. This description is followed by a return to the problem of the constitution, which suggests that in the complete book the military section was a digression arising out of the main discussion.

In order to demonstrate the merits of the Roman constitution Polybius feels obliged to compare it—using the traditional device

---

[11] vi. 4. 7–13, 5. 1–9. 9.
[12] vi. 9. 10–11.
[13] vi. 9. 12–14.
[14] vi. 9. 10.
[15] vi. 10.
[16] vi. 11 a.
[17] vi. 11–18.
[18] So Ziegler, col. 1493 n. 1.
[19] vi. 19–42.

of the σύγκρισις[20]—with other highly praised constitutions; and fourteen chapters[21] are devoted to a comparison of the constitution of Rome with those of Sparta, Crete, Mantinea, Carthage, Athens, Thebes, and of Plato's *Republic*, though some of these are no sooner mentioned than dismissed, including the *Republic*, which, he points out,[22] hardly provides a valid basis for comparison, being merely a blue-print for a constitution and rather like a statue compared with a living person. Finally he rounds off the book with some remarks on the likely future development of Rome[23] and an anecdote[24] illustrating the high moral standards which existed there at the time of Cannae—which brings him conveniently back to the chronological point at which he inserted this formidable digression.

I have sketched the outline of book vi in order to indicate how complicated a pattern it presents, and how many different elements have been brought together in it. It is in fact even more complicated than the account I have just given might suggest, since the concepts of the mixed constitution and the *anacyclosis* themselves draw on a very rich and varied tradition of theory and speculation concerned not only with political forms but also with cultural origins. I shall return to this point shortly.

2.

It seems clear that from the moment he planned his *Histories* Polybius envisaged the writing of book vi. The definition which I have already quoted—'how and thanks to what kind of constitution Rome rose to world power'—implies this. How she rose was described in the work as a whole: 'thanks to what kind of constitution' could only be answered by book vi or something like it. It has however been widely argued that in the form in which it has come down to us the book embodies a change in Polybius' beliefs. There is an apparent contradiction between those parts in which Polybius stresses the stability of the mixed constitution and its built-in capacity for resisting threats of change, and several passages[25] which indicate clearly that Rome too will ultimately

---

[20] See on this F. Focke, 'Synkrisis', *Hermes*, 58 (1923), 348 ff.; for Polybius' use of the comparative method see Pédech, *Méthode*, 405–31 (especially 425–31 on the comparison of constitutions); Petzold, *Studien*, 34–90.

[21] vi. 43–56.   [22] vi. 47. 7–10.

[23] vi. 57.   [24] vi. 58.

[25] vi. 9. 10–14, 10. 7 (keeping the second ἐπὶ πολύ), 51. 3–8, 57.

slide back upon the inexorable wheel of constitutional change. As De Sanctis wrote,[26] the question at issue here is 'whether these contradictory views are innate in Polybius' political philosophy and in his judgement on Rome, or whether they represent two successive stages in his thought and two successive drafts of book vi'.

This is a subject on which I must confess to being a little sensitive, since I have at different times espoused both sides in this controversy.[27] But all I have read on the problem since 1954—and a good deal has been written[28]—has reinforced my conviction that there is no evidence compelling the belief that any part of book vi was composed substantially later than the book as a whole, and that there is nothing in it which requires the hypothesis of a date later than around 150 B.C. for its composition. Contradictions are certainly there: but they seem to arise not from any change in Polybius' views about the stability of Rome, but out of the difficulty which he experienced in coordinating several different concepts to form a rational whole. To reconcile the mixed constitution with the *anacyclosis* was not perhaps too difficult, since it could be conceived as a device for putting a brake on the wheel of change. But in addition Polybius repeatedly asserts that political development, like the world of nature, is subject to a kind of biological law which requires all things to have their birth, growth, prime, decay and end;[29] and this is by no means easy to reconcile with the *anacyclosis*, which has no very clear prime, and which, once started, represents perpetual change rather than coming-into-being and perishing. Since however this biological scheme was the scheme of nature,[30] and the development of Rome was, more than any other state, one that had developed 'according to nature', κατὰ φύσιν,[31] somehow the two had to be reconciled. In order to see this problem in its proper perspective it will be necessary first to look at some of the other elements in Polybius' construction, and in particular to consider how far they derive from earlier traditions.

[26] iii. 1. 205–9.
[27] Walbank, 'Polybius on the Roman constitution', *CQ*, 37 (1943), 73–89; Brink and Walbank, 'The construction of the sixth book of Polybius', *CQ*, 4 (1954), 97–122.
[28] See above, p. 130 n. 3, for bibliography.
[29] Cf. vi. 4. 11–13, 9. 11–14, 43. 2, 51. 3–8, 57.
[30] See Brink and Walbank, 'The construction of the sixth book of Polybius', *CQ*, 4 (1954), 110.
[31] vi. 9. 13–14, κατὰ φύσιν ἀπ' ἀρχῆς ἔχουσαν τὴν σύστασιν καὶ τὴν αὔξησιν, κατὰ φύσιν ἕξειν καὶ τὴν εἰς τἀναντία μεταβολήν.

3.

The idea that a mixed constitution might possess merits and stability which the simple political forms did not was one of some antiquity. Our earliest reference to such a political device is in Thucydides,[32] who praises Theramenes' constitution as 'a discreet fusion of the few and of the many', μετρία. . .ἐς τοὺς ὀλίγους καὶ τοὺς πολλοὺς ξύγκρασις, and since that constitution was conceived amid the realities of fifth-century politics it had of course no place in it for kingship.[33] Aristotle[34] mentions a political system proposed by Hippodamus of Miletus which may fairly be described as an attempt 'though', as Newman[35] says, 'a crude one' at a mixed constitution, and Aristotle[36] also remarks that some people—and he is probably referring to the Athenian conservatives who wanted to modify the Athenian democracy in the early fourth century[37]— interpreted Solon's constitution as mixed, the Areopagus being the oligarchic, the elected officers the aristocratic and the popular law courts the democratic element. It is interesting to find the triple arrangement here but still without kingship; though incidentally Aristotle himself disagreed with this view of Solon's constitution. The first reference to a mixture of political abstractions—of βασιλεία, ἀριστοκρατία and δημοκρατία—is to be found in Plato's *Menexenus*,[38] and from then onwards the notion is common; though its first appearance in Isocrates is, curiously, not until 339.[39] In the *Laws* Plato has a defence of the mixed constitution,[40] linking it with Sparta in a passage which Aristotle cites in his *Politics*.[41] Aristotle himself is also interested in mixtures, but would like to secure a constitutional blending, preferably inside the various elements—the deliberative, the executive and the judicial[42]—rather than a constitution which was itself a combination of monarchy, aristocracy and democracy.

[32] Thucyd. viii. 97. 2; for Theramenes' constitution as a democracy reserving certain privileges to the rich see G. E. M. de Ste. Croix, 'The constitution of the five thousand', *Historia*, 5 (1956), 1–23.   [33] Cf. Aalders, *Theorie*, 27.

[34] *Pol.* ii. 12, 1267 b 22 ff.   [35] Newman, i. 384.   [36] *Pol.* ii. 12, 1273 b 35 ff.

[37] Cf. Barker, *Politics*, 88 n. 1; Larsen, 'Cleisthenes and the development of the theory of democracy at Athens', *Sabine essays*, 13.

[38] Plato, *Menex.* 238 cd; cf. Aalders, *Theorie*, 31–4.

[39] In the *Panathenaicus*; see Aalders, *Theorie*, 35–7; P. Cloché, 'Isocrate et la politique théraménienne', *LEC*, 5 (1936), 394 ff.

[40] *Laws*, iv. 712 de.   [41] *Pol.* ii. 6, 1265 b 33 f.

[42] *Pol.* vi (iv). 14, 1297 b 41 f.; Aalders, *Theorie*, 54–69.

Whence Plato derived the notion is not known. Stobaeus[43] records fragments of a work *On Law and Justice* attributed to Archytas of Tarentum and containing an account of a mixed state like Sparta as the ideal, and on the strength of this it has been claimed that Plato was drawing on the Pythagoreans. Archytas' work is almost certainly spurious, as Aalders has recently demonstrated,[44] but, as he himself argues, the theory may well have arisen in a context of practical politics and against a background of sophistic and (possibly Pythagorean) discussion. Thucydides' comment on Theramenes' constitution perhaps supports this prudent view.

A slightly later advocate of the mixed constitution was Dicaearchus of Messana, Aristotle's pupil, who composed a work entitled Τριπολιτικός.[45] According to Photius,[46] the anonymous Byzantine author of a dialogue *On Politics* referred to the εἶδος πολιτείας Δικαιαρχικόν, which was a mixed constitution.[47] The suggestion has often been made that Polybius derived his views about the virtues of the mixed constitution from Dicaearchus. Although he was undoubtedly acquainted with Dicaearchus' geographical work, it is perhaps rather rash to make him Polybius' source for a concept which was by this time so widespread. For example, Areius Didymus, Augustus' teacher, who shows knowledge of it,[48] will almost certainly have had it from a Peripatetic source; but it was also accepted by the Stoics,[49] whether Polybius' contemporary Panaetius or the earlier Chrysippus, and by the mid-second century it was sufficient of a commonplace for the Elder Cato to

[43] Stobaeus, iv. 1. 132, 135–8; iv. 5. 61 = Wachsmuth–Henze, iv. 79, 82, 218.

[44] *Theorie*, 13 ff.

[45] Cf. Cicero, *Att.* xiii. 32. 2; Athen. iv. 141 a (cf. Wehrli, *Dikaiarchos*, fg. 70 and 72).

[46] Phot. *Bibl.* 37. 69 c (cf. Wehrli, *Dikaiarchos*, fg. 71).

[47] See Aalders, *Theorie*, 72–3, for full discussion and references to earlier work. He rightly rejects the view, upheld by Hirzel and Wilamowitz, that δικαιαρχικόν here referred not to the author, but to the 'rule of justice' or 'rule of the just'; but against his view that the Τριπολιτικός was the source of Aelius Aristides' references to the Roman imperial government as a mixed constitution in his Εἰς 'Ρώμην, 90–1, see my criticisms in *CR*, 19 (1969), 315.

[48] Cf. Stobaeus, ii. 7. 26 = Wachsmuth–Henze, ii. 150, a passage of interest because it contains the two words ὀχλοκρατία and μικτή which both feature in Polybius vi. Areius Didymus' source will be Peripatetic; but it cannot be identified more closely.

[49] Cf. Diog. Laert. vii. 131, πολιτείαν δ' ἀρίστην τὴν μικτὴν ἔκ τε δημοκρατίας καὶ βασιλείας καὶ ἀριστοκρατίας. For the view that his source is Panaetius see Pohlenz, *Stoa*, ii. 102; but it is more likely on the whole to be Chrysippus (von Arnim, *SVF*, iii, fg. 700).

mention it in connection with the constitution of Carthage.[50] With such a broad choice, it seems therefore wiser to treat the question of where Polybius derived his theory of the mixed constitution as virtually unanswerable.

4.

When we turn to the *anacyclosis*, the difficulties are still greater, since this theory is even more complicated in its origins. In the form in which Polybius describes it,[51] social organisation begins when, after some general cataclysm due to flood, famine or the like, the survivors, a savage horde without arts and crafts, gather together out of weakness and appoint as leader some man who is pre-eminent in strength and physique—as happens among birds and beasts. The next step comes with the birth of children, and the natural expectation of dutifulness from them and a sense of out-rage on the occasions when it is not forthcoming. From this and similar situations arises a notion of duty and hence of justice; and with the growth of ethical concepts the primitive monarch yields place (or develops into) a king ruling by moral force. How-ever in due course the king's descendants, who have grown up in luxury and privilege, begin to indulge their appetites in acts of violence against their subjects. Conspiracies arise and at length the best men, supported by the commoners, overthrow the kings who have become tyrants and set up an aristocracy. But when with the passing of time their children too are corrupted by their privileged position, having had no experience of misfortune and not yet knowing the meaning of civil liberty and equality—per-haps, as has recently been suggested,[52] because this was a concept which was only to arise with the next political form—they in turn resort to acts of violence, often of a sexual character, until the people rise, expel them and set up a democracy. But once again with the passing of the first and second generations, freedom and equality are so common that they cease to be valued; lust for power, corruption of the people and the growth of bribery lead to the rule of violence, massacres, plunder and eventually complete savagery, from which the only saviour will be the monarch,[53] who sets the cycle off once more.

[50] Cf. Serv. ad *Aen.* iv. 682.   [51] vi. 5. 4–9. 9.
[52] By D. Musti, 'Polibio e la democrazia', *Annali di Pisa*, 36 (1967), 193.
[53] Cf. Walbank, 'Polybius and the Roman state', *GRBS*, 5 (1964), 246.

It is clear that this strange sequence is an amalgam drawing on several traditions.[54] It derives in part from a theory about the origins of culture; but it also incorporate s atheory about the causes of corruption in states, which accounts for the fact that the conditions which lead to the downfall of kingship, aristocracy and democracy are virtually the same for each phase. These two threads may be considered separately before we turn to the question of who combined them and what was his relationship to Polybius.

In Polybius' version primitive, savage men—like other living things—gathered together through weakness.[55] This is the 'naturalistic' explanation which we find illustrated in the fable about the creation of man which Plato put into the mouth of Protagoras;[56] men being preyed on by beasts came together and founded cities—but could only live peaceably in them after Zeus had given them *Aidos* and *Dike*. The idea is clearly sophistic in origin, and it may derive from Democritus,[57] as indeed Cole has argued with ingenuity in his recent book on Democritus and the sources of Greek anthropology.[58] Parallels can be traced between Polybius' account and one to be found in the first book of Diodorus,[59] and this common tradition may well go back ultimately to Democritus. Cole argues that other elements in Democritus' theory of cultural origins appear elsewhere, for example his account of technological progress in various passages in Diodorus, Tzetzes, Vitruvius, Lucretius and Poseidonius, and his view about the origins of language in Diodorus, Vitruvius and Lactantius.[60] He also traces a close parallel between Polybius' account of early social development and a version to be found in book iii of Plato's *Laws*,[61] which he also claims for Democritus. I cannot discuss his theory in detail here. It depends upon the comparison of a large number of pas-

---

[54] For detailed discussion see my *Commentary*, i. 643 ff.; I owe a good deal to the analysis in Ryffel, 189 ff.

[55] Cf. vi. 5. 7, τότε δήπου, καθάπερ ἐπὶ τῶν ἄλλων ζῴων, καὶ ἐπὶ τούτων συναθροιζομένων—ὅπερ εἰκός, καὶ τούτους εἰς τὸ ὁμόφυλον συναγελάζεσθαι διὰ τὴν τῆς φύσεως ἀσθένειαν.   [56] Plato, *Protag.* 322 ab.

[57] See my *Commentary*, i. 651 on vi. 5. 7.

[58] See above, p. 130 n. 3.

[59] Diod. i. 8. 1–2; cf. K. Reinhardt, 'Hekataios von Abdera und Demokrit', *Hermes*, 47 (1912), 492 ff., reprinted in *Vermächtnis der Antike, Gesammelte Essays zur Philosophie und Geschichtsschreibung* (Göttingen, 1960), 114–32; E. Norden, *Agnostos theos* (Berlin, 1913), 399; Cole, *Democritus*, 174–92.

[60] His view is summarised, *Democritus*, 130.

[61] Plato, *Laws*, iii. 677 a–683 a; Cole, *Democritus*, 97 ff.

sages and the detection of similarities, not all of which are equally convincing. To take an example, one of the main features of Plato's theory is the gradual growth of society from the individual to the herd and thence to larger and larger groups, ultimately culminating in cities, alliances and nations. But, after the first stage, this is wholly absent from Polybius' version. Similarly, the argument[62] that both Polybius and Democritus have the same account of the establishing of relations between parents and children rests on an analogy between two passages which in fact say quite different things—Democritus that men, in comparison with animals, are unique in having developed the practice of getting some enjoyment from their children, Polybius that it is as a result of their resentment at their children's ingratitude (and of similar situations) that men are led to formulate general concepts of what is good and bad. I quote these two examples (which could be multiplied) to show that there are sufficient uncertainties in this thesis to render it no more than a possibility—though, I would concede, quite a strong one—that Polybius' naturalistic view of human cultural development derives ultimately from Democritus. It is clear that this naturalistic view is in contrast to the one expressed in book ii of Plato's *Republic*,[63] which derives society from an innate political instinct 'since men cannot be sufficient each to himself'. On the other hand, the two views of social origins— primitive weakness and a 'political' instinct—are not mutually exclusive, for Cicero mentions both in the *de re publica*,[64] even if like the Stoics he assigns more importance to the second.

5.

To his theory of social origins Polybius in his *anacyclosis* adds another about constitutional change and corruption; and here too, in spite of his remarks that it has been expounded in detail 'by Plato and certain other philosophers',[65] the identification of his sources remains uncertain. The germ of the idea may go back to

---

[62] Cole, *Democritus*, 112 ff.; the two passages which Cole compares are vi. 6. 2–5 and Diels–Kranz, *Frag. Vorsokr.* i. 68 B 278.

[63] Plato, *Rep.* ii. 369 b, γίγνεται τοίνυν... πόλις, ὡς ἐγῷμαι, ἐπειδὴ τυγχάνει ἡμῶν ἕκαστος οὐκ αὐτάρκης, ἀλλὰ πολλῶν ⟨ὢν⟩ ἐνδεής.

[64] Cicero, *rep.* i. 39, 'eius autem prima causa coeundi est non tam imbecillitas quam naturalis quaedam hominum quasi congregatio'; this I take not to exclude *imbecillitas* as a cause of combining, but to make it secondary to the social instinct.   [65] vi. 5. 1.

Solon's theory[66] that lawlessness leads to tyranny. But we first find a 'sequence of constitutions' in the *Republic*,[67] where the best form—aristocracy or kingship—is followed by the so-called Cretan or Laconian state, and then oligarchy, democracy and tyranny, with the implication at any rate that they develop one into another.[68] It was this passage which Aristotle criticised in the *Politics*,[69] on the grounds first that Plato never explained how the changes took place, and secondly that all kinds of alternative sequences of constitution are possible—a criticism which, as Ernest Barker pointed out,[70] can be turned against Aristotle's own sequence in *Politics* iii.[71] It is perhaps significant that as a *reductio ad absurdum* Aristotle goes on to say that the logic of Plato's argument would require his tyranny to change back into the first, ideal constitution: 'for in this way', he says, 'there would be a complete circle'. It is this complete circle, which Plato never produces, either in the *Republic* or in his further development of the theory in the *Laws* and the *Politicus*,[72] nor Aristotle himself in his discussion of constitutional forms in book viii of the *Nicomachean Ethics*,[73] that constitutes the novel feature of Polybius' *anacyclosis*. This, as we have seen, succeeds in closing the circle, thanks to its combination of the two theories of constitutional change and cultural origins.

That it was Polybius himself who linked the two theories together and closed the gap to form the circle is possible,[74] but somewhat unlikely; and I find confirmation of this view in the fact that in his account of the *anacyclosis* Polybius uses the word μόναρχος in a different sense from the one he usually gives to it in the remaining parts of his *Histories*.[75] There μόναρχος means 'a tyrant', and μοναρχία is 'tyranny'; thus for example Aratus' object was to expel the Macedonians from the Peloponnese and to dissolve the tyrannies, τὰς δὲ μοναρχίας καταλῦσαι;[76] and when several tyrants laid down their authority the phrase used is ἀποθέμενοι τὰς μοναρχίας.[77] The tyranny of Molpagoras of Cius is described as

---

[66] Cf. Herod. i. 59. 3 ff.; Ryffel, 80.   [67] Plato, *Rep.* viii. 544 c.

[68] Cf. Plato, *Rep.* v. 449 a, ἐγὼ μὲν ᾖα τὰς ἐφεξῆς ἐρῶν, ὥς μοι ἐφαίνοντο ἕκασται ἐξ ἀλλήλων μεταβαίνειν.   [69] *Pol.* vii (v). 12, 1316 a 1 ff.

[70] Barker, *Politics*, 143 n. 2.   [71] *Pol.* iii. 15, 1286 a 1 ff.

[72] *Laws*, iii. 677 a ff.; iv. 709 a ff.; *Polit.* 291 de; cf. *Epist.* vii. 326 b ff.

[73] *Eth. Nic.* viii. 10. 12, 1160 b 10 f.

[74] So von Fritz, *Mixed constitution*, 60–75; Erbse, 'Polybios-Interpretationen', *Phil.* 101 (1957), 275; and Pédech, *Méthode*, 303 f.

[75] See Walbank, 'Polybius on the Roman constitution', *CQ*, 37 (1943), 76 ff.

[76] ii. 43. 8.   [77] ii. 44. 6.

μοναρχικὴ ἐξουσία;⁷⁸ and examples could be multiplied. There are, it is true, a few places⁷⁹ where μόναρχος is used more neutrally to describe an autocratic ruler, even a legitimate one, like Philip V of Macedonia; but usually μόναρχος for Polybius means a tyrant. This usage is found in several places in book vi; for example in the account of the corruptions of the simple forms in chapter 3,⁸⁰ the degraded form of kingship consists of μοναρχικὰς καὶ τυραννικὰς... πολιτείας, and in the next chapter Polybius says that not every μοναρχία can be called kingship, just as not every oligarchy can be called aristocracy.⁸¹ In fact μοναρχία is the corruption of βασιλεία.⁸² However, in the section describing the *anacyclosis*⁸³ his usage is different; for here monarchy is specifically the primitive monarchy based on the rule of strength, which with the growth of moral concepts changes into kingship. When in turn kingship is corrupted, it gives place to tyranny: ἐγένετο ἐκ τῆς βασιλείας τυραννίς.⁸⁴ From this follows the whole *anacyclosis* until the people, having deteriorated into a state of chaos and savagery, once again find a δεσπότης καὶ μόναρχος and the process begins anew.⁸⁵

This use of the word μόναρχος for the primitive ruler, and of τυραννίς (not μοναρχία) for tyranny, points to a source whose vocabulary Polybius has taken over without adaptation, and weighs against the view that the *anacyclosis* was Polybius' own invention. But on the identity of that source there is no agreement. Most scholars, perhaps wisely, are content to speak of Platonic or Peripatetic traditions.⁸⁶ Some have gone so far as to hazard a name such as Theophrastus or Dicaearchus; and it used to be fashionable to think of the Stoic philosopher, Panaetius of Rhodes,⁸⁷ despite the fact that he was younger than Polybius and not likely to have been

---

⁷⁸ xv. 21. 2.

⁷⁹ E.g. viii. 8. 4 (monarchs generally and Philip V in particular), 8. 7 (Philip II and Philip V).   ⁸⁰ vi. 3. 9–10.   ⁸¹ vi. 4. 2–3.

⁸² vi. 4. 6; for further examples of this pejorative sense of μόναρχος and μοναρχικός (as well as of the use of these words in a neutral sense) in book vi see Walbank, 'Polybius on the Roman constitution', *CQ*, 37 (1943), 77.

⁸³ vi. 4. 7–9. 14.   ⁸⁴ vi. 7. 8.   ⁸⁵ vi. 9. 9.

⁸⁶ E.g. Ryffel, 201 n. 360; Regenbogen, *RE*, Suppl.-B. vii, 'Theophrastus', col. 1519, suggests Theophrastus, and Erbse, 'Zur Entstehung des poly-bianischen Geschichtswerkes', *Rh. Mus.* 94 (1951), 160 n. 1 (following Zeller), Dicaearchus. See too Gelzer, reviewing von Fritz, *Mixed constitution*, *Kl. Schr.* iii. 195, 'zu den 5. 1 erwähnten Philosophen kann Theophrast sehr wohl gehört haben'.

⁸⁷ For references see Walbank, 'Polybius on the Roman constitution', *CQ*, 37 (1943), 85.

acquainted with him at the time the latter was writing book vi.[88] Polybius, it is true, uses Stoic terms occasionally in his account of the *anacyclosis*,[89] but at a time of philosophical eclecticism this is not firm proof of a Stoic origin for the theory. Indeed, if we are to seek a source for it in one piece, it is probably in a less exalted milieu that we should look. However, before pursuing this point further there is another aspect of Polybius' theory that is due to be considered.

6.

In several places[90] Polybius describes the *anacyclosis* as exemplified by the natural development of states, and the various stages of their growth, perfection, change and end. In doing so he is invoking what we may call the biological pattern, which runs right through nature to ensure that all mortal things have their birth, rise, acme, decline and end. It is a fairly obvious concept derived from observation and it can be traced back in its general outline to Anaximander,[91] after whom it quickly became a commonplace; as Thucydides remarks:[92] πάντα...πέφυκε καὶ ἐλασσοῦσθαι, 'it is in the nature of all things also to dwindle'. In the Hellenistic age this pattern came to be identified with Fate, εἱμαρμένη.[93] To Polybius it is a law of nature, and accordingly the *anacyclosis*, which is also natural, must be brought into relation with it. How the two are to be logically reconciled is a long-standing problem: but it seems as though it is the common concept of operating κατὰ φύσιν that provides the general link between them.[94]

[88] Cf. Brink and Walbank, 'The construction of book vi of Polybius', *CQ*, 4 (1954), 103 n. 3.

[89] E.g. vi. 5. 5, ὁ λόγος αἱρεῖ (but the Stoic sense was different), 5. 10, ἔννοια...τοῦ καλοῦ καὶ δικαίου (cf. Cicero, *fin.* iii. 21, 'quam appellant ἔννοιαν illi'), 6. 7, ἔννοια...τῆς τοῦ καθήκοντος δυνάμεως, 6. 11, διανεμητικὸς ...τοῦ κατ' ἀξίαν ἑκάστοις (cf. von Arnim, *SVF*, iii fg. 262; but the phrase is also found in Aristotle). See my *Commentary*, i. 651–5, ad locc., however, for doubts concerning several examples.

[90] vi. 4. 11–13, 9. 11–14, 57. 1–4. But which states are supposed to exemplify its operation is never made clear. vi. 3. 1 seems to suggest that something like it occurred widely in Greece, but not universally there (ὅσα...εἴληφε).

[91] Diels–Kranz, *Frag. Vorsokr.* i. 12 B 1.   [92] Thucyd. ii. 64. 3.

[93] Cf. Phot. *Bibl.* 249, 1584 B, where τὸ ἐκ παιδὸς εἰς μειράκιον ἐλθεῖν καὶ τὰς καθ' ἑξῆς ἡλικίας οἰκείως διελθεῖν exemplifies εἱμαρμένη (the source is perhaps Agatharchides).

[94] Cf. for example vi. 4. 7 φυσικῶς, 4. 9, 4. 11, 4. 13 κατὰ φύσιν, 5. 8 φύσεως ἔργον ἀληθινώτατον and 9. 10 φύσεως οἰκονομία (both referring to the *anacyclosis*), 9. 13, 9. 14, 51. 4 κατὰ φύσιν, 57. 1 ἡ τῆς φύσεως ἀνάγκη.

The difficulties are apparent immediately one begins to look at the details. The biological pattern is a single curve demanding an acme, a high point; but where is the acme in the *anacyclosis*? To this question there are various possible answers, all relatively unsatisfactory. One solution is to take the *anacyclosis* as a whole and to identify its beginnings with primitive society, its growth with monarchy, its acme with kingship, and its decline with the decay into tyranny. But such a scheme does not really fit, since it ignores the further stages of the cycle. Another alternative is to treat aristocracy as the acme; but although in his account of Rome Polybius believes the predominant role of the senate to be a reason for regarding its constitution as superior to that of Carthage,[95] this is not because he considers aristocracy to be the best constitution but because inside a mixed constitution (such as Rome by definition at that time possessed) deliberation is properly the business of the aristocratic element.[96] Yet another possibility is to regard the biological scheme as applying to each of the constitutional forms in turn, so that in fact there are three acmes consisting of kingship, aristocracy and democracy;[97] and in fact Polybius uses the words ἀρχὴ καὶ γένεσις in relation to both kingship and aristocracy.[98] But, against this, it is clearly not to the parts but to the whole of Roman history that Polybius intends the biological pattern to apply; 'for', he says,[99] 'it is especially in reference to the Roman state that this way of considering it (i.e. the method of the *anacyclosis*) will enable us to arrive at the knowledge of its formation, growth, and acme, and likewise of the change for the worse which will one day follow.'

Nevertheless, it is plain that, despite the difficulty of interpreting the *anacyclosis* in terms of the biological scheme of birth, acme and decline, Polybius regards the two as being closely linked and in fact that, as the natural process peculiar to constitutions, the *anacyclosis* is somehow to be taken as the expression of the biological law. It has been observed that there are other second-century

[95] vi. 51. 5–6, cf. 57. 8.

[96] On this see Brink and Walbank, 'The construction of book vi of Polybius', *CQ,* 4 (1954), 117–18. It is clear that under the mixed constitution deliberation on policy was carried out at Rome by the Senate (vi. 12. 3) and indeed the Senate took all decisions of this kind (vi. 13); this does not however make Rome an aristocracy.   [97] So Ryffel, 217, argues.

[98] Cf. vi. 7. 1, 8. 1 (but there is no αὔξησις or ἀκμή mentioned: see above, p. 131 n. 10).   [99] vi. 9. 12–14; cf. 4. 13.

treatises which show a similar concern to illustrate a natural law of biological change in various contexts. A product of popular philosophy which has come down under the name of Ocellus Lucanus provides one such example.[100] This work distinguishes various levels in the universe, all of which except the highest are subject to various forms of such a law; thus at the second level the four elements move in a Heracleitean flux described as ἀντι-περίστασις, at the third level plants move in a cycle of seed, fruit, seed, called ἐπανάκαμψις; and at the fourth level men and other living creatures pass through a succession of ages. Thus each level reveals the special form of the biological law appropriate to it; and it is in some such milieu as this, it has been suggested,[101] that the *anacyclosis* was put forward as the form of the law appropriate to constitutions. Now there is of course no evidence directly linking the *anacyclosis* with Ocellus Lucanus; but the rather elaborate scheme with its own special piece of jargon—for the word *ana-cyclosis* is very rare elsewhere and is nowhere used in precisely this sense—is sufficiently like the schemes there sketched, containing such words as ἀντιπερίστασις and ἐπανάκαμψις, as to render plausible the hypothesis that it took its rise in a similar context of popular philosophy. Whether this was linked with the second-century Peripatos, as Harder suggested,[102] and to what extent it was affected by Stoicism, can perhaps scarcely now be determined.

7.

The ambiguity about where the acme in this process was really located was not too serious a problem for Polybius, since in the case of Rome he had already placed it outside the cycle proper in the mixed constitution, the acquisition of which brought the circular movement to a halt. It is indeed as an answer to the problem of political instability that the mixed constitution finds its place in book vi. Primarily Polybius is concerned to explain the reason

[100] See my *Commentary*, i. 644–5; on Ocellus see Harder, *Ocellus*, and Thesleff, *Texts*, and *Writings*; W. Theiler, *Gnomon*, 1 (1925), 151; 2 (1926), 151–3, 590 ff.

[101] Cf. Ryffel, 203 ff. Links between Polybius and Ocellus (and also between Polybius and the fragments of ps.-Hippodamus preserved in Stobaeus) had already been indicated by von Scala, 223 ff., 240 ff.; cf. Pöschl, *Römischer Staat*, 89 n. 84, 100.

[102] Harder, *Ocellus*, 149–53; see my *Commentary*, i. 644–5.

for Roman success—'how and by virtue of what kind of constitution' Rome has in so short a time become mistress of the Mediterranean world; and it is only as a very secondary issue that he is concerned with the question whether the Roman constitution will itself in due course decline.

Logically, of course, since it is a natural phenomenon that has developed essentially κατὰ φύσιν, it must like all other human affairs be subject to the law of change and decay; and in four passages[103] Polybius speaks of the mixed constitution, in Sparta or Rome, in terms implying that its duration is finite. Like Plato's ideal republic[104] it too will one day fall and decay; and indeed it is this fact which makes it somewhat easier for Polybius to reconcile it with those parts of his theory which stress either constitutional change or biological growth, acme and decline. The analysis of the mixed constitution was essential to the didactic purpose of book vi; but obviously the association of this ideal form with a particular historical period—'Lycurgan' Sparta or third- and second-century Rome—explicitly raised the question of its growth and implicitly the question of its decline; in the case of Sparta the latter could clearly be seen as a contemporary issue,[105] but in the case of Rome it still lay well in the future and was only incidental and peripheral to Polybius' main purpose. For the analysis of the

---

[103] vi. 10. 7, 10. 11, 10. 14, 11. 1.

[104] Plato, *Rep.* viii. 456 a.

[105] Polybius regarded Cleomenes III, Machanidas and Nabis as tyrants; cf. iv. 81. 12–14; but in vi. 49–50 he puts the beginning of Spartan troubles earlier, since he associates it with overseas expeditions, and evidently is thinking of those of Agesilaus in the early fourth century. His treatment of Sparta is in fact confused. On the one hand, he does not distinguish between two separate problems, that of the relationship between the mixed constitution set up by Lycurgus and the *anacyclosis*, against the effects of which it was to offer protection, and that of the influence of Spartan social institutions on citizens in their relationship to the state. He nowhere attempts to relate the ἀγωγή and the δίαιτα, those peculiar features of Spartan life, to the mixed constitution; and moreover he seems unaware of how paradoxical it is to treat Cleomenes both as the restorer of *Lycurgi leges moresque* (Livy, xxxviii. 34. 3, based on Polybius), which ought to have been the foundation of the highly prized mixed constitution, yet at the same time as the tyrant who subverted the *patrios politeia*, or ancestral constitution. See on this B. Shimron, 'Polybius and the reforms of Cleomenes III', *Historia*, 13 (1964), 147–55; Walbank, 'The Spartan ancestral constitution in Polybius', *Ancient Society*, 303–12, with bibliography in n. 1 (on p. 305 lines 18–20 'There is no evidence... Lycurgan regime' should be deleted: a survival from an earlier draft of this article, they are in clear contradiction to the evidence from Livy cited in nn. 36 and 37).

growth of the Roman constitution the *anacyclosis* provided an invaluable framework, since the three constitutional forms which made up the mixed constitution were all there present consecutively in the moving cycle; and the early history of Rome seemed in itself to furnish a demonstration of the relevance and accuracy of the scheme. That the *anacyclosis* implied ultimate change and decay was also no difficulty, since Polybius was by no means committed to the thesis of Roman perfection; indeed, to anticipate a topic with which I shall deal more fully in the final chapter, he had already been confronted with the issue of Roman deterioration long before he came to write his sixth book. In so far as the Roman constitution and Roman society showed signs of decay, the *anacyclosis* would provide an explanation of their significance; but this was marginal to the main issue. Briefly, then, the mixed constitution fits into the general scheme by providing the acme which it was difficult to locate anywhere within the *anacyclosis* itself. Rome had come to it by way of the early stages of the cycle, and in so doing she had temporarily succeeded in establishing an equilibrium which put her outside the range of the forces which would normally have made for change. Thus, in one sense, the Roman mixed constitution causes a break in the *anacyclosis* pattern, which was the natural order, κατὰ φύσιν. Yet by providing an acme absent from the continuous pattern of the cycle it brings this more closely into relation with the biological concept of origin, growth, acme and decline, and so from that point of view makes the development of Rome essentially 'natural'. This helps to explain the apparent paradox when Polybius insists[106] that Rome more than any other state has developed naturally, κατὰ φύσιν, though thanks to the mixed constitution she had made an almost unique breach in the 'natural' rhythm of the *anacyclosis*. Clearly there is a contradiction here: but it is one that lies firmly embedded within the complicated set of propositions which Polybius has attempted with some— though not complete—success to combine within a single theory— and is not, as has been sometimes supposed, the result of clumsy revision designed to take account of a substantial change in Polybius' views.[107]

[106] vi. 9. 13.
[107] As those scholars assume who believe in the existence of two or more 'layers' in the composition of book vi; for recent examples see my *Commentary*, i. 636; add Petzold, *Studien*, 40–90.

8.

If what I have so far said is correct, it was important for Polybius' theory to demonstrate how Rome had succeeded in making the transition from the moving cycle of political change to the comparative stability of the mixed constitution. It is especially unfortunate, therefore, that we have almost completely lost one of the organic elements of book vi, the survey of early Roman history which followed the exposition of the constitutional theory and preceded, quite logically, the analytical account of the detailed elements that made up the mixed constitution. Of this historical section, which Polybius had already foreshadowed earlier in the book,[108] when he spoke of Greek ignorance of early Roman history (τὴν ἄγνοιαν τῶν προγεγονότων), only ten fragments survive, and those are mainly of an antiquarian character; though some—like the explanation of how any breach of the rule which forbade a Roman matron to drink wine was immediately detected, thanks to another rule which obliged her to kiss all her male relatives and relatives-in-law up to second cousins upon first meeting them each day[109]—illustrate an interest in those ἔθη καὶ νόμοι, customs and laws, which Polybius elsewhere insists[110] are fundamental in any constitution. There has been a long debate on how far Polybius' argument can be reconstructed from Cicero's account of early Roman history in book ii of the *de re publica*.[111] The version which he there puts into the mouth of Scipio Aemilianus shows the Roman constitution gradually evolving through a kind of mixed monarchy, mixed kingship and mixed aristocracy to culminate in the fully balanced constitution which he goes on to describe; and it has been argued that this interpretation is taken directly from Polybius. In fact Scipio is there made to express his debt to Cato,[112] and Laelius goes out of his way to praise Scipio's account as novel and nowhere to be found in Greek books, *nova ad disputandum ratio, quae nusquam est in Graecorum libris*. Moreover, it has been shown by Pöschl[113] that Cicero used other sources besides Polybius in order to construct a picture of Roman development that was essentially his own; and it is clearly dangerous to

---

[108] vi. 3. 3.   [109] vi. 11 a. 4.
[110] vi. 47. 1.
[111] Cicero, *rep.* ii. 1–63; see above, p. 22 n. 111.
[112] Cicero, *rep.* ii. 1.   [113] *Römischer Staat*, 42. ff.

lean too heavily on the hypothesis that Polybius' account of early Rome can be reconstructed *in toto* from Cicero.

What is clear from the first words[114] following Polybius' *archaeologia* (to use what is now the traditional and convenient name for this section, although it has no ancient authority in this context) is that the decisive date in the development of the constitution was thirty-*x* years after Xerxes' crossing into Greece; and however one fills up the lacuna—to read thirty-two, or even thirty-four or thirty-five[115]—it is beyond doubt that the reference is to the decemvirate, or the consulship following it. From 449 onwards Rome possessed a mixed constitution, which gradually reached its perfection by the time of the Hannibalic War,[116] and the *archaeologia*

[114] vi. 11. 1.

[115] Ed. Meyer, 'Untersuchungen über Diodor's römische Geschichte', *Rh. Mus.* 37 (1882), 622–3, read ⟨τέτταρσι⟩ or ⟨πέντε⟩ καὶ τριάκοντα and De Sanctis, ii. 41 n. 1, ⟨δύο⟩. The date from which Polybius is reckoning is 'Xerxes' crossing into Greece'. This event was canonised in Greek chronology (cf. Pédech, *Méthode*, 315 n. 50) and although Xerxes crossed the Hellespont in spring 480 (i.e. Ol. 74. 4), wherever (as for instance in Eratosthenes, *FGH* 241 T 1, or the Parian Marble, *FGH* 239 A 51) 'Xerxes' crossing' is used in this way, it implies the year of Salamis, i.e. Ol. 75. 1 = 480/79 (cf. Dion. Hal. ix. 1; Diod. xi. 1; Leuze, *Jahrzählung*, 148–9; my *Commentary*, i. 340 on iii. 22. 2). Hence, if De Sanctis' ⟨δύο⟩ is accepted, by inclusive reckoning from Ol. 75. 1 thirty-two years brings us down to Ol. 82. 4 = 449/8, and this could well be equated with A.U.C. 305 = 449, in the course of which L. Valerius Potitus and M. Horatius took over the consulship from the Decemvirs.

[116] Following von Fritz, *Mixed constitution*, 366, 468–9, I interpret vi. 11. 1 to mean: 'after the details (τῶν κατὰ μέρος) of the Roman political order had, from this time onwards, and prior to the Hannibalic War (προ- in προδιευκρινουμένων), continued to be ever more well arranged'. This rendering has been criticised by Büchner, *Cicero*, 196 f., on the grounds that it would require an aorist participle, and also that it would imply *two* high points for the Roman constitution, one in 449 and a second one at the time of the Hannibalic War. To meet these objections Eisen, 79–83, proposes to translate προδιευκρινουμένων 'to judge correctly in advance' and he offers two alternative translations: *either* (*a*) 'the Roman constitution was constantly in the hands of people who took the right decisions on each detail in advance' (possessive genitive), *or* (*b*) 'individual issues being always correctly appreciated and decided in advance as they arose' (genitive absolute). Of these the second is open to the same objection that Büchner raised against von Fritz's version, viz. that one might have expected an aorist, and not a present participle; and the first would in fact require τῶν ⟨τὰ⟩ κατὰ μέρος προδιευκρινουμένων. But, what is perhaps more serious, Polybius tells us (vi. 10. 14) that the Romans achieved their mixed constitution as a result of the discipline of many struggles and always choosing the best in the light of experience gained in disaster. This belief is hardly to be reconciled with the Romans' always having taken the right decision in advance. There are moreover other objections to Eisen's rendering (see my review in *CR*, 17 (1967), 35–6), and on the whole von Fritz's version still seems

must therefore have described how she gradually passed through the earlier stages of the *anacyclosis* in order to attain this. If we cautiously take a few hints from Cicero, it seems that Polybius' account (which he may have derived from Fabius Pictor or C. Acilius),[117] made Romulus the monarch, the elder Tarquin and Servius Tullius kings,[118] Superbus the tyrant, the early republic the aristocracy, and the decemvirate the oligarchy. Without pressing the parallels from Cicero unduly, it is clear that the aristocracy of the early republic must have retained in it a monarchical element, in as much as it possessed the consulship—which Polybius regards as the monarchical part of the later mixed constitution. But whether he also pointed to institutions (for instance the tribunate) which anticipated the later democratic element, is unknown. It is not impossible; on the other hand the *anacyclosis* must have remained the fundamental basis of his narrative, since if it was not, it is difficult to see what function it had at all in book vi. After all, it was the 'natural' scheme of development for states and Rome had developed naturally.

9.

After the account of Rome's early development comes an analysis of the actual working of the mixed constitution. This section[119] is very carefully organized from the formal aspect: it contains eight chapters, one introductory and one a summary at the end, and between them three chapters dealing each in turn with the powers of the consuls, the senate and the people, and three more indicating for each of these constitutional elements the checks imposed by the other two—except that there is no mention of any restrictions exercised by the consuls upon the Senate. This section of the book contains a great deal of important factual information, organised to fit the pattern which Polybius has imposed on the Roman state. It also throws light on the way he interpreted

to me the most likely way to take this passage. But the present participle is certainly awkward, and perhaps we should reckon with the possibility that this sentence has been compressed and distorted seriously by the excerptor, as both Büttner-Wobst and Hultsch alleged ('ab epitomatore temere in brevius contracta sunt').

[117] So M. Gelzer, 'Der Anfang römischer Geschichtsschreibung', *Kl. Schr.* iii. 97 n. 18 (Fabius); reviewing von Fritz, *Mixed constitution*, ibid. 196 (C. Acilius).

[118] Cf. vi. 7. 1–2 for the hereditary principle.

[119] vi. 11. 11–18. 8.

the mixed constitution. It was in fact not a mixed constitution in the sense of one in which the various elements were mingled, but rather a balance in which the three parts were held in a kind of tension, through the checks exercised on each by the other two. Aristotle[120] had praised the mixture of elements within the separate branches of government and had regarded a balanced constitution as dangerous and unstable, and for that reason had sought to give a preponderance of power to the middle class, the μέσοι; and in his *de re publica* Cicero[121] distinguished clearly between a mixture and a balance, since he asserted that under the kings at Rome the three elements, royal, aristocratic and democratic, were mixed but not at all in a balanced way 'ita mixta fuerunt. . .ut temperata nullo fuerint modo'. There is no indication that Polybius made this distinction at all, and when he speaks of the Roman mixed constitution he is in fact describing a balanced constitution in which the three elements are kept in place by a system of automatic checks.

10.

The section on the Roman army and encampment comes next[122] and after it the discussion of various constitutions,[123] and their comparison (up to a point) with Rome. Polybius' choice of examples seems to be based largely on traditional considerations. There were established conventions about which constitutions merited discussion; as Polybius remarks,[124] 'nearly all authors have recorded as constitutions of outstanding excellence those of Sparta, Crete, Mantinea and Carthage', and this statement can be confirmed by reference to the surviving works dealing with such topics. The question has been asked why Polybius makes no reference in this section to the Achaean constitution which he praises so highly in book ii. Various answers have been suggested. In his book on the mixed constitution in antiquity von Fritz[125] has given two: first, that in calling Achaea a democracy Polybius has used the word in a rather different sense from that given to it in book vi, and one more related to current Hellenistic practice. This

---

[120] *Pol.* vi. (iv). 11. 10, 1295 b 35 ff.
[121] Cicero, *rep.* ii. 42.   [122] vi. 19–42.
[123] vi. 43–56.
[124] vi. 43. 1; see my *Commentary*, i. 724 for details.
[125] *Mixed constitution*, 7–9.

seems to be true but is no real obstacle to a discussion of Achaea in book vi. Secondly he argues that the political structure of Achaea depended largely on 'extra-constitutional circumstances, which could not be described in terms of definite political agencies and their official competences'. But in fact book vi gives a good deal of emphasis incidentally to extra-constitutional features, and this again hardly seems to explain Polybius' silence. More recently Cole has put forward another solution[126]—that his account of the mixed constitution was in reality based on that of Achaea, and that to introduce Achaea into book vi would be to strip the veil from his pretence that it was something else. This view depends on what has not, I think, been proved—that Polybius' account of the mixed constitution is the Achaean constitution in disguise, and in any case, as an Italian critic has observed,[127] as an explanation it is far too abstract. There is, I think, a more simple solution to the problem: in the first place Achaea, partly because it was a federal constitution, did not appear in the traditional roster of constitutions for discussion, and secondly Polybius had no reason to involve himself in an embarrassing comparison of Rome and Achaea, which could hardly have been satisfactorily concluded by an Achaean patriot analysing the causes of Roman success while living in a slightly privileged form of detention in Italy.[128]

In general then Polybius preferred to stick to the traditional list of constitutions; but besides those I have mentioned, some authors had included Thebes and Athens. These Polybius rejects out of hand on the grounds that the success of both was due to chance and circumstances, and took the form of a sudden flash of glory following an abnormal growth, and quickly extinguished.[129] Thebes, moreover, owed all her success to two men, Epaminondas and Pelopidas, not to the merits of her constitution; and Athens, once Themistocles had gone, resembled a ship without a steersman. In both cases the process of growth (τὰς αὐξήσεις) was irrational, the period of bloom (τὰς ἀκμάς) was brief, and the changes (τὰς μεταβολάς) too violent. Polybius here appears to be thinking of the process of the *anacyclosis* or at any rate of the biological scheme

---

[126] 'The sources and composition of Polybius vi', *Historia*, 13 (1964), 485 n. 114.

[127] D. Musti, 'Problemi polibiani, 1950–64', *Parola del passato*, 104 (1965), 395.

[128] See my remarks in a review of von Fritz, *Mixed constitution*, in *JRS*, 45 (1955), 150.   [129] vi. 43. 2 ff.

generally, though indeed the growth κατὰ λόγον, which he looks for, is not perhaps precisely the same as growth κατὰ φύσιν.[130] In addition it appears to militate against both states that their constitutional growth is so much the work of individuals[131] and not an organic development like that of Rome.

Mantinea is never mentioned again,[132] but Crete is given greater attention since various authors had commended it and compared it to Sparta. Polybius mentions four—Ephorus, Xenophon, Callisthenes and Plato. Of these, Xenophon says nothing about the Cretan constitution in any surviving work, nor is it known where if anywhere Callisthenes dealt with this topic.[133] Plato certainly associated Crete with Sparta in several places in the *Laws*, and also in the *Republic*; but Ed. Meyer long ago demonstrated[134] that it is in fact Ephorus whom Polybius is attacking here. The evidence is worth recalling. Strabo has transmitted Ephorus' account of Crete in book x,[135] and Diodorus, book vii,[136] contains a summary version of his account of Sparta. Polybius accuses Ephorus of describing the Spartan and Cretan constitutions in the same words, and this allegation is confirmed by a comparison of the two versions, which show identity both in sentiment and even vocabulary. Both stress that freedom, ἐλευθερία, is a prize to be won by rulers, not ruled, and that it can be achieved only by concord and courage (ὁμόνοια and ἀνδρεία). Since both theories play a prominent part in Polybius' discussion,[137] the probability is that he is using Ephorus here, and that the other names are intended mainly to impress. Ephorus' commendation of Crete is rejected, a little unjustly indeed, for in fact he had admitted some deterioration in Cretan affairs, and had pointed out that older conditions were not to be deduced from the current situation;[138] but for Polybius a decisive consideration is the fact that 'it would be rare to find personal conduct more treacherous or public policy more

---

[130] See Brink and Walbank, 'The construction of the sixth book of Polybius', *CQ*, 4(1954), 119, 'Polybius here attributes to nature that conformity to rule and reason which Greek rationalists liked to discover in nature and dub λόγος.'

[131] vi. 44.

[132] He probably mentioned it only because it was one of the cities the constitutions of which were normally discussed (cf. Jacoby on *FGH*, 70 F 54).

[133] See my *Commentary*, i. 726 f.

[134] See Ed. Meyer, *Forschungen*, i. 218 n. 1; Jacoby, commenting on *FGH*, 70 F 149.   [135] Strabo, x. 476–84; cf. *FGH*, 70 F 33, 147–9.

[136] Diod. vii. 14. 3; cf. Jacoby commenting on *FGH*, 70 F 148.

[137] vi. 46. 7, 48. 3–5.   [138] Strabo, x. 481.

unjust' than in Crete,[139] and, as he says, the customs and laws (ἔθη καὶ νόμοι) of a people are a good indication of the merits of the state.

Plato's *Republic* is excluded from the comparison as being a purely intellectual exercise, not a real state.[140] Lycurgan Sparta, on the other hand, is highly praised as a genuine mixed constitution, which, as I have just said, secured concord and courage, and through these freedom for its people; but it failed in respect of foreign policy, since it neither rendered the Spartans contented and willing to stay at home, nor yet provided them with the means of implementing a policy of aggression.[141] 'If anyone', Polybius remarks[142] 'esteems it finer and more glorious...to be the leader of many men, and to lord it over many and have the eyes of the world upon him, it must be admitted that from this point of view the Spartan constitution is defective, while that of Rome is superior and better formed for the attainment of power.' In view of the main purpose of Polybius' *Histories*, to explain the rise of the Roman world empire, this is of course a decisive criticism; and it leaves only Carthage in the field.

The comparison between Rome and Carthage is in fact the real heart of the σύγκρισις; for these are the two powers that had faced each other at Cannae. Polybius concludes that although Carthage was also a mixed constitution, at the time of the Hannibalic War this had already passed its prime. By then the masses had gained the chief voice in deliberation, whereas at Rome the Senate still kept control over this vital aspect of policy.[143] This conclusion is followed by a detailed examination of the two rival states,[144] taking account of their skill in fighting both by land and by sea, and of their morals; and Polybius adds some interesting information on Roman customs, on the attitudes of the two peoples towards acquiring wealth and on Roman religious observances. This all contributes to the general picture of Roman *mores*, and underlines the superiority of Rome.

In these chapters the basis of comparison is broadened to include general questions of *morale*, ἔθη καὶ νόμοι,[145] which adds to the

[139] vi. 47. 5.
[140] vi. 47. 7–8.
[141] vi. 48–9.
[142] vi. 50. 3–4.
[143] vi. 51.
[144] vi. 51–6.

[145] vi. 47. 1, where ἔθη καὶ νόμοι are the two criteria in every state by which one judges its true quality and form (δυνάμεις...καὶ...συστάσεις). See further Roveri, *Studi*, 191 ff.

realism of a book in which at times theory may seem to preponderate; and in one comment[146]—that in contrast to the Spartans the Romans by gaining world dominion were able to command an abundance of material wealth which served to support their freedom—Polybius points to a significant connection between liberty and economic strength.

11.

Early in book vi Polybius contrasts Rome with Greek states.[147] In their case, he says, it is an easy matter both to describe their past and to pronounce upon their future; but the Roman constitution is so complicated that it is hard to explain how it has come to be what it is, and equally hard to foretell the future, because of Greek ignorance about Roman public and private life.[148] One purpose of book vi is thus to open up the way to prognostication about the future of Rome.[149] In the penultimate chapter of the book as we now have it Polybius briefly reverts to this point and, without specifically mentioning Rome—perhaps out of tact—he indicates the probable ultimate fate of all states, that attain to supremacy and uncontested sovereignty and the well-being conse-

---

[146] vi. 50. 6.

[147] vi. 3. 1. Polybius contrasts Rome, not with all Greek states, but only with 'such as have frequently risen to greatness, and have frequently experienced a complete change of fortune'. This seems to imply that taken individually states which fall in this category have had these frequent ups and downs. One can compare Plato, *Laws*, iii. 676 bc, which says much the same. But it is very hard to discover what particular states Polybius is thinking of, which have had not one rise and fall but many; and if, arguing back from his statement that it is easy to describe their past and pronounce upon their future, one deduces that they are states that follow the normal pattern of the *anacyclosis*, the problem becomes no easier, since in practice it proves very difficult to find any state (other than Rome) which can be shown to have followed this very schematic line of development. Petzold, *Studien*, 66 n. 2, thinks the Lycurgan and, with limitations, the Cretan constitutions are indicated; but there is no evidence of *frequent* ups and downs in their case, and they are mentioned in vi. 45–47. 6 as 'traditionally good' states, not as states which followed the evolutionary process.   [148] vi. 3. 1–4.

[149] Several scholars (e.g. De Sanctis, iii. 1. 208; Petzold, *Studien*, 67) regard the reference to prognosis as belonging to a later stage in the development of the book. In my opinion it is an *integral* but *minor* part of the plan from the outset; Polybius was concerned primarily to explain Roman success, but his analysis logically brought with it the possibility of foretelling Roman decline. See my *Commentary*, i. 638; Brink and Walbank, 'The construction of the sixth book of Polybius', *CQ*, 4 (1954), 108–10; Walbank, 'Polybius and the Roman state', *GRBS*, 5 (1964), 252 ff.

quent upon this; their prosperity corrupts them and their leaders are led by extravagance and ambition to flatter the populace, as a result of which the latter no longer consent to obey or even to be the equals of the ruling caste. When this happens, the state will decline into what is in reality mob-rule, no matter under what fine-sounding name it is disguised. Rome under her mixed constitution is not of course situated at any stage in the *anacyclosis*; hence the process envisaged cannot be described entirely in terms of that sequence, and Polybius prefers to use the more general vocabulary of the biological scheme—though the reference to ὀχλοκρατία at the end links up firmly with the *anacyclosis*. However, all this is set in the future, and there is no suggestion that Rome has already begun this constitutional decline. Indeed the somewhat vaguely phrased prognostications of this chapter suggest that Polybius is issuing only the most general of warnings, and do not upset the impression that the real business of book vi is to explain the nature of Roman success and supremacy, and that prophecies of doom are only incidental.

12.

The sixth book is a remarkable work. For the first time Greek political theory has been used to interpret the realities of the Roman state. There is of course some creaking. As a definition of the Roman government of the late third and early second centuries the mixed constitution is too formal and too abstract.[150] Yet, it is an analytical tool which enables Polybius to lay his finger on one aspect of the Roman character, its genius for compromise. At the same time, with its mirage of divided powers and its almost mechanical system of checks and balances, the doctrine of the mixed constitution blinded him, to an extraordinary degree, to the elaborate texture of political life which throughout this period ensured the domination of the *nobiles*; and this is remarkable in a highly intelligent man who enjoyed close relations with one of Rome's leading families. The real mainspring of imperial success

[150] He perhaps came nearer the truth in xxiii. 14. 1, P. Scipio Africanus φιλοδοξήσας ἐν ἀριστοκρατικῷ πολιτεύματι...περιεποιήσατο παρὰ μὲν τοῖς ὄχλοις εὔνοιαν παρὰ δὲ τῷ συνεδρίῳ πίστιν...; this extract comes from the Suda, but can be accepted as representing Polybius' own words, for there is a clear contrast between Philopoemen, whose greatness was achieved in a democratic state (xxiii. 12. 8), and Scipio who achieved his in the aristocratic state of third- and second-century Rome.

lay in the direction and doggedness of the senatorial order, and in the flexibility and capacity for growth and innovation—borrowing rather than inventing—which had so impressed Philip V of Macedonia that in a letter which he sent to the Thessalian town of Larisa in the summer of 215,[151] urging the authorities to create new citizens, he commented on the way in which the Romans gave citizenship to their liberated slaves and asserted (incorrectly as it happens) that thanks to this they had already sent out about 70 colonies.[152]

This potentiality for growth, which is real enough, does not fit easily into Polybius' patterns, for the biological scheme spoke only of birth, growth, acme and decline, and the *anacyclosis* simply went round and round; while the mixed constitution was a typical product of Greek political speculation in that it identified perfection with immobility and saw political evolution as the road to disorder and ruin. As an Achaean land-owner Polybius was no doubt disposed by tradition to accept this somewhat pessimistic view of human society. However in one particular he succeeded in going outside his theories and achieved a remarkably accurate formulation of the Roman genius. The Roman constitution, he observed, was the fruit of a long period of political development attained 'not by any process of reasoning'—not, he implies, thanks to some νομοθέτης, or lawgiver, in the Greek fashion—'but by the discipline of many struggles and troubles and always choosing the best in the light of experience gained in disaster'.[153] This is an acute diagnosis which gets closer to the heart of Roman success and fully justifies Polybius' claim to be the interpreter of Rome to his fellow-countrymen. In the final chapter I propose to consider in greater detail how Polybius' views on Rome took shape and how far they were the reflection of his own experience.

[151] *Syll.* 543; on the letters to Larisa see J. M. Hannick, 'Remarques sur les lettres de Philippe V de Macédoine à la cité de Larissa (*IG* ix. 2. 157)' in *Antidorum W. Peremans sexagenario ab alumnis oblatum* (Louvain, 1968), 97 ff. On the date of the two letters (September 217—year 5, not year 2, as the re-reading of the stone makes clear—for the first, and August 215 for the second) see C. Habicht, 'Epigraphische Zeugnisse zur Geschichte Thessaliens', *Ancient Macedonia*, 273–8. On the Macedonian calendar see Werner, *Republik*, 50–1 n. 4.

[152] Cf. Salmon, *Roman colonisation*, 69, who suggests that Philip may have been thinking of *fora et conciliabula*.

[153] vi. 10. 13–14; see above, p. 132.

VI

Polybius and Rome

1.

As we have already seen, Polybius' *Histories* were intended to explain 'how and under what kind of constitution' the Romans had in so short a time made themselves masters of the *oecumene*.[1] Explaining implies a theory of causality; and before turning to the question of Polybius' attitude towards Rome and Roman imperial power I want to say something about his notion of causes. In a recent study of Polybius' historical method, Pédech[2] has distinguished four kinds of phenomena which occupy a predominant place as causative factors in Hellenistic writers, including Polybius himself. The first is the influence of individuals, and especially of counsellors on kings—here one thinks of the pressure exerted by Aratus, Apelles, Demetrius and Heracleides on Philip V,[3] of Agathocles at Alexandria,[4] or Hermeias on the young Antiochus III.[5] A second is the character of political institutions and military expertise—and book vi of Polybius is an excellent illustration of both. Thirdly Pédech points to the geographical milieu: I have already said something about this in an earlier chapter.[6] And finally there is the role of *Tyche* or Fortune, and this too is also familiar in Polybius.[7]

In all this Polybius adheres closely to the general pattern of his age. But his theme required him to devote particular attention to wars, and it is to explain primarily why specific wars break out that he propounds a more schematic and more detailed theory of

[1] See above, p. 130 n. 1 for references.
[2] *Méthode*, 70 ff.
[3] Cf. Walbank, *Philip V*, 261–2; see above, pp. 93–4 with n. 175, on the theme of the 'evil counsellor'.   [4] Cf. v. 63. 1; xiv. 11. 1; xv. 25 ff.
[5] Cf. v. 41. 1–56. 13; Polybius' source is strongly prejudiced against Hermeias.
[6] See above, pp. 115 ff.
[7] See my *Commentary*, i. 16–26; above, pp. 60 ff.

causation. The passage in which this theory is most fully enunciated is in book iii.[8] We must distinguish, he explains, between three concepts—ἀρχαί, αἰτίαι and προφάσεις. Two of these words are familiar to us from Thucydides,[9] who distinguished αἰτίαι, 'grievances', and so 'immediate causes' of the Peloponnesian War, from the 'truest explanation', the ἀληθεστάτη πρόφασις.[10] But Polybius uses the words differently. For him an αἰτία is anything that contributes to the decision of the individual (or individuals) responsible to make war. The πρόφασις[11] or 'pretext' is whatever is alleged—apparently on either side—as the reason for making war, whether true or not; and the ἀρχή is the first action of the war itself. Clearly this formula is more mechanical and more superficial than that of Thucydides. In the first place the αἰτίαι, though they eventually lead to decisions, are in themselves something external to these; they are 'the events that shape in advance our purposes and decisions', but they do not include these, as some scholars have mistakenly assumed.[12] These formative events are often plain historical facts,[13] the march of the 10,000 or Agesilaus' expedition in Asia,[14] which persuaded the Greeks and Philip II that Persia was vulnerable. But they can also include states of mind, for example the anger of the Aetolians,[15] which Polybius regards as an αἰτία of the war between Rome and Antiochus, or the wrath of Hamilcar Barca,[16] which was the first cause of the Hannibalic War—the other two being the Roman behaviour over Sardinia,[17] and the success of the Carthaginians in Spain, which gave them

---

[8] iii. 6. 1 f.   [9] Thucyd. i. 23. 6.

[10] Cf. L. Pearson, 'Prophasis and aitia', *TAPA*, 83 (1952), 205–23.

[11] Viewed objectively, this is sometimes called the ἀφορμή, 'jumping off point'; cf. iv. 13. 6, where Polybius mentions the αἰτία, ἀφορμή and ἀρχή of the Social War. See Pédech, *Méthode*, 91; Petzold, *Studien*, 139.

[12] iii. 6. 7, αἰτίας δὲ (sc. εἶναί φημι) τὰς προκαθηγουμένας τῶν κρίσεων καὶ διαλήψεων, where τὰς προκαθηγουμένας is attracted into the gender of αἰτίας. The phrase is taken differently by Pédech, *Méthode*, 78–9, who makes τῶν κρίσεων καὶ διαλήψεων a partitive genitive and translates 'les antécédents en matière de jugements et réflexions' or 'jugements et conceptions préalables'; this leads him to regard κρίσεις and διαλήψεις themselves as causes and so to make Polybius' theory of causality far more of an intellectual affair than it really was (cf. his *Polybe i*, p. xxiv, 'les causes sont toujours des opérations intellectuelles'). See my remarks in *CR*, 16 (1966), 38 and the useful comments of Petzold, *Studien*, 11 n. 1.

[13] Cf. Momigliano, 'Some observations on causes of war in ancient historiography', *Secondo contributo*, 20.   [14] iii. 6. 10–11.

[15] iii. 7. 1.   [16] iii. 9. 6.

[17] iii. 10. 4.

confidence to embark on a second war with Rome.[18] But in this there is no notion of causes operating at a deeper level. It is all shallow and rational. 'While Thucydides is too vague', Momigliano remarks,[19] 'Polybius is too simple.'

The scheme I have just described is not easily adapted to explaining anything else but wars; and in fact it is not always applied to them. In a recent study of the προκατασκευή, that is the introduction to the *Histories* contained in books i and ii, Petzold has drawn attention[20] to Polybius' emphasis on causality in this part of his work, and his concern 'to leave no possible obscurity in his account of the causes'.[21] But notwithstanding this stress on causation, the scheme involving αἰτίαι, πρόφασις and ἀρχή is not applied to the First Punic War or the war between Achaea and Cleomenes III of Sparta. Not is it systematically adduced for all the wars in the main part of the *Histories*; it is for example only incidentally[22] that we learn of the Aetolian pretext for fighting Achaea and Macedonia in the First Macedonian War, and then only through the mouth of a neutral envoy. In one place[23] Polybius seems to have his causal scheme in mind when analysing the Roman constitution, since, he says, the character of the constitution is the chief cause, or αἰτία of political success or failure—presumably because this above all shapes in advance the decisions of those living under it; but clearly the full scheme of αἰτία, πρόφασις and ἀρχή cannot easily be applied to the solution of such a general problem as 'Why were the Romans politically successful?' That is why, when he is discussing the reasons for Achaean success in book ii,[24] Polybius points to the remarkable democracy of the confederation as an αἰτία, but makes no attempt to apply his causal scheme in detail.

The scheme has a further disadvantage. Not only is it limited to the context of explaining wars, but it is rigid and unilateral even in its application to them. The definition of αἰτίαι as whatever helps to shape decisions in advance means that, before he can apply the scheme, the historian has to decide who took the decisions; and implicitly this means branding one party as responsible for the war,

---

[18] iii. 10. 6.

[19] Art. cit. (p. 158 n. 13), 20.   [20] Petzold, *Studien*, 17.

[21] i. 12. 6, τοῦ μηδὲν ἀπόρημα καταλιπεῖν ὑπὲρ τῶν κατὰ τὰς αἰτίας ἀποδείξεων.

[22] xi. 5. 1, 4; it was nominally to free the Greeks from Philip, according to the speaker (a certain Thrasycrates, according to a marginal gloss).

[23] vi. 2. 8–10.   [24] ii. 38. 5.

whereas in reality many wars are the result of a gradual build-up of hostile feeling and will to war on both sides. There is some indication of this dilemma in the discussion of the causes of the Roman war against Perseus,[25] where the responsibility is laid at the door of the previous king, Philip V, who 'first conceived the notion of entering on the last war against Rome and had prepared everything for the purpose',[26] yet the pretexts (προφάσεις) to which Polybius refers—Perseus' expulsion of Abrupolis from his kingdom in Thrace, his invasion of Dolopia, and his journey to Delphi—are all such as the Romans, not Perseus, would allege as reasons for making war. True, Polybius nowhere says that the προφάσεις can only be alleged by the party guilty of the war: but it is more than a little odd that in this case all three προφάσεις are such as one would expect to find in a war in which the Romans took the initiative. Some of our difficulties might disappear if we possessed Polybius' text in a fuller form; but equally they might well increase. What, for example, should we make of the Sixth Syrian War, for which we have to fall back on accounts in later authors[27] who derive from Polybius? According to Livy,[28] not only was Antiochus IV threatening Egypt and planning to use Coele-Syria as an excuse, but the tutors of Ptolemy VI were preparing for war against Antiochus, also alleging Coele-Syria as a reason. This looks very much like a war for which both sides were responsible; and, indeed, why not? But in that case it is not easy to see how Polybius can have applied his scheme of αἰτίαι, ἀρχαί and προφάσεις to account for it.[29]

2.

I have spent a little time on this question of causality, because it is relevant when we turn to Polybius' views on how Rome gained her empire during the years covered by his *Histories*. The Hannibalic War marked an important stage in that enterprise; and

[25] xxii. 18; cf. Pédech, *Méthode*, 123–40.

[26] xxii. 18. 10.

[27] The only surviving fragments are xxvii. 19–20; xxviii. 1, 18–23; xxix. 23–7. Otherwise his account can only be recovered through Livy (xlii. 6. 4–12, 29; xlv. 11–12. 8), Diodorus (xxix. 29, 32; xxx. 2, 14–18; xxxi. 1–2), Porphyry (Hier. *Dan.* xi. 21–45 = *FGH*, 260 F 49–56) and Josephus (*BJ*, i. 1; *AJ*, xii. 4. 11–5. 3). See Pédech, *Méthode*, 147–8.

[28] Livy, xlii. 29. 5–7.

[29] Pédech, *Méthode*, 147 ff., tries to work out a scheme, but he does not face the difficulties raised by this over-motivated war.

although in one passage in book iii[30] he seems to suggest that it was her victory in that war that caused Rome to conceive an ambition to rule the world (τῆς τῶν ὅλων ἐπιβολῆς), it is clear from several other passages[31] that the war with Hannibal was itself already the first step in such a plan. In fact, the clash with the Carthaginians followed a period of expansion in Italy from the time of the truce made with the Gauls in 387 B.C.,[32] an event which Polybius takes as the starting point for his introductory account in books i and ii, and as the beginning of Roman growth (οἷον ἀρχὴν τῆς συναυξήσεως). Indeed having defeated the Latins, Etruscans, Celts and Samnites, the Romans 'now for the first time attacked the rest of Italy, not as if it were a foreign country, but as if it right-fully belonged to them'.[33]

Polybius does not trace the causes behind each of these wars, for they lay well outside his main *Histories*; but they are clearly regarded as forming the pattern of expansion which later brought Rome into conflict with Carthage, the state with which she was eventually to dispute the empire over the world.[34] To understand that conflict meant understanding first what were the policies and secondly what were the material resources on which the Romans relied (ποίοις διαβουλίοις ἢ ποίαις δυνάμεσι καὶ χορηγίαις χρησά-μενοι).[35] Although it was alarm at seeing the Carthaginians masters of the island and in occupation of Messana, a convenient base against Italy, that first tempted the Romans into Sicily,[36] only the capture of Agrigentum led them to enlarge their aims and seek to possess the whole island;[37] and the experience of the First Punic War and their victory in it gave the Romans both the courage to aim at universal dominion and the ability to achieve it. If Polybius does not actually say that the Romans conceived this aim immediately after the victory of 241,[38] he certainly implies that there was a continuous process and pattern leading forward from the conquest of Italy to the intervention in Sicily; and elsewhere, in book vi,[39] the conquest of Italy is linked closely with the conquest of the whole world.

It was the Gallic Wars, which Polybius describes at some

[30] iii. 2. 6.
[31] i. 3. 6; xv. 9. 2, 10. 2.
[32] i. 6. 3.
[33] i. 6. 6.
[34] i. 3. 7.
[35] i. 3. 9.
[36] i. 10. 5–9.
[37] i. 20. 1–2.
[38] So, correctly, Petzold, *Studien*, 175 n. 4.
[39] vi. 50. 6.

length,[40] that had given the Romans the psychological and the military schooling for their clash with Pyrrhus and, later, with Carthage.[41] When, in 232, C. Flaminius proposed dividing up the *ager Gallicus*, the Gauls concluded that the Romans were no longer concerned merely with sovereignty over them, but were intending to exterminate them completely[42]—a policy which the Romans did indeed adopt after their victory at Telamon.[43] This stepping up of aims reminds us of the changes of objective in Sicily which Polybius attributed to the Romans after their seizure of Agrigentum,[44] and though in either case the charge is psychologically credible, it may well be, as Heuss has suggested, that Polybius is here giving a rationalized interpretation of Roman expansion in terms of how men are apt to behave.

Such an interpretation might well see each episode as growing out of the one before, and contributing cumulatively to a single overall pattern of expansion; and this is precisely the pattern which Polybius formulates in a passage in book iii.[45] 'I regard the war with Antiochus', he writes, 'as deriving its origin from that with Philip, the latter as resulting from that with Hannibal, and the Hannibalic War as a consequence of that for Sicily, the intermediate events, however many and various their character, all tending to the same purpose.' Behind this pattern lies the conscious aim at world dominion.[46] When Polybius discusses the treatment of Syracuse after the suppression of its revolt during the Hannibalic War, he justifies the seizure of gold and silver by the Romans because 'it was impossible for them to aim at world empire with-

[40] ii. 14–35.   [41] ii. 20. 8–10.
[42] ii. 21. 9.   [43] ii. 31. 8.
[44] i. 20. 1–2; on this see A. Heuss, 'Der erste punische Krieg und das Problem des römischen Imperialismus', *Hist. Zeitsch.* 169 (1949–50), 487–8.
[45] iii. 32. 7.
[46] Pédech, *Polybe i*, p. xvii, argues that Polybius 'ne prête pas aux Romains un plan de conquête conçu et réalisé par tranches successives; il ne considère pas davantage leurs conquêtes comme l'effet d'une force se développant d'elle-même par un dynamisme interne. Elles seraient plutôt de l'ordre logique et s'appelleraient les unes les autres comme les diverses propositions d'un sorite ou comme un étage d'une maison appelle l'étage suivant.' I do not wholly follow this. The second storey of a building only appears on the first storey because someone decides to put it there; and surely the view that the stages in the Roman world-conquest are related to each other, in Polybius' view, only as a logical sequence cannot be reconciled with his references to the Romans *aiming* at world empire (e.g. iii. 2. 6, ἔννοιαν σχεῖν τῆς τῶν ὅλων ἐπιβολῆς; ix. 10. 11).

out weakening the resources of other peoples and strengthening their own'.[47] It follows that in his view they had already conceived such an aim.

Earlier I referred to the role which Polybius attributed to *Tyche*, Fortune, and the difficulty of reconciling the concept of Roman world-dominion as the handiwork of Fortune with the idea that the Romans owed it to rational planning and the proper exploitation of their growing resources.[48] There is however yet another and perhaps more serious contradiction in Polybius' account of Roman imperialism. For the odd thing is that where we have his detailed narrative of the events leading up to the major wars which serve as stages in the progress of Rome to universal empire, the responsibility for the war seems invariably to rest with the other side. For the wars before 220 we cannot expect much detail, since in books i and ii Polybius is giving an introductory survey. But as we have seen, he is interested in causes and he goes into the events leading up to the First Punic War with some care, making it clear that the Senate was in no haste to accede to the Mamertine appeal, but carefully weighed the possible moral obloquy against the practical advantage, so that it was only in fact when the matter was referred to the people, and they responded to the consuls' appeal to their greed, that the decision was taken.[49] The First Illyrian War, which contributed greatly to the formation and growth of the Roman dominion,[50] was forced on Rome when the Queen Teuta, 'with a woman's shortness of view'—this feminine influence is a typical Hellenistic motif—set out on a career of piracy and plunder[51] which led to the robbing and killing of Italian traders,[52] and followed it up with the murder of Roman envoys.[53]

The Second Punic War emerges clearly as the handiwork of the Barca family,[54] who left Rome no alternative to avenging the

---

[47] ix. 10. 11.

[48] See above, pp. 60 ff.   [49] i. 10–11.

[50] ii. 2. 2, τὴν αὔξησιν καὶ κατασκευὴν τῆς Ῥωμαίων δυναστείας.

[51] ii. 4. 6 ff.; on this war see G. Walser, 'Die Ursachen des ersten römisch-illyrischen Krieges', *Historia*, 2 (1953/4), 316; Badian, 'Notes on Roman policy in Illyria (230–201 B.C.)', *Studies*, 1–33; N. G. L. Hammond, 'Illyris, Rome and Macedon, 229–205 B.C.', *JRS*, 58 (1968), 4 ff.; H. Dell, 'The origin and nature of Illyrian piracy', *Historia*, 16 (1967), 344–58; K.-E. Petzold, 'Rom und Illyrien', *Historia*, 20 (1971), 199–223.

[52] ii. 8. 2–3.   [53] ii. 8. 12–13.

[54] iii. 9. 6–10. 6.

attack on her ally Saguntum; and in any case the invasion of Italy by Hannibal clinched the matter. The First Macedonian War, too, was plainly forced on Rome by the compact between Philip V and Hannibal.[55] For the Second Macedonian War we are reduced to conjecture, since if Polybius analysed its causes, the passage has not survived. Bickerman has argued[56] that any such passage would necessarily have laid the responsibility at the door of the Romans; I doubt that very much, and can only say that if it were so, this would be the only major war between 264 and 172 for which Polybius did hold Rome responsible. For, as we saw, the war with Antiochus was due to the anger of the Aetolians,[57] and that against Perseus had already been planned long before by Philip.[58]

It can be shown that the picture of Rome as an aggressive imperial power with Machiavellian intentions was one commonly held in Greece; I have collected the evidence elsewhere and I will not repeat it here.[59] But there can be no doubt, I think, that Polybius' careful analysis of the causes of Rome's wars, at any rate down to the war with Antiochus, bears a closer relationship to Roman aims and policies than his schematic picture of a power advancing logically and forcibly from victory to victory. It is true that his detailed analysis of the events which in each case preceded the outbreak of war is probably influenced at points by the Roman theory of the just war,[60] which implied that Rome was never in any circumstances the aggressor; Polybius may have derived this doctrine in part from Fabius Pictor, and partly too from the milieu of the Aemilii and the Scipios with whom he was closely connected at Rome. Nevertheless, as Holleaux demonstrated convincingly over fifty years ago,[61] the realities of Roman foreign policy were far more uncertain and hesitating than contemporary Greeks believed. Holleaux's famous thesis, I need hardly say, has since been modified in several particulars;[62] we know more now about

---

[55] Cf. vii. 9; Livy, xxiii. 33–4.

[56] 'Bellum Philippicum: some Roman and Greek views concerning the causes of the Second Macedonian war', CP, 40 (1945), 137–48, especially 148.

[57] See above, p. 158 n. 15.   [58] See above, p. 160 n. 26.

[59] See Walbank, 'Polybius and Rome's eastern policy', JRS, 53 (1963), 1–12.

[60] Cf. Gelzer, 'Römische Politik bei Fabius Pictor', Kl. Schr. iii. 56 nn. 31, 91.

[61] Rome, la Grèce et les monarchies hellénistiques (Paris, 1921), passim.

[62] For a discussion of some of these see Walbank, 'Polybius and Rome's eastern policy', JRS, 53 (1963), 2–4.

early links between Italy and Greece, and we no longer see the Senate as quite so uniform in its ambitions and reactions as it appears in Holleaux's work. But his contention that down to the end of the third century Rome had no imperialist aims in the east still seems substantially sound; and more recently Badian has convincingly interpreted the war with Antiochus as the sequel to a cold war which erupted into a struggle unwanted by either side.[63] The later events—the war with Perseus and the developments down to the destruction of Carthage and Corinth in 146—present a somewhat different situation about which I shall say something more when I discuss Polybius' attitude towards Rome.[64]

The contradiction between Polybius' detailed narrative and his schematic interpretation of Rome as an expansionist power with imperial ambitions requires some explanation. There are, I would suggest, several factors involved.[65] In the first place, a Greek familiar with the details of his own history would be likely to assume that powerful states normally attempted to expand: as Thucydides makes the Athenians remark at Melos, 'of the gods we believe and of men we know that by a necessary law of their nature they rule wherever they can'.[66] Further, Polybius decided to write his account of the rise of Rome to world power after he came to Rome in 168; by then the earlier wars were well in the past. Rome was established in her position of dominance, and in retrospect the successive stages of her rise to power may have seemed far more inevitable than they in fact were at the time. But above all, I suspect that the real element of distortion lies in the concept of *Tyche* or Fortune, which plays so big a part in shaping the *Histories*. As we have already seen, Polybius' theory of *Tyche* is at variance with his emphasis on a rational analysis of motives and causes. By superimposing a general pattern on events, it creates the presumption that a process in which the Romans played the leading role, and from which they emerged as the ultimate beneficiaries, was one which they themselves had planned. In this way Polybius was perhaps led to postulate a development with a logical inevitability, which ignored the detailed analysis of events and the specific motives of those active in them. The result is a contradic-

[63] Cf. Badian, 'Rome and Antiochus: a study in cold war', *Studies*, 112–39.
[64] See below, pp. 166 ff.
[65] See on this Walbank, 'Polybius and Rome's eastern policy', *JRS*, 53 (1963), 11–13.   [66] Thucyd. v. 105. 2.

tion of which he does not himself appear to be aware; and it is one
for which the historian must be grateful, for it allows us to use the
detailed account of the relations between Rome and the other
states with far more confidence than we could do, had Polybius
attempted to force the evidence to match his schematic picture
of Roman imperial advance.

3.

Rome lies at the centre of Polybius' work. But this does not mean
that his attitude towards Rome remained unchanged throughout his
long life, or even throughout the years when he was composing his
Histories. To trace the changes in his views is not however a simple
matter, since we have to rely on his own testimony, and are in some
uncertainty about the dates at which various passages were composed. For example, the account of the escape of the Seleucid prince
Demetrius from Rome is generally assumed to have been written
in the form of a memorandum shortly after it happened, though it
appears in its appropriate place in book xxxi, which was composed
after 146;[67] and this suggests that it was Polybius' habit to make
such memoranda for future use. Whether upon incorporating
these in his *Histories* he might at the same time alter judgements
contained in them we cannot of course tell.

As we saw earlier,[68] Polybius was confronted with the problem
of Rome as an element in Achaean foreign policy from his early
youth. It seems clear that between 198 and 182, when Philopoemen
died, Polybius' father Lycortas,[69] and Polybius himself as he grew
older, were supporters of him rather than of Aristaenus. The
interesting comparison between the policies of the two men which
Polybius makes in book xxiv[70] ends with the conclusion that while
both were safe, that of Aristaenus was plausible (εὐσχήμων) and
that of Philopoemen was honourable (καλή); but that Aristaenus
got the reputation of being more well-disposed towards Rome.
The issue between them was precisely that of how best to cope
with a dominant power, nominally an ally. Aristaenus, we are told,

[67] xxxi. 11–15; see above, p. 9. For the importance of this passage as a
clue to Polybius' technique of composition see p. 9 n. 41 and the work by
Gelzer quoted there.

[68] See above, p. 7.

[69] Cf. Gelzer, 'Die Achaica im Geschichtswerk des Polybios', *Kl. Schr.* iii.
149–50; Errington, *Philopoemen*, passim; Deininger, 112–13.

[70] xxiv. 11–13; cf. Deininger, 109 ff.

went out of his way to anticipate and comply with Roman wishes, whereas Philopoemen collaborated within the strict conditions of the laws and the alliance, but refused to bend the terms of either. Polybius was probably only in his teens when Philopoemen died.[71] I think it can be assumed that whenever he actually wrote the passage, his judgement on Aristaenus and Philopoemen reflects the views with which he was familiar in the home and circle of Lycortas, and in this context it is perhaps worth recalling his comments[72] on the policy of Hiero of Syracuse, who had realised the importance of preserving Carthage. 'We should never', he says, 'contribute to the attainment by one state of a power so preponderant, that none dare dispute with it even for their acknowledged rights.' It has recently been suggested by Petzold,[73] however, that this comparison between the policies of Philopoemen and Aristaenus— which does not appear in Plutarch's *Life of Philopoemen* and therefore, it is argued, did not appear in Polybius' own *Life of Philopoemen*—represents a later insertion in the *Histories*, dating to a time when Polybius had become convinced of the importance of ethical factors in history. But this conclusion is not compelling, and that Polybius became interested in ethical criteria only in his later years seems to me to be a dubious hypothesis.

In 170/69 Polybius was hipparch of the Achaean confederation and found himself personally responsible to a high degree for the adoption of a correct policy towards Rome. His account of the events of that year, when the Romans were already making war on Perseus of Macedonia, survives only fragmentarily; but book xxviii[74] contains an interesting record of a discussion at an Achaean assembly immediately preceding Polybius' entry into office, in which Lycortas advocated a policy of neutrality, but Polybius more cautiously followed that of Archon, who had spoken in favour of a fuller measure of collaboration with the Romans. No doubt this represented a judgement of political tactics rather than any fundamental change in attitude towards Rome; but it certainly indicates that Polybius recognised that the Roman attitude towards the Greeks was hardening.

---

[71] Philopoemen died in spring 182 (Errington, *Philopoemen*, 241–5) and Polybius was born a little before 200 (see above, p. 6 n. 26).

[72] i. 83. 4.   [73] *Studien*, 49 n. 1.

[74] xxviii. 6–7; see now Pédech, 'Polybe hipparque de la confédération achéenne (170–169 av. J.-C.)', *LEC*, 37 (1969), 252–9.

With his deportation to Italy after the war Polybius' relationship to Rome was completely changed. It was no longer merely the dominant power seen from an Achaean perspective. It was his new home for sixteen years, and, after the establishment of a congenial relationship with the young Scipio Aemilianus, increasingly Rome became the background of his thought and very soon dominated his interest. It was now that he began his *Histories* and, as we have seen,[75] he wrote at least the first fifteen books and published a good many of them during his detention. But at the same time it is plain that he was carefully watching events, making memoranda, questioning visitors not only about what had happened during the years before Pydna, but also about contemporary issues and policies; and during this period his attitude towards Rome was gradually undergoing a change. Our evidence comes from the later books, xxx to xxxiii, which he wrote after 146, but clearly with the aid of the memoirs which he had made at the time.[76] It is largely from these books that we have to deduce Polybius' attitude towards Rome during the early years of his stay in Italy.

When one considers his position and the treatment he and his fellow Achaeans had received and continued to receive at the hands of the Senate, it would be surprising if his account of what was happening during those years was very favourable towards Rome; and it is not. Indeed books xxx to xxxiii, covering the years 167 to 153, furnish us with an almost unbroken run of cynical comments on Roman policy. Thus when King Eumenes of Pergamum sent his brother Attalus as envoy to Rome in 168/7, certain unnamed Romans tried to tamper with his loyalty;[77] and when the plot failed the Senate broke its promise to hand over Aenus and Maronea to Pergamum, and instead liberated those Thracian towns. A year later Prusias II of Bithynia (who had earlier greeted a Roman embassy dressed as a freedman) came to Rome and there behaved in an utterly abject fashion, prostrating himself at the Senate's door and addressing the senators as 'saviour-gods';[78] for this reason he was well received, thus demonstrating that servility paid dividends at Rome.

Shortly afterwards Eumenes himself arrived in Italy, but the Senate, embarrassed by this untimely visit by their former favourite, passed a decree debarring all kings from entering Rome, and sent

---

[75] See above, pp. 18–19.   [76] See above, pp. 74–5 with n. 37.
[77] xxx. 1–3.   [78] xxx. 18. 1–7.

a quaestor to Brundisium to usher him out of Italy.[79] In so humiliating him they hoped, says Polybius, to encourage the Galatians to attack him—perhaps an over-subtle interpretation of the Senate's policy, but clearly one believed in the circles Polybius frequented. The same winter an Athenian embassy arrived in Rome to ask for the cession of Delos, Lemnos and Haliartus.[80] Polybius (who did not like Athens)[81] denounces the claim to Haliartus as unjust and unworthy of the Athenians; but in recording the Senate's decision in their favour, he merely remarks that the transaction proved less advantageous to the Athenians than they had hoped. Clearly Polybius disapproved; but he leaves it open whether the Senate was being Machiavellian or the dupes of Athenian persuasiveness.

In 158/7 Ariarathes of Cappadocia came to Rome, and also his enemies Diogenes and Miltiades; these men were successful in gaining senatorial support since 'falsehood won the day without trouble'.[82] The suggestion is that the Senate were hoodwinked, just as they were on another occasion by the Seleucid envoy Heracleides,[83] who persuaded them to pass a *senatus consultum* in favour of Laodice and Alexander by means of charlatanry (ταῖς γοητείαις), and as Ti. Sempronius Gracchus had been in 167/6 when he was sent out to investigate the affairs of Syria.[84] But the Romans were not merely naïve. Sometimes they just did not care about justice. For instance, when in the late 150's the Prienians appealed to Rome about Ariarathes' demand that they should hand over to him the money deposited with them by Orophernes, the Romans paid no attention.[85] Worse still, on numerous occasions they let men like Charops of Epirus and Callicrates of Achaea persuade them not to allow the Greek exiles to return home.[86] In

---

[79] xxx. 19. 1–13.   [80] xxx. 20.

[81] See for example v. 106. 6–8, criticising her isolation from Ἑλληνικαὶ πράξεις (i.e. the Hellenic Symmachy) and her subservience to the kings; vi. 44 (criticism of the Athenian constitution: Athens is like a ship without a skipper). Polybius' dislike probably springs from a combination of irritating factors— radical democracy (in the fifth and in some degree the fourth centuries); hostility to Epaminondas and later Philip II; resistance to Aratus and refusal to join the Achaean confederation in the third century; and a reputation in the Hellenistic courts which still brought her more renown than that of Achaea.

[82] xxxii. 10.   [83] xxxiii. 18. 10 (153/2).

[84] xxx. 27, 30. 7–8.   [85] xxxiii. 6. 8.

[86] xxx. 32 (164); xxxii. 3. 14–17 (159); xxxiii. 1. 3–8, 3 (155), 14 (153); see above, p. 10 n. 45.

such cases blindness and carelessness had led the Romans to bad decisions; but frequently, as in the expulsion of Eumenes, Polybius explicitly attributes Machiavellian motives to the Senate.

4.

Thus in 164/3 Demetrius, who was a hostage at Rome, appealed to be restored to the Seleucid throne. The Senate rejected the appeal because, ὡς ἐμοὶ δοκεῖν, says Polybius, they preferred the youth and incapacity of Antiochus IV's son.[87] When, the next year, the younger Ptolemy came to Rome asking for a revision of the agreement between himself and his elder brother, the Senate agreed, since this matched their interests.[88] 'Many Roman decisions are now of this kind', Polybius comments; 'profiting by others' mistakes they effectively (πραγματικῶς) increase and build up their own power, simultaneously doing a favour and appearing to confer a benefit on the guilty party'. Self-interest was now usual in Roman decisions. In the many appeals from Carthage and Masinissa, the Carthaginians always came off second best, 'not because they had not right on their side, but because the judges were convinced that it was in their own interest to decide against them'.[89]

The same cynical attitude, this *nova sapientia*, as some of the more old-fashioned senators had recently styled it,[90] also appears in Roman declarations of war. In 157/6 war was declared on the Dalmatians. There were good grounds, but the real reason for the decision, according to Polybius, was that the Senate judged the time opportune, both because the army was growing slack after twelve years' peace (since Pydna) and because it was high time to resume activity in Illyria. By fighting the Dalmatians they hoped to frighten the Illyrians into submission. 'But to the world at large', says Polybius, 'they said it was because of the insult to their ambassadors.'[91] He interprets the preliminaries of the Third Punic War in the same way. The Romans, he says,[92] had long ago

---

[87] xxxi. 2. 1–7.   [88] xxxi. 10.   [89] xxxi. 21. 6.

[90] Livy, xlii. 47. 9; on this see Walbank, 'A note on the embassy of Q. Marcius Philippus, 172 B.C.', *JRS*, 31 (1941), 82–93; J. Briscoe, 'Q. Marcius Philippus and *nova sapientia*', *JRS*, 54 (1954), 66–77.   [91] xxxii. 13. 9.

[92] xxxvi. 2; in 2. 1 the phrase πάλαι δὲ τούτου κεκυρωμένου βεβαίως ἐν ταῖς ἑκάστων γνώμαις must mean that they had decided on war; cf. Walbank, 'Political morality and the friends of Scipio', *JRS*, 55 (1965), 6; Gelzer, 'Nasicas Widerspruch gegen die Zerstörung Karthagos', *Kl. Schr.* ii. 43 ff.

decided on their policy, but they were looking for a suitable occasion and a pretext that would appeal to foreign nations (πρόφασιν εὐσχήμονα πρὸς τοὺς ἐκτός)—for the Romans, he adds, paid great attention to this aspect, and rightly. He then quotes a saying of Demetrius of Phalerum that 'when a war seems to be just (δικαία ...εἶναι δοκοῦσα), it increases the profits of victory and reduces the evil results of failure, while if it is thought to be unjust, this has the opposite effect'. So strongly were the Romans convinced of this that their arguments about the effect on opinion abroad nearly made them refrain from going to war.[93]

In retailing all this, Polybius gives no indication of his own approval or disapproval. Clearly, in many instances he was personally involved, either because they concerned the Achaean exiles, or because they were in some way connected with the Aemilii; for example the splendid example of high principle set by the Romans on the occasion of the visit of the unspeakable Charops to Rome[94] was sparked off by the refusal of M. Aemilius Lepidus and L. Aemilius Paullus to let him enter their houses. But this does not necessarily mean that he condemned pragmatism in politics when he felt free to view an incident dispassionately. The *nova sapientia* of Q. Marcius Philippus who employed a piece of diplomatic sharp practice at the outset of the war with Perseus in order to steal a march on the king,[95] is condemned by the older senators, who remain mindful of *mos antiquus* and hark back to the moral standards of olden times. We are not entitled to assume that Polybius judged it in the same way.

In fact, it is by no means easy to be sure what Polybius' real views were about Machiavellianism in politics. But the importance of the question can be seen from the passage in book iii,[96] in which he gives his reasons for extending the *Histories* to cover the years from Pydna down to 146 B.C. The passage has already been

---

[93] Whether Polybius recorded the debate between Cato and Scipio Nasica on whether war should be declared on Carthage (cf. Livy, *per.* 48; App. *Lib.* 69; Plut. *Cato mai.* 27. 2; Diod. xxxiv. 33. 3; Flor. i. 31. 5) is not known; there is no reference to it in the surviving fragments, but these contain nothing inconsistent with Polybius' having mentioned it (cf. Gelzer, art. cit. (n. 92)). See also p. 4 n. 16 above. I am not convinced by the arguments of W. Hoffmann, 'Die römische Politik des 2. Jahrhunderts und das Ende Karthagos', *Historia*, 9 (1960), 340 ff., against the historicity of the famous debate. See also Astin, 48 ff., 270–81; 'Scipio Aemilianus and Cato Censorius', *Latomus*, 15 (1956), 159 f.   [94] xxxii. 6. 4 ff.

[95] See above, p. 170 n. 90.   [96] iii. 4. 1 f.

mentioned earlier:[97] the relevant words read as follows. 'If from their success or failure alone we could adequately judge how far states and individuals merit praise or blame, I could here bring my narrative to a close...in accordance with the plan set out at the beginning of my work...[98] But since judgements regarding either victors or vanquished based purely on the actual struggle are by no means final...I must append...an account of the subsequent policy of the conquerors and how they exercised their universal rule, as well as of the various opinions...entertained by the rest about their rulers, and finally I must describe what were the prevailing and dominant tendencies and ambitions of the various peoples in their private and public life...Contemporaries will thus be enabled to see clearly whether Roman rule is acceptable or not and future generations whether Roman government should be considered to have been worthy of praise and admiration or rather of blame.'

The rise of Rome to world-empire reflected a transcendental plan, the work of Fortune. But evidently this did not absolve the Romans from submitting their subsequent exercise of power to the judgement of present and future generations. In the circumstances his readers are naturally anxious to learn what was Polybius' verdict. Was he in the long run adverse or favourable to Rome? Obviously there was a problem and one very relevant to his contemporaries. From his own pages and from the Polybian parts of Livy one can easily assemble a long list of occasions from the time of the Hannibalic War onwards, when Greeks had accused Rome either of aggressive aims or of exploiting the supposed grievances of allies in order to further their imperial ambitions.[99] It has been argued[100] that in extending his *Histories* to cover the next two decades after Pydna Polybius was himself concerned to pass such moral judgements on Rome and to link them with the moral deterioration which appeared once the Romans became involved in wars overseas. Such a view seems to me over-simplified. First, as I have already observed, there is no reason to suppose that Polybius became especially sensitive to moral issues and moral

[97] See above, pp. 27 ff.

[98] iii. 4. 1, κατὰ τὴν ἐξ ἀρχῆς πρόθεσιν; on the meaning of this phrase (which refers back to i. 1. 5–6) see H. Erbse, 'Polybios-Interpretationen', *Phil.* 101 (1957), 227 ff. That plan involved going down only to Pydna.

[99] See the evidence which I have assembled in 'Political morality and the friends of Scipio', *JRS*, 55 (1965), 3.   [100] Cf. Petzold, *Studien*, 60 f.

deterioration only in his more advanced years. His criticism of Philip V and his discussion of the influence of Aratus, Apelles and Demetrius of Pharos[101] on him clearly show him alert to questions of morals at an early date; and his discussion of the Roman constitution in book vi lays full emphasis on ἔθη καὶ νόμιμα.[102] Equally he was aware from the time he came to Rome that there had been some moral decline in its people. He could hardly not have been. Cato's censorship in 184 had been celebrated by the erection of a temple of Salus with an inscription saying that 'when the Roman state was tottering to its fall, he was made censor and by helpful guidance, wise restraints and sound teaching restored it again'.[103] This moral restoration had however been incomplete; for almost twenty years later, about the time of Polybius' arrival in Rome, the virtue of the youthful Scipio Aemilianus was already something exceptional. No doubt Polybius exaggerates this in order to flatter his friend. But he records[104] that at this time most youths gave themselves up to paederasty or the company of prostitutes; they spent their time at concerts and dinner-parties and generally led lives of extravagance, paying a talent for a catamite and 300 drachmas for a jar of caviare. Scipio by contrast possessed the moral virtues: moderation, generosity, financial integrity, and courage[105]—which was what a state needed both to keep its political stability in the face of internal or outside threats, and to build an empire.[106] Without these qualities in its citizens a state would be in peril, and that is largely the reason Polybius condemns immorality. But clearly these moral shortcomings were not new, nor had they necessarily any connection in his eyes with the use of Machiavellian policies by an imperial state.

5.

Polybius' extension of his *Histories* covered the years 168 to 146/5, but he divides it into two parts. 'The final end achieved by my history', he writes,[107] 'will be to learn what was the condition of each people after the struggle for supremacy was over and all

---

[101] See above, p. 157 n. 3.

[102] See my *Commentary*, i. 733 on vi. 47. 1–6; above, pp. 147 (with n. 110), 153–4 (with n. 145).

[103] Plut. *Cato mai.* 19. 3; see my *Commentary*, i. 647–8.

[104] xxxi. 25. 3.   [105] xxxi. 25. 2, 25. 9, 29. 1.

[106] Cf. vi. 50. 3–6, 56. 1–5; and book vi passim.

[107] iii. 4. 12–13.

had fallen under the domination of Rome, down to the disturbed and troubled time that afterwards ensued. About this latter...I was induced to write as if starting on a new work, both because of the importance of the actions and the unexpected character of the events which it contained, and also because I not only witnessed most of these but also took part in or actually directed others.' This fresh start applies, not to the period after 168/7, as some scholars have thought,[108] but only to the years of 'confusion and disturbance'; and, as I have already observed,[109] although the line of demarcation is somewhat confused, it seems to come more or less around the year 152/1, where the geographical survey of book xxxiv interrupts the narrative. Read strictly, Polybius seems to suggest that it is the period from 167 to 152 that is to facilitate judgements on victors and vanquished by contemporaries and later generations.[110] But in practice the two periods are not clearly demarcated, either chronologically—as we saw earlier—nor in the function assigned to them, since the most extended and elaborate discussion of Roman policy (in the surviving fragments) is introduced in connection with the Third Punic War,[111] which falls in the later period. It may be useful to consider this discussion in some detail.

Four arguments are recorded.[112] The first defends the Roman destruction of Carthage as a wise and statesmanlike act in defence of the Empire. Carthage had been a constant menace, had frequently disputed Roman hegemony and might do so again. To secure one's own rule, one's ἀρχή, was the act of sensible men who took the long view.[113] A second group argued on the contrary that hitherto it had been Roman policy to fight only until their opponents submitted and agreed to obey; this new policy, which had just made itself apparent in the elimination of the Macedonian kingdom, was one of annihilation—and that despite the readiness of Carthage to accept all the conditions laid upon her. In thus

---

[108] Most recently Petzold, *Studien*, 55 n. 4; but see also R. Thommen, 'Über die Abfassungszeit der Geschichten des Polybios', *Hermes*, 20 (1885), 199; Susemihl, ii. 108 n. 104.

[109] See above, pp. 29–30; 'Political morality and the friends of Scipio', *JRS*, 55 (1965), 4.   [110] Cf. iii. 4. 12.

[111] xxxvi. 9.

[112] I take the ἔνιοι of 9. 13 to be a subdivision of those mentioned in 9. 11: otherwise one would have to speak of five views.

[113] xxxvi. 9. 3–4.

following in the footsteps of Athens and Sparta Rome was likely to end as they had ended—and by this Polybius means, I think, as a tyrant city.[114] The third view is really a variant on the second, and virtually too an echo of the criticism levelled against Q. Marcius Philippus by the older senators.[115] The ancient Romans had excluded all kinds of deceit and sharp practice from the declaring and waging of war; but both had been used against Carthage in a manner which could only be characterised as impiety and treachery (ἀσέβημα καὶ παρασπόνδημα). This line of attack is one that sets the Roman action against Rome's own professed policy and the background of the *iustum bellum*; Polybius develops it at some length so that it occupies sixteen lines in his text.[116]

The reply, put into the mouths of a fourth group, is allowed just over thirty lines, thus indicating the seriousness of the charge and also, I suggest, where Polybius' own sympathies lay. To the moral charge the defenders of Rome reply with arguments based on legal definitions. Because the Carthaginians had made an act of *deditio*, they had surrendered every right to challenge Roman orders; thus there could be no question of impiety or treachery. The definition of the two words ἀσέβημα and παρασπόνδημα is then analysed, and it is shown that the Romans had not committed any act which fell under either head. On the contrary, it was the Carthaginians who had committed a παρασπόνδημα when they broke the terms of their treaty and attacked Masinissa. The Romans had then accepted their submission and had resorted to

[114] xxxvi. 9. 5–8; but, as Hoffmann, 'Die römische Politik des 2. Jahrhunderts und das Ende Karthagos', *Historia*, 9 (1960), 311 ff., points out, neither Athens nor Sparta maintained her empire for long—that of Sparta lasted only twelve years (Polyb. i. 2. 3)—so he may also be thinking of this.

[115] In xiii. 3, an attack on Philip V for treacherous behaviour in making war (κακοπραγμοσύνη), Polybius contrasts οἱ ἀρχαῖοι, who even avoided using ἐκήβολα, weapons thrown through the air, and the laying of ambushes, and always declared war and announced their intention to fight a battle. He speaks approvingly of such traces of this behaviour as survived among the Romans, in contrast to the excessive (ὑπὲρ τὸ δέον) use of treacherous methods then generally prevalent; and Livy, xlii. 47, seems to derive from a similar passage, now lost, in book xxvii, in which 'veteres et moris antiqui memores' complain that the Romans have lapsed from these principles in their dealings with Perseus. However, Polybius' whole-hearted admiration for the burning of the Punic camps by Scipio Africanus (xiv. 4–5) is not easily reconciled with the comments in xiii. 3. It is perhaps not irrelevant that, as in the fall of Carthage in 146, it was a Scipio who was concerned.   [116] xxxvi. 9. 9–11.

force only when the Carthaginians declined their orders.[117] From this argument the intangibles—the long series of adverse decisions, the Numidian provocation, the atmosphere in which Carthage was led to take a false step and then buoyed up with illusory hopes of generous treatment—are all left out; and thanks to their omission the Romans are placed in a logically impregnable position.

It must have been along these lines that the supporters of a harsh policy towards Carthage countered the charge that her destruction had been organised in a way discreditable to Rome's reputation as a state founded on moral principles. This harsh policy was advocated and implemented by Scipio Aemilianus, and it is hard to believe that Polybius, who followed its execution from headquarters, did not sympathise with it. The fall of Carthage was one of the events which he describes as constituting the time of disturbance and trouble, ταραχὴ καὶ κίνησις; others were the Spanish war, where Aemilianus had had to set an example of patriotism to the demoralised youth of Rome,[118] the revolt of the pretender Andriscus in Macedonia, and the Achaean War. These events are παράδοξα; policy no longer obeys the rule of reason. Thus in Macedonia the story of Andriscus, the false Philip, seems at first sight quite unbelievable (οὐδ' ἀνεκτός).[119] This 'Philip fallen from the sky' (ἀεροπετὴς Φίλιππος) quite incredibly and irrationally won victory after victory; and the Macedonians, after being well treated at the hands of Rome, which had brought them, as all confessed, freedom instead of slavery[120] and put an end to internal conflicts, now rushed to fight for an impostor who exiled, tortured and murdered them in large numbers. In this situation one could only speak of a heaven-sent infatuation (δαιμονο-βλάβεια).[121]

The Greek disaster is discussed in similar terms.[122] This was a catastrophe both universal and discreditable, with none of the

[117] xxxvi. 9. 12–17.
[118] xxxv. 4. 7–14; this was in 151. The war had broken out in 154 (cf. xxxv. 1. 1–6, which should more correctly stand in book xxxiii; see above, pp. 124–5 n. 147).   [119] xxxvi. 10.
[120] On the attitude in Macedonia see P. McKay, 'The coinage of Macedonian republics, 168–146 B.C.', Ancient Macedonia, 258–64, who argues that the settlement of 167 was successful and popular, and revolts rare.
[121] xxxvi. 17. 12–15.
[122] On the Achaean War see J. Deininger, 220–38; RE, Suppl.-B. xi, 'Diaios', cols. 521–6; 'Kritolaos und die Eröffnung des achaischen Krieges', Phil. 113 (1969), 287–91. A. Fuks, 'The Bellum Achaicum and its social aspect',

redeeming features which in the case of earlier Greek disasters had justified feelings of consolation and pride; in this almost unprecedented misfortune 'the whole country was visited by an unparalleled attack of insanity, with people flinging themselves into wells and over precipices'.[123] Such was men's behaviour and to such an extent was everyone a victim of madness and demoralised confusion, of a kind scarcely to be encountered among barbarians, that one could only attribute the fact that Greece did ultimately emerge to the successful intervention of some kind of resourceful and ingenious fortune. The parallel with Macedon hits one in the eyes. Madness and infatuation are the terms used to describe policies Polybius could neither approve nor understand; for he was, by then, an active and interested party. As it happened, the change in the character of events around 152 had coincided with a change in the character of his own fortunes. On the one hand a long period of minor conflicts and diplomatic manoeuvres had suddenly burst out into violent warfare in Spain, Macedonia, Greece and Africa; and simultaneously, sixteen years' enforced detention, devoted to historical composition, now gave way for Polybius to a time of long journeys by land and sea, participation in wars alongside Scipio, and eventually an influential and even decisive role in the settlement of Achaea—this perhaps one of the more important achievements of that 'resourceful and ingenious fortune'!

It is not surprising therefore that Polybius speaks of beginning his account of those years 'as if starting on a new work', nor that the somewhat cynical and detached comments on Roman policy, recorded in the memoranda which he made between 168 and 153, and still to be read in his account of those years, now gave way to comments more violent and more partisan.

Indeed the violence of Polybius' remarks about the enemies of Rome at this time is most striking and perhaps deserving of a little

JHS, 90 (1970), 78–89, argues that despite Polybius' attack on the leaders, the war was widely supported and a genuine national rising. This is, I believe, true. Deininger also regards it as a movement of the πλῆθος against Rome, and although Fuks shows that the economic measures taken were equivalent to a moratorium on debts rather than (as has often been alleged) their cancellation, such a moratorium, along with the liberation of slaves, must have appeared to the richer class as part of the much feared revolutionary programme—which is no doubt one reason why Polybius is so hostile towards the movement and its supporters.   [123] xxxviii. 16. 7.

attention. Thus the followers of Diaeus and Critolaus in Achaea are the 'worst men from each city, the most god-forsaken and the greatest corruptors of the nation'.[124] At Carthage Hasdrubal is a vacuous braggart wholly lacking in the qualities of a statesman or a soldier; Polybius despises him for his folly in failing to realise that Carthage was finished, and he goes out of his way to describe his unlovely appearance—his large paunch and face red from ill-timed feasting at the height of his country's ordeal.[125] There is an element of ruthlessness in Polybius at all times: he has little sympathy for those who choose the wrong course.

The *Histories*, which tell of the world power of Rome, constitute a 'success-story'; and Polybius is apt to identify success with moral worth. For him politics is a dangerous game—no doubt it always was in Greece—and if, like those Greeks who made the mistake of backing Perseus, you lost, then the proper course was to accept the situation and perish bravely;[126] no one, he observes, could approve men like the brothers Hippocritus and Hippomedon of Cos, or Deinon and Polyaratus of Rhodes, who were known to have done all they could to help Perseus, and yet could not bring themselves to commit suicide—thus leaving to posterity not the slightest ground for pitying or pardoning them. A general who stakes all on victory but fails and then cannot make up his mind to die on the field—as Hasdrubal did so admirably at the Metaurus[127]—adds disgrace and shame to disaster. In his account of the capture of Abydus by Philip V, Polybius recounts the oath of the citizens, to slaughter all the women and children and die fighting; he then goes on to tell how after the most appalling scenes of carnage two leaders called together a few of the older men and 'sacrificed in the hopes of personal advantage all that was splendid and praise-worthy in the resolution of the citizens by deciding to save the women and children alive and to send out...the priests and priest-esses to Philip to beg for mercy and surrender the city to him'.[128]

These examples clearly illustrate the general temper of Polybius' mind, ruthless, hard and realistic. But in his account of the events of 152 to 146 there is a violence and an emotion in his comments on those who opposed the Roman cause, which perhaps suggests some basic uneasiness. For if, as seems likely, he accepted the

---

[124] xxxviii. 10. 8.   [125] xxxviii. 7. 1, 20.
[126] xxx. 7. 2–4.   [127] xi. 2. 1–11.
[128] xvi. 31–3.

Roman case over Carthage—and in view of his relations with Aemilianus the alternative is barely credible,[129] then it seems likely too that he also accepted the 'new diplomacy' and all that it implied, as the legitimate instrument of an imperially-minded state; and what it implied was, in the last resort, the elimination of dangerous or intransigent enemies. It has been convincingly argued by Gelzer that this view finds support in a passage of Diodorus xxxii,[130] almost certainly derived from Polybius, which asserts that 'those whose object is to attain hegemony over others use courage and intelligence to get it, moderation and considera-tion for others to extend it widely, and paralysing terror to secure it against attack'. Two chapters later Diodorus illustrates this doctrine from Macedonian and Roman history, and from the latter he points to the razing of Corinth, the rooting out of Perseus of Macedonia and the destruction of Carthage and Numantia. The fall of Numantia was not of course included in Polybius' *Histories*; but it can easily have been added by Diodorus,[131] if he remembered that just as his father Aemilius Paullus had crushed Perseus (and carried out a policy of terrorism in Epirus) so too Scipio Aemilianus himself had been the executioner of both Car-thage and Numantia—the latter on his own initiative without waiting for the decision of the Senate. Polybius had himself dealt with that operation in his Numantine monograph.[132] The destruc-tion of Corinth had indeed nothing to do with Scipio,[133] but it was the sequel to a policy in Achaea which Polybius condemns in violent terms, and the prelude to the period of reconstruction which redounded so greatly to his own credit.

If Gelzer's hypothesis is correct, it would seem that when Polybius set about writing the extension to his *Histories* at some un-

[129] Contra Petzold, *Studien*, 62–3, who seems to identify the Greek criticism of Rome in xxxvi. 9. 5–8, with Polybius' own judgement; on this see below, pp. 180 f.

[130] Diod. xxxii. 2 and 4; on this passage see Gelzer, 'Nasicas Widerspruch gegen die Zerstörung Carthagos', *Kl. Schr.* ii. 64 ff.; F. E. Adcock,' Delenda est Carthago', *CHJ*, 8 (1946), 127–8; A. E. Astin, *Scipio*, 280–1; 'Scipio Aemilianus and Cato Censorius', *Latomus*, 15 (1956), 180; H. Strasburger, 'Poseidonius on the problems of the Roman Empire', *JRS*, 55 (1965), 46 n. 58.

[131] Or even by Polybius himself after 133; but it is likely that the *Histories* were substantially complete by then (see above, p. 22).

[132] Cicero, *fam.* v. 12. 2; see above, p. 12 n. 60, p. 15 n. 74.

[133] On the hostility between Q. Caecilius Metellus Macedonicus, a political associate of Scipio, and L. Mummius, see Astin, *Scipio*, 73–4.

known date after 145, using the material which he had sedulously
collected while in Rome and drawing on his own first-hand
experience for the years of disturbance following 152, he suffered
some embarrassment in reconciling his earlier views with his later.
In accepting a Roman policy which was realistically directed to
maintaining the empire, he was in fact going back on opinions
which he had already expressed in the earlier part of his work.
I have sketched the different points of view which Polybius mentions in connection with the Third Punic War.[134] The second group
of those mentioned had argued that the danger of Rome's becoming
a tyrant city was illustrated by her policy of annihilating first
Perseus' kingdom and then Carthage.[135] They were in fact appeal-
ing to a tradition which had in the past been widely approved at
Rome. Thus Flamininus, at the conference after Cynoscephalae,
had asserted[136] that the Romans never exterminated their adver-
saries after a single war,[137] and brave men ought to be tough in
battle, if beaten courageous and high-minded, and if victorious
moderate, gentle and humane. Moreover Polybius, speaking in
his own person in an earlier book,[138] following the death of the two
Scipios in Spain remarks that the Carthaginians made the mistake
of treating the Spaniards in an overbearing manner, imagining
'that there is one method by which power should be acquired and
another by which it should be maintained; they had not learnt
that those who preserve their supremacy best are those who adhere
to the same principles by which they originally established it'.

Polybius could in fact claim some justification for his change of
front. In the case of the Spaniards humane treatment is advocated
on utilitarian grounds; if an imperial power intends to go on
governing a defeated people—as the Romans had done in Italy
and proposed now to do in Spain—a generous policy of *parcere
subiectis* would yield the best results. But there was an alternative,
no less logical—the one employed at Carthage and Numantia.
If the criterion to be invoked was utility, the policy of extermina-
tion where feasible might prove no less efficacious, and involve
fewer risks. The reply of the second group of Rome's critics had
been based, however, not on utility but on ethical grounds: to wipe

[134] See above, pp. 174–6.   [135] xxxvi. 9. 5–8.
[136] xviii. 37. 2, 37. 7.
[137] In the case of Carthage it was of course the third war.
[138] x. 36. 2 f.

out a defeated enemy was to behave like a tyrant, and to behave like a tyrant was wrong. Earlier, Polybius had said the same. In phrases which are, it is true, somewhat rhetorical, and reminiscent of those of the sophists, he had condemned Philip V's destruction of the Aetolian centre at Thermum[139] during the Social War on the grounds that 'good men should not make war on wrongdoers with the object of destroying and exterminating them, but with that of correcting and reforming their errors'. Clearly this worthy and sententious observation was not easily reconciled with the realities of imperial policy at Carthage seventy years later.

6.

The ambiguity which thus appears in Polybius' attitude towards Roman policy during the two decades after Pydna has yet a further aspect. As I have already mentioned,[140] in summarising his reasons for extending his *Histories* to cover this period, Polybius invites his readers to draw conclusions on whether Roman rule is acceptable or not, and whether deserving of praise or blame. The implication of this remark is novel. The criterion invoked is that of the subject peoples of the empire—and if one bears in mind that when he propounded it Polybius was writing as a Greek, once more established in his home at Megalopolis, it is not perhaps a wholly strange one. But it carried with it other more searching questions. What in fact is the end of imperial action? What further test of empire can there be beyond the subjection of states and the preservation in safety of what has been won?

The strange thing is that Polybius propounds this problem but never makes any attempt to answer it.[141] If I am right, the contradiction between his detached attitude towards Roman policy during the years of his detention and his committed policy during the years of ταραχή καὶ κίνησις which follow will go a long way towards explaining his apparently objective account of the various Greek views of the rights and wrongs of Roman policy at Carthage —so objective in fact that readers can still disagree about what his own opinions were. But it is that same swing over to the Roman point of view which prevents him from developing any theory of

[139] v. 11. 5; see my *Commentary*, i. 549 ad loc.
[140] Above, pp. 171–2.
[141] Cf. Strasburger, 'Poseidonius on problems of the Roman empire', *JRS*, 55 (1965), 46, 'a development of this theme is not to be found anywhere in the surviving part of his work'.

imperial justification based on the advantage or disadvantage of the ruled. To the question he has raised Polybius has no answer. One was given later, and we can find it adumbrated in the *de republica*, where Cicero puts it in the mouth of C. Laelius;[142] St Augustine later discusses it in the *De Civitate Dei*.[143] Briefly that answer was that imperial rule is justifiable, as is the rule of god over man, the mind over the body, reason over passion; it follows a universal law equally beneficial to rulers and ruled. This doctrine has been attributed to Panaetius;[144] but Strasburger has exposed the fragility of that view,[145] in an important discussion of Poseidonius, who certainly made some contributions to its development. However, this does not concern us here. The point is that Polybius himself goes no further than generalities.

7.

Polybius' last ten books thus furnish a curious contrast to the parts of his *Histories* which belong to the original plan. In those he has a clear thesis to propound and to explain, and he does so with a fair degree of success. 'How and thanks to what kind of constitution Rome became the ruler of the world' is the question— and the *Histories* provide a systematic answer. But for the last ten books the question has become 'Was Roman rule acceptable?', and to this question there is no clear answer and indeeed no attempt to work out what an acceptable criterion of empire should be. The contrast is so striking that one is led to wonder if the purpose which Polybius alleges for adding two decades to his *Histories* is really the true one. If one considers his position after he had returned to Greece in 145, one may be led to a different conclusion. His main work was perhaps still to be finished—as we saw,[146] we cannot be sure that he had written beyond book xv while at Rome—and this he would no doubt now complete. But he had in addition a mass of material assembled at Rome covering

[142] Cicero, *rep*. iii. 33–41, especially 36.

[143] *Civ. Dei*, xix. 21.

[144] See W. Capelle, 'Griechische Ethik und römischer Imperialismus', *Klio*, 25 (1932), 86–113; it was thought that Panaetius put it forward in a work on politics mentioned by Cicero, *leg*. iii. 14. Earlier I accepted this view ('Political morality and the friends of Scipio', *JRS*, 55 (1965), 13–14), but Strasburger's arguments against it seem cogent.

[145] Strasburger, 'Poseidonius on problems of the Roman empire', *JRS*, 55 (1965), 40–53.

[146] See above, p. 19.

the years after 168 and he had—what was more important—a personal story to tell of his voyages and political activity from 151 to 146. He could have turned this story into a monograph, like the later *Numantine War*, for it was, as he says, virtually a separate work.[147] But in that case he would have had to jettison the material assembled during the years 167 to 152. In the event he decided on a simple solution—to add a new section to his universal history; but having decided on this, he had to justify it.

What I am suggesting is that Polybius wrote his main *Histories* under the stimulus of an idea, but that he wrote the last ten books mainly because he had material to hand and a personal story to tell: in that case the 'programme'—to enable his readers to pass judgement on Roman rule—may be more of an after-thought, and if so this may help to explain why it is hardly fulfilled in the work itself.[148] The *Histories* begin by being focused on Rome, they end by being focused on Polybius, perhaps an anti-climax, but one which throws some light on the man who wrote them.

[147] iii. 4. 13, οἷον ἀρχὴν ποιησάμενος ἄλλην.

[148] It is interesting to note that Polybius does not refer to this secondary purpose in the epilogue (xxxix. 8), although the terminal point there mentioned is 146/5.

Abbreviations and Select Bibliography

The following list is intended primarily as a convenient key to the main books and journals referred to in an abbreviated form in the notes. It also serves as a select bibliography, which can easily be supplemented from those in the more recent works on Polybius mentioned in it, especially the *RE* article of K. Ziegler, the study of Polybius' methods of composition by P. Pédech and my *Commentary*.

Aalders, *Theorie* = G. J. D. Aalders, *Die Theorie der gemischten Verfassung im Altertum.* Amsterdam, 1968.

AJP = *American journal of philology.*

Altheim Festschrift = *Beiträge zur alten Geschichte und deren Nachleben: Festschrift für Franz Altheim zum 6. 10. 1968.* Ed. Ruth Stiehl and H. E. Stier. Vol. 1. Berlin, 1969.

Ancient Macedonia = *Ancient Macedonia: Papers read at the first international symposium held in Thessaloniki, 26–29 August 1968.* Ed. B. Laourdas and Ch. Makaronas. Thessaloniki, 1970.

Ancient society = *Ancient society and institutions: studies presented to Victor Ehrenberg.* Ed. E. Badian. Oxford, 1966.

Annali di Pisa = *Annali della scuola normale superiore di Pisa: lettere, storia e filosofia.*

Annuaire = *Annuaire de l'institut de philologie et d'histoire orientale de l'université de Bruxelles.*

Astin, *Scipio* = A. E. Astin, *Scipio Aemilianus.* Oxford, 1967.

Athen. = *Athenaeum: studii periodici di letteratura e storia dell'antichità.*

Avenarius = G. Avenarius, *Lukians Schrift zur Geschichtsschreibung.* Diss. Frankfurt, 1954.

Aymard, *Assemblées* = A. Aymard, *Les Assemblées de la confédération achaienne.* Bordeaux, 1938.

Aymard, *Études* = A. Aymard, *Études d'histoire ancienne.* Paris, 1967.

Aymard, *Rapports* = A. Aymard, *Les Premiers rapports de Rome et la confédération achaienne.* Bordeaux, 1938.

Badian, *Studies* = E. Badian, *Studies in Greek and Roman history.* Oxford, 1964.

Barker, *Politics* = E. Barker, *The Politics of Aristotle.* Oxford, 1946.

Beloch, *RG* = K. J. Beloch, *Römische Geschichte.* Berlin–Leipzig, 1926.

Bickerman, *Chronology* = E. Bickerman, *Chronology of the ancient world.* London, 1968.

Birt, *Buchwesen* = T. Birt, *Das antike Buchwesen.* Berlin, 1882.

Brown, *Timaeus* = Truesdell S. Brown, *Timaeus of Tauromenium.* Berkeley–Los Angeles, 1950.

Bruns, *Persönlichkeit* = I. Bruns, *Die Persönlichkeit in der Geschichtsschreibung der Alten.* Berlin, 1898.

Brunt = P. A. Brunt, *Italian manpower, 225 B.C.–A.D. 14.* Oxford, 1971.

BSR = *Papers of the British School at Rome.*

Büchner, *Cicero* = K. Büchner, *Studien zur römischen Literatur.* ii. *Cicero.* Wiesbaden, 1962.

Büttner-Wobst = Th. Büttner-Wobst, *Polybii historiae.* 5 vols (vol. 1, ed. 2). Leipzig, 1889–1905.

Bull. ép. = *Bulletin épigraphique,* published by J. and L. Robert in *REG.*

Bull. Inst. Class. Stud. = *Bulletin of the institute of classical studies (London).*

Bung, *Fabius* = P. Bung, *Q. Fabius Pictor, der erste römische Annalist.* Diss. Cologne, 1950.

Burck, *Erzählungskunst* = E. Burck, *Die Erzählungskunst des T. Livius.* Berlin, 1934; ed. 2, 1964.

Bury, *Historians* = J. B. Bury, *The ancient Greek historians.* New York–London, 1958 (reprint of 1909 edition).

Carpenter, *Pillars* = Rhys Carpenter, *Beyond the Pillars of Heracles: the classical world through the eyes of its discoverers.* New York, 1966.

CHJ = *Cambridge historical journal.*

CIL = *Corpus inscriptionum latinarum.*

Class. et med. = *Classica et mediaevalia.*

Cole, *Democritus* = T. Cole, *Democritus and the sources of Greek anthropology.* American Philological Association, 1967.

Collingwood, *Idea* = R. G. Collingwood, *The idea of history.* Oxford, 1946.

CP = *Classical philology.*

CQ = *Classical quarterly.*

CR = *Classical review.*

CRAI = *Comptes rendus de l'académie des inscriptions et belles-lettres.*

Cuntz = O. Cuntz, *Polybios und sein Werk.* Leipzig, 1900.

Deininger = J. Deininger, *Der politische Widerstand gegen Rom in Griechenland, 217–86 v. Chr.* Berlin–New York, 1971.

De Sanctis = G. De Sanctis, *Storia dei Romani,* i–iv. 1, Turin, 1907–1923; iv. 2–3, Florence, 1953–64.

Diels–Kranz, *Frag. Vorsokr.* = H. Diels–W. Kranz, *Fragmente der Vorsokratiker.* 3 vols. Ed. 11. Zürich–Berlin, 1964.

Eisen = K. F. Eisen, *Polybiosinterpretationen: Beobachtungen zu Prinzipien griechischer und römischer Historiographie bei Polybios.* Heidelberg, 1966.

Erkell = H. Erkell, *Augustus felicitas fortuna: lateinische Wortstudien.* Göteborg, 1952.

Errington, *Philopoemen* = R. M. Errington, *Philopoemen.* Oxford, 1969.

FGH = F. Jacoby, *Fragmente der griechischen Historiker.* 3 parts in 15 volumes. Berlin–Leiden, 1923–58.

Fougères, *Mantinée* = G. Fougères, *Mantinée et l'Arcadie orientale.* Paris, 1898.

Gelzer, *Kl. Schr.* = M. Gelzer, *Kleine Schriften.* 3 vols. Wiesbaden, 1962–4.

GGM = C. Müller, *Geographi graeci minores.* 2 vols. Paris, 1855–61.

Gomme, *Thucydides* = A. W. Gomme, *A historical commentary on Thucydides.* Vols. i–iii. Oxford, 1945–56.

Graeber, *Mischverfassung* = E. Graeber, *Die Lehre von der Mischverfassung bei Polybios.* Bonn, 1968.

GRBS = *Greek, Roman and Byzantine studies.*

Hansen, *Attalids* = E. V. Hansen, *The Attalids of Pergamum.* Ed. 2. Ithaca, N.Y., 1971.

Harder, *Ocellus* = R. Harder, 'Ocellus Lucanus', *Text und Kommentar.* Berlin, 1926; reprint Dublin–Zürich, 1966.

Harv. stud. = *Harvard studies in classical philology.*

Hercod = R. Hercod, *La Conception de l'histoire dans Polybe.* Diss. Lausanne, 1902.

Herodot = *Herodot: die Bemühungen um sein Verständnis* (Wege der Forschung, 26). Ed. W. Marg. Darmstadt, 1962; ed. 2, 1965.

Hirzel, *Cicero* = R. Hirzel, *Untersuchungen zu Ciceros philosophischen Schriften*. Vol. 2. Leipzig, 1882.

Histoire et historiens = *Histoire et historiens dans l'antiquité* (Entretiens Hardt, 4). Vandœuvres–Geneva, 1958.

History and theory = *History and theory: studies in the philosophy of history.*

Hist. Zeitsch. = *Historische Zeitschrift.*

Holleaux, *Études* = M. Holleaux, *Études d'épigraphie et d'histoire grecques*. Ed. L. Robert. 6 vols. Paris, 1938–68.

Howald = E. Howald, *Vom Geist antiker Geschichtsschreibung*. Munich–Berlin, 1944.

HRF = *Historicorum romanorum fragmenta*. Ed. H. Peter. Leipzig, 1883.

IG = *Inscriptiones graecae.*

IG² = *Inscriptiones graecae*: editio minor.

Insch. Olymp. = W. Dittenberger and K. Purgold, *Olympia...die Ergebnisse der Ausgrabung. Textband* v. *Die Inschriften*. Berlin, 1896.

Jacoby, *Abhandlungen* = F. Jacoby, *Abhandlungen zur griechischen Geschichtsschreibung*. Ed. H. Bloch. Leiden, 1950.

Jacoby, *Atthis* = F. Jacoby, *Atthis, the local chronicles of ancient Athens*. Oxford, 1949.

Jahrbücher = *Jahrbücher für Philologie und Pädagogik*. 1826–30; other variants of the title subsequently.

JHS = *Journal of Hellenic studies.*

Jones, *Democracy* = A. H. M. Jones, *Ancient democracy*. Oxford, 1957.

JRS = *Journal of Roman studies.*

Kahrstedt, *Karthager* = U. Kahrstedt, *Geschichte der Karthager von 218 bis 146*. (Vol. 3 of Meltzer's *Geschichte der Karthager*.) Berlin, 1913.

Klotz = A. Klotz, *Livius und seine Vorgänger*. Berlin–Leipzig, 1940–41.

La Bua, *Filino* = V. La Bua, *Filino-Polibio, Sileno-Diodoro*. Palermo, 1966.

Laistner = M. L. W. Laistner, *The greater Roman historians*. Berkeley–Los Angeles, 1947.

Laqueur = R. Laqueur, *Polybius*. Leipzig, 1913.

Larsen, *Federal states* = J. A. O. Larsen, *Greek federal states*. Oxford, 1968.

Larsen, *Representative government* = J. A. O. Larsen, *Representative government in Greek and Roman history*. Berkeley–Los Angeles, 1955.

Latin historians = *Latin historians*. Ed. T. A. Dorey. London, 1966.

LEC = *Les études classiques.*

Lehmann, *Untersuchungen* = G. A. Lehmann, *Untersuchungen zur historischen Glaubwürdigkeit des Polybios*. Münster, 1967.

Leo = F. Leo, *Geschichte der römischen Literatur*. Berlin, 1913.

Leuze, *Jahrzählung* = O. Leuze, *Die römische Jahrzählung*. Tübingen, 1909.

Lorenz, *Untersuchungen* = K. Lorenz, *Untersuchungen zum Geschichtswerk des Polybios*. Stuttgart, 1931.

Mauersberger = A. Mauersberger, *Polybios-Lexicon*. Berlin, 1956– . (3 fascicules, covering α to κ, so far published.)

Meloni, *Perseo* = P. Meloni, *Perseo e la fine della monarchia macedone*. Rome, 1953.

Mette, *Sphaeropoiia* = H. J. Mette, *Sphaeropoiia: Untersuchung zur Kosmologie des Krates von Pergamon*. Munich, 1936.

Meyer, *Forschungen* = E. Meyer, *Forschungen zur alten Geschichte*. 2 vols. Halle, 1892–9.

Mioni = E. Mioni, *Polibio*. Padua, 1949.

Momigliano, *Secondo contributo* = A. D. Momigliano, *Secondo contributo alla storia degli studi classici*. Rome, 1960.

Momigliano, *Studies* = A. D. Momigliano, *Studies in historiography*. London–New York, 1966.

Momigliano, *Terzo contributo* = A. D. Momigliano, *Terzo contributo alla storia degli studi classici e del mondo antico*. 2 vols. Rome, 1966.

Mommsen, *Chronologie* = T. Mommsen, *Die römische Chronologie bis auf Cäsar*. Ed. 2. Berlin, 1859.

Mommsen, *RG* = T. Mommsen, *Römische Geschichte*. Ed. 8. 4 vols. Berlin, 1889.

Mommsen, *Staatsrecht* = T. Mommsen, *Römisches Staatsrecht*. Ed. 3. 3 vols. Leipzig, 1888.

Moore = J. M. Moore, *The manuscript tradition of Polybius*. Cambridge, 1965.

Müllenhoff = K. V. Müllenhoff, *Deutsche Altertumskunde*. Ed. 2. Berlin, 1890.

Newman = W. L. Newman, *The Politics of Aristotle*. 4 vols. Oxford, 1887–1902.

Nilsson, *Religion* = M. P. Nilsson, *Geschichte der griechischen Religion*. Ed. 2. Munich, 1961.

Ninck, *Entdeckung Europas* = M. Ninck, *Die Entdeckung Europas durch die Griechen*. Basel, 1945.

Nissen, *Untersuchungen* = H. Nissen, *Kritische Untersuchungen über die Quellen der vierten und fünften Dekade des Livius*. Berlin, 1863.

Nitzsch = K. W. Nitzsch, *Polybius: zur Geschichte antiker Politik und Historiographie*. Kiel, 1842.

Norden, *Urgeschichte* = E. Norden, *Die germanische Urgeschichte in Tacitus' Germania*. Leipzig, 1920.

OCD = *Oxford classical dictionary*. Ed. 2; ed. N. G. L. Hammond and H. H. Scullard. Oxford, 1970.

OGIS = *Orientis graeci inscriptiones selectae*. Ed. W. Dittenberger. 2 vols. Leipzig, 1903–5.

Pearson, *Lost histories* = L. Pearson, *The lost histories of Alexander the Great*. American Philological Association, 1960.

Pédech, *Méthode* = P. Pédech, *La Méthode historique de Polybe*. Paris, 1964.

Pédech, *Polybe* = P. Pédech, *Polybe, Histoires, Livre i, texte établi et traduit*. Paris, 1969. *Livre ii, texte établi et traduit*. Paris, 1970. *Livre xii, texte établi, traduit et commenté*. Paris, 1960.

Petzold, *Studien* = K.-E. Petzold, *Studien zur Methode des Polybios und zu ihrer historischen Auswertung*. Munich, 1969.

Phil. = *Philologus*.

Phil. Woch. = *Philologische Wochenschrift*.

Pöschl, *Römischer Staat* = V. Pöschl, *Römischer Staat und griechisches Staatsdenken bei Cicero*. Berlin, 1936.

Pohlenz, *Stoa* = M. Pohlenz, *Die Stoa: Geschichte einer geistigen Bewegung*. 2 vols. Göttingen, 1948–9.

Πρακτικά ἀρχ. ἐτ. = Πρακτικά τῆς ἐν ᾿Αθήναις ἀρχαιολογικῆς ἐταιρείας.

Pritchett, *Studies* = W. K. Pritchett, *Studies in ancient Greek topography*. 2 vols. Berkeley–Los Angeles, 1965–9.

Proc. Camb. Phil. Soc. = *Proceedings of the Cambridge Philological Society*.

RE = Pauly–Wissowa, *Real-Encyclopädie der classischen Altertumswissenschaft*. 1893–

REA = *Revue des études anciennes*.

REG = *Revue des études grecques*.

Rh. Mus. = *Rheinisches Museum für Philologie*.

Riv. fil. = *Rivista di filologia e d'istruzione classica*.

Rostovtzeff, *Hellenistic world* = M. I. Rostovtzeff, *The social and economic history of the Hellenistic world*. 3 vols. Oxford, 1941.

Roveri, *Studi* = A. Roveri, *Studi su Polibio*. (Studi pubblicati dall'Istituto di filologia classica, Università degli studi di Bologna, Facoltà di lettere e filosofia, 17). Bologna, 1964.

Ryffel = H. Ryffel, Μεταβολὴ πολιτειῶν: *der Wandel der Staatsverfassungen*. Bern, 1949.

Sabine essays = *Essays in political theory presented to George H. Sabine*. Ed. M. R. Konvitz and A. E. Murphy. Ithaca, N.Y., 1948.

Salmon, *Colonisation* = E. T. Salmon, *Roman colonisation under the republic*. London, 1969.

Schmitt, *Antiochos* = H. H. Schmitt, *Untersuchungen zur Geschichte Antiochos des Grossen und seiner Zeit*. (Historia, Einzelschrift 6.) Wiesbaden, 1964.

Schweighaeuser = J. Schweighaeuser, *Polybii Megalopolitani Historiarum quidquid superest recensuit, digessit, emendatiore interpretatione, varietate lectionis, adnotationibus, indicibus, illustravit.* 8 vols (8. 2 contains a *Lexicon Polybianum*). Leipzig, 1789–95.

SEG = Supplementum epigraphicum graecum.

Siegfried, *Studien* = W. Siegfried, *Studien zur geschichtlichen Anschauung des Polybios.* Berlin, 1928.

Sommella = P. Sommella, *Antichi campi di battaglia in Italia.* Rome, 1968.

Strachan-Davidson = J. L. Strachan-Davidson, *Selections from Polybius.* Oxford, 1888.

Strasburger, *Wesensbestimmung* = H. Strasburger, *Die Wesensbestimmung der Geschichte durch die antiken Geschichtsschreiber (Sitzungsberichte der wissenschaftlichen Gesellschaft an der Johann Wolfgang Goethe-Universität, Frankfurt/Main, 5 (1966) no. 3).* Pagination according to the separate edition.

Stuart, *Epochs* = D. R. Stuart, *Epochs of Greek and Roman biography.* Berkeley, 1928.

Studi alessandrini = Miscellanea di studi alessandrini in memoria di Augusto Rostagni. Turin, 1962.

Susemihl = F. Susemihl, *Geschichte der griechischen Literatur in der Alexandrinerzeit.* 2 vols. Leipzig, 1891–2.

SVF = H. F. von Arnim, Stoicorum veterum fragmenta. 4 vols. Leipzig, 1903–24.

Syll. = Sylloge inscriptionum graecarum. Ed. W. Dittenberger. Ed. 3. 4 vols. Leipzig, 1915–24.

Symb. Osl. = Symbolae Osloenses.

TAPA = Transactions and proceedings of the American philological association.

Thesleff, *Texts* = H. Thesleff, *The Pythagorean texts of the Hellenistic period.* Åbo, 1965.

Thesleff, *Writings* = H. Thesleff, *An introduction to the Pythagorean writings of the Hellenistic period.* Åbo, 1961.

Thukydides = Thukydides (Wege der Forschung, 98), ed. H. Herter. Darmstadt, 1968.

van Gelder, *Galatarum res* = H. van Gelder, *Galatarum res in Graecia et Asia gestae usque ad medium secundum saeculum ante Christum.* Diss. Amsterdam, 1888.

von Fritz, *Geschichtsschreibung* = K. von Fritz, *Die griechische Geschichtsschreibung,* i. 2 vols. Berlin, 1967.

von Fritz, *Mixed constitution* = K. von Fritz, *The theory of the mixed constitution in antiquity: a critical analysis of Polybius' thought.* New York, 1954.

von Scala = R. von Scala, *Die Studien des Polybios.* Stuttgart, 1890.

Walbank, *Commentary* = F. W. Walbank, *A historical commentary on Polybius.* 2 vols. so far published (out of 3). Oxford, 1957–67.

Walbank, *Philip V* = F. W. Walbank, *Philip V of Macedon.* Cambridge, 1940 (reprint, Camden, Conn., 1969).

Walbank, *Speeches* = F. W. Walbank, *Speeches in Greek historians.* Oxford, n.d. (1965).

Wehrli, *Aristoxenos* = F. Wehrli, *Die Schule des Aristoteles: Texte und Kommentar.* ii. *Aristoxenos.* Ed. 2. Basel, 1967.

Wehrli, *Dikaiarchos* = F. Wehrli, *Die Schule des Aristoteles: Texte und Kommentar.* i. *Dikaiarchos.* Basel, 1944.

Werner = H. M. Werner, *De Polybii vita et itineribus quaestiones chronologicae.* Diss. Leipzig, 1877.

Werner, *Republik* = R. Werner, *Der Beginn der römischen Republik.* Munich, 1963.

Woodhouse, *Aetolia* = W. J. Woodhouse, *Aetolia, its geography, topography and antiquities.* Oxford, 1897.

Wunderer, *Forschungen* = C. Wunderer, *Polybios-Forschungen.* 3 vols. Leipzig, 1898, 1901, 1909.

Zegers, *Wesen* = N. Zegers, *Wesen und Ursprung der tragischen Geschichtsschreibung.* Diss. Cologne, 1959.

Ziegler = K. Ziegler, Pauly–Wissowa, *RE,* vol. xxi. 2, cols. 1440–578, 'Polybios'.

Index

II AUTHORS AND PASSAGES

The figures in bold type indicate pages of this book